Why Philosophy?

Why Philosophy?

Edited by
Paolo Diego Bubbio and Jeff Malpas

DE GRUYTER

ISBN 978-3-11-064933-8
e-ISBN (PDF) 978-3-11-065099-0
e-ISBN (EPUB) 978-3-11-064924-6

Library of Congress Control Number: 2019934867

Bibliografic information published by the Deutsche Nationalbibliothek
The Deutsche Nationalbibliothek lists this publication in the Deutsche Nationalbibliografie;
detailed bibliografic data are available on the Internet at http://dnb.dnb.de.

© 2021 Walter de Gruyter GmbH, Berlin/Boston
This volume is text- and page-identical with the hardback published in 2019.
Cover image: Auguste Rodin's "Le Penseur" in a graphic elaboration by Paolo Diego Bubbio
Printing and binding: CPI books GmbH, Leck

www.degruyter.com

Table of Contents

Acknowledgements —— VII

Paolo Diego Bubbio and Jeff Malpas
Introduction: Why Philosophy? —— IX

I. What Is Philosophy?

Jacob Graham
Doing Philosophy —— 3

Patrick Stokes
The House Always Wins: Why Philosophy Isn't Optional —— 15

Paolo Diego Bubbio
Why We Need Philosophy – and Philosophers —— 27

David Macarthur
Irreverent Thoughts on the Relevance of Philosophy —— 41

II. What can Philosophy Contribute?

Lisa Bortolotti and Katherine Puddifoot
Philosophy, Bias, and Stigma —— 51

Jon Askonas and Katherine Withy
Thinking Failure in the War in Iraq: The Cultural Turn and the Concept of "World" —— 65

Paul Redding
The Role of Philosophy in "Post-Truth" Times —— 81

III. What can Philosophy do?

Robert Frodeman
A Robot Took My Boyfriend and My Job: Positioning Philosophy for a Resurgence —— 105

Babette Babich
Good for Nothing: On Philosophy and its Discontents —— 123

Jeff Malpas
On Thinking in a Thoughtless Time —— 151

Contributors —— 173

Index of Names —— 177

Index of Subjects —— 181

Acknowledgements

Timely though we believe this book to be, it was not a book for which it was easy to find a publisher. The difficulty seemed unrelated to any question of the quality of the material it contained, but almost purely a matter of publishers' uncertainty as to its potential readership. The book does not address a well-established topic within the philosophical curriculum—either of teaching or research—and although intended to be accessible to a general audience, publishers seemed unconvinced (and unable to be convinced) that there was an audience with an interest in the question of philosophy's significance or relevance. We are thus extremely grateful to De Gruyter for their willingness to take the project on board.

We would like to thank our contributors for participating in the volume, and so also for viewing the project, seemingly against the current of publishing opinion, as a worthwhile one. We would also like to give special thanks to Randall Lindstrom who became involved in the project at a very late stage in order to ensure the final editing and formatting was done to an appropriate standard. Randall's editorial brief was to ensure consistency and accuracy of formatting and bibliographic detail, and to leave style and content to one side—any infelicities in the latter respects are thus the responsibility of the authors alone. We are extremely grateful to Randall for taking us, as well as the original typescript, in hand, and thereby ensuring that everything got to the publisher in good order and in reasonable time. Our thanks also go to our potential readers who we hope will be attracted to the book's title, not out of a desire to abandon philosophy, but precisely because of the desire—and the necessity—to return to it. Last of all, we want to express our gratitude to those, like Irma Sartori (the grandma of Paolo Diego Bubbio—see chapter 3), for whom philosophy—which is to say that form of thinking and questioning that is genuinely concerned for the world and looks to make a difference in it—is always to be valued, all the more so when it seems to be ignored or derided.

Paolo Diego Bubbio and Jeff Malpas
Introduction: Why Philosophy?

In 423 BC, *The Clouds*, a comedy written by the ancient Greek playwright Aristophanes, was staged for the first time. The two main characters in the play, Strepsiades and his son Pheidippides, go to the Thinkery, an imaginary school, in the hope that they might learn from the philosopher Socrates how to turn poor arguments into winning arguments, with the aim of beating their creditors in court. In the Thinkery, students are engaged in a series of seemingly absurd and pointless activities, like inventing a unit of measurement for calculating the distance jumped by a flea (a flea's foot), and the exact cause of the buzzing noise of a gnat. Then the philosophy master Socrates makes his appearance, floating on to the stage in a basket, so that he can contemplate the sun. In the end, it is not Strepsiades, but only his son Pheidippides who benefits from Socrates' teaching—learning how to use dishonest speech to his own ends and even being influenced by Socrates to attack his father Strepsiades—something for which the now-learned Pheidippides is able to provide a supposedly rational justification.

In *The Clouds*, we already find all the classic stereotypes that are usually invoked to mock philosophy and affirm its futility. Philosophy is presented as a technique to win otherwise hopeless and meritless arguments thanks to conceptual tricks; philosophy students loose time in pointless experiments that have no practical implications; the philosopher himself (in this case Socrates) effectively floats in the air with his head in the clouds, removed from concrete reality; and not only do philosophers not do anything useful, but they influence young people to question sensible customs and reasonable traditions, and encourage them to rebel against authority. Twenty-three years after the first representation of *The Clouds*, the real Socrates was indeed found guilty of impiety and corruption of the youth, and sentenced to death.

Attacks against philosophy and, as a consequence, philosophers' attempts to defend themselves and the discipline they practice, are as old as philosophy itself—which is to say, almost as old as Western culture. There is thus a sense in which there is nothing new in increasing attacks that, in the past few years, have been directed against philosophy—attacks that came from scientists, politicians, and public figures in general. It seems that every generation of philosophers is called to respond to such attacks, and justify their existence over and over again. From this point of view, this volume can be considered as a repetition of this ongoing and seemingly endless debate.

There is, however, a sense in which philosophy is currently experiencing a crisis for which there is no precedent. Philosophy has always been constituted in terms of the search for the truth. Even when some philosophical approaches question the very idea of truth (here one can think of Gianni Vattimo's book, *Farewell to Truth*), this move is made in the name of a supposedly superior "truth"—not a theoretical truth, but a practical "truth," such as love or charity. Yet the criticism of philosophy has typically been directed at philosophy's supposed inability or unwillingness to reach the truth—thus Aristophanes depicts Socrates as someone who teaches people how to use conceptual tricks and rhetoric to turn "wrong" arguments into convincing ones. Truth becomes the rod with which to beat philosophy—even though the truth as seen by someone like Aristophanes is the "truth" that is grounded on traditional values and customs, on what we might think of as "common-sense" (so part of what is also at issue in Aristophanes is the ridiculing of any "truth" apart from the truth that is already known and commonly acknowledged).

Nowadays, however, not only philosophy, but truth itself seems to be under attack, along with academia more generally—insofar as universities are the institutions whose goal is, or should be, the search of the truth. While we were in the process of collecting the essays that constitute this volume, in 2016, "post-truth" was chosen as the Oxford Dictionaries Word of the Year—the term being said to relate or denote "circumstances in which objective facts are less influential in shaping public opinion than appeals to emotion and personal belief." The choice of this word was, no doubt, connected with its frequent use in analyses of the Brexit referendum in the United Kingdom and the 2016 presidential election in the United States of America. Here we have neither the space nor the competence (another word which seems under attack today) to engage in analyses of this particular rhetorical-political phenomenon, its impact on politics and communication more generally, and its implications. As philosophers, we are not only concerned, and certainly not primarily so, with the fact that some politicians and public commentators tend to appeal to emotions and personal prejudices rather than rational thought (has that not always been the case?), but also that the spread and use of social media facilitates a cultural environment in which facts that do not fit a particular narrative are disregarded or ignored. These are indeed very worrying phenomena. A more urgent and pressing concern for us, as philosophers, is that so many people do not see these phenomena as a source of concern at all—even that they barely even recognize them as phenomena. It seems that what we face is actually a paradigm shift, though one that is seldom acknowledged, that effectively breaks with the twenty-five centuries old tradition that has hitherto been so central to Western and European culture, and that has its analogues in many other cultures: namely, the tradition that takes the search for truth (conceived, as remarked earlier, in a very broad sense) as a value in itself, beyond personal or collective interests, emotions, and beliefs. This tradition seems now to be viewed as almost irrelevant in many circles or at least to be almost entirely disregarded. If something along these lines is happening, then philosophy today is facing a radically new challenge—one that calls upon philosophy to reposition in relation to a new task: not only to defend itself and its own value and legitimacy, but also, and more fundamentally, to defend one of the core ideals on which our entire civilization has been built.

In *Why Philosophy?*, we have asked philosophers from different countries, some of whom have already engaged, in one way or another, in public debates about these issues, to write essays providing their answers to the range of questions that the contemporary situation of philosophy gives rise. Such questions include: Why should we have, or do, philosophy? Is philosophy valuable, and why? What kind of contributions can philosophy offer in dealing with the challenges that we, as human beings, face? The resulting essays explore these questions from different angles, and emphasize different aspects, according to each individual author's sensibility, concerns, and philosophical standpoint. Although there is considerable diversity in the essays themselves, there are some broad themes and continuities across them, and in response to this, we have organized the essays into three main sections. In the first section, "What is Philosophy?," our authors look to the over-arching reasons why philosophy has been, and still remains, valuable. In the second section, "What Can Philosophy Contribute?," the focus is more specifically on the value and relevance of philosophy in particular domains and field of inquiry or with respect to particular problems. In the third and final section, "What Should Philosophy Do?," the authors offer their (sometimes diverging) views and insights into the future of philosophy and the agenda that philosophy might set for itself. Admittedly, the division into three sections is somewhat artificial: since all three of these broad topics inevitably overlap with one another, answers in one area typically imply answers in another. Yet the division into these three sections does reflect a difference in overall orientation and emphasis among the essays contained here, and it provides some landmarks by which the reader may begin to navigate through the material.

The first section, "What is Philosophy?," opens with an essay by Jacob Graham entitled "Doing Philosophy" In this essay, Graham maintains that philosophical questions can be therapeutic. Graham defends his claim by arguing that, despite the common perception of philosophy as an abstract discipline, philosophy is actually "embodied and fully grounded," and that it can help us in understanding and managing our emotions and feelings. In "The House Always Wins: Why Philosophy Isn't Optional," Patrick Stokes takes into consideration some recent attacks against philosophy by scientists, such as the famous (or infamous) claim by Stephen Hawking that "philosophy is dead," and shows how any attack against philosophy is inevitably philosophical—hence, philosophy is unavoidable. Paolo Diego Bubbio, in his "Why We Need Philosophy—and Philosophers," develops an argument along similar lines, showing that philosophy is everywhere, whether one realizes or not. Together with this, Bubbio advances a conception of philosophy as ongoing conversation that is, simultaneously, an interpretation of the world and an attempt to change the world.

David Macarthur, in his "Irreverent Thoughts on the Relevance of Philosophy," while also offering an account of philosophy, goes on to outline some of the most significant contributions that philosophy has offered, and still offers, in several different areas. Macarthur's essay thus paves the way for the second section of the volume.

Focusing on the question "What Can Philosophy Contribute?," the second section begins with Lisa Bortolotti and Katherine Puddifoot's essay, "Philosophy, Bias, and Stigma." Bortolotti and Puddifoot consider the potential contribution of philosophy in providing solutions to the problems raised by implicit bias (when, for instance, group members are associated with traits in virtue of their social group membership) and mental health stigma (when people with a known psychiatric diagnosis are discriminated against for the mere reason that they experience mental health issues). On this basis, they argue that philosophical discussion can contribute to developing practical solutions to otherwise difficult yet pressing problems—all the more significant in a world in which bias and stigma are both so prevalent and so damaging. The second essay of this section moves to another realm of philosophical applications—the cultural/political. In "Failure in the War in Iraq: The Cultural Turn and the Concept of 'World,'" Jon Askonas and Katherine Withy argue that the actions of the U.S. Army in Iraq, vis-à-vis the locals and inevitable interactions with them, could have been more informed and successful if they had employed a concept of "world," such as the one advanced by the philosophical school of phenomenology, rather than a standard concept of "culture." Here the focus is on the value of a specific concept but also, therefore, on the value of the thinking that gives rise to that concept. The value of philosophical analysis and discussion in the public realm is also the object of the third essay of this section, "The Role of Philosophy in 'Post-Truth' Times," by Paul Redding. Here, the issue of the role of philosophy in the public realm is addressed from a different angle, and with a broader scope. Redding looks to contextualize events such as Brexit and the election of Donald Trump in terms of a more general shift in the balance between "the universal" and "the particular" that is also at play in the apparent flight from "truth" and that can be seen to be closely tied to changes in the operation of contemporary politics and changes in the nature of political allegiance. Redding concludes that philosophy plays a crucial role in clarifying the conception of ourselves and the problematic situations in which we find ourselves—but that it is left up to us to come up with solutions.

In the third section of the volume, we ask the question "What Should Philosophy Do?." When we try to answer such a question, disagreement among philosophers is unavoidable. However, rather than being a sign of weakness or instances of navel-gazing debates, such disagreements are evidence of the vitality and vigor of a discipline that exercises the passion of thought to deal with any possible problem—including those problems that threaten its own existence. Richard Frodeman's "A Robot Took My Boyfriend and My Job: Positioning Philosophy for a Resurgence" and Babette Babich's "Good for Nothing: On Philosophy and its Discontents," represent two alternatives in the debate over how philosophy should position itself in the current landscape and vis-à-vis circumstances that seem to jeopardize its very existence. Frodeman maintains that developments in science and technology are creating opportunities for philosophy to become central to societal concerns that are ethical, epistemic, and metaphysical in nature, such as issues in artificial intelligence, nanotechnology, and genetic manipulation; he therefore calls on philosophers to reposition themselves, both within academia and across society. This requires, Frodeman argues, a greater attention paid to the rhetorical elements of persuading different audiences in order to reach the public sphere. Babich holds a different view and, in an almost direct dialogue with Frodeman (as she mentions *Socrates Tenured*, a book that Frodeman co-authored with Adam Briggle in 2016), she argues that the answer does not reside in "colonizing other disciplines," or in "appointing philosophers to political roles" so that their views are "heard by public agencies"—strategies that all come down, in her view, to "seeking 'impact'" and "getting philosophy funded" (on the assumption that philosophy knows "the answer to the question of what is to be done"). Rather than being primarily concerned with the issue of how to generate "public interest," Babich argues that philosophers should start listening to one another, and engaging more with one another's work. This is itself, she contends, a "step on the way to the public as such." We should, Babich concludes, "listen to the older voices" of the great philosophers of the past "before they vanish completely"—not out of some form of nostalgia, but because we need their insights to deal with contemporary problems. Finally, in "On Thinking in a Thoughtless Time," Jeff Malpas suggests that we should ask not so much what philosophy can do as what can be done without philosophy, without thinking. Taking up issues of value and truth, Malpas connects the origins of "post-truth" (and what might also be thought of as "post-ethical") to earlier shifts in media, management, and organization that are evident in developments over the last thirty to forty years, including the undermining of professional authority, all of which implied the establishing of the dominance of instrumentalist over other considerations and a genericization of judgment and expertise.

As editors, and philosophical editors at that, we cannot help but take sides in the debate that the volume takes up—all the more so inasmuch as the debate itself shows the necessity and inevitability of philosophy. The irony of such a debate is that, as so many of our authors point out, the very asking of the question "why philosophy" is itself a move *within philosophy*—one does not escape philosophy by questioning philosophy, but indeed only moves more into its orbit. Aristophanes, then, cannot be seen as simply the dramatist standing against the follies of the philosopher, but is already, in the very form of the play, taking a stand on what is essentially a philosophical question concerning the value and worth of philosophy. The disagreement, then, can never be over philosophy as such, but only over the manner in which it is pursued.

In the 1748 essay "Answering the Question: What is Enlightenment?," Immanuel Kant employed the Latin phrase *Sapere aude* ("Dare to know," or "Dare to think for yourself") as the motto of his own philosophy, and for the Enlightenment in general. Today, we might question whether the ideal of reason appealed to in the Enlightenment era is still valid, and we might debate over its limits (already, in itself, a philosophical question), but if we take the injunction it captures in a broad sense, then there is surely no doubt about its validity. In a time like ours, in which emotions, prejudices, biases, and a narrow (and often short-sighted) conception of "usefulness" seem to exercise priority over thought, it is the task of philosophy to affirm the centrality of an activity on which our entire civilization, and perhaps our very humanity, is grounded: *thinking*. If, with this volume, we have managed to draw attention toward this task, then the volume will have gone a long way to having achieved its goal.

I. What Is Philosophy?

1. What is Philosophy?

Jacob Graham
Doing Philosophy

Abstract: Doing philosophy—and I mean "philosophy" in its etymological sense, "loving wisdom"—can be a fully integrated part of one's life, a way of living life, a life's orientation. If this is true, then there can be no question as to philosophy's usefulness or relevance. Whether we are asking questions about the nature of reality, or questions about the nature of knowledge, these inquiries already stem from and are directed back towards a life, namely, the life of the one who asks the questions. Indeed, these questions even enrich and improve the overall life of the questioner.

1 Introduction

Given the circumstances, you might hear someone say, "She does philosophy" or, "I do philosophy" or, someone might ask, "You do philosophy?" What "do" means depends upon the circumstances. I am a professional philosopher; that is, I teach philosophy. So, I might say that I do philosophy and that this doing consists of teaching. Or, "do" might be more akin to the actual activity of philosophical thought. My point here is not to enumerate all the senses of "do" in the phrase "doing philosophy," in part because I'd like for you to feel inspired to continue reading my chapter. Nor do I want to undertake the hefty task, if it's possible at all, of providing an exhaustive definition of exactly what I do mean. I will be satisfied to provide a general *sense* of what I mean. So, I'll start by saying that I intend a holistic, practical sense when I talk in this chapter about "doing philosophy." That is, I aim to show that doing philosophy—and I mean "philosophy" in its etymological sense, "loving wisdom"—can be a fully integrated part of one's life, a way of living life, a life's orientation. If this is true, then there can be no question as to philosophy's usefulness or relevance since its usefulness and relevance unfolds and plays out directly in one's life, in one's living.

The great historian of ancient western philosophy, Pierre Hadot, has shown that philosophy for the ancient Greeks and Romans was a way of life, a life practice. When philosophers talk about practical philosophy, if they are not talking about pragmatism, they are likely talking about ethics. Ethics has to do with praxis, action, doing. I want to suggest that all major branches of philosophy can have an ethical orientation, where "ethics" is construed broadly. That is, whether we are asking metaphysical questions (questions about the nature of re-

https://doi.org/10.1515/9783110650990-003

ality or being) or epistemological questions (questions about the nature of knowledge), these inquiries and whatever revelations they might hold already stem from and are directed back towards a life, namely, the life of the one who asks the questions. Indeed, these questions even enrich the overall life of the questioner.

Moreover, since ethics has to do with the realm of human action, and since action plays out in a political context—that is, action is always in some way situated in our social being—there are also political ramifications of doing philosophy. Really, I'm just retelling an old, old story. It's the same one that Socrates (469–399 B.C.E.) told. For him, the life of philosophy is the best life and the unexamined life is not worth living.[1] This is the sort of ethical orientation that I intend. It is a broad construal of ethics, influenced by ancient philosophy, that asks about what makes for a good life. The examined life, to some degree or another, is part of a good life. Also like Socrates, I suggest that if, in our age when philosophy and the humanities are more and more denigrated, others find philosophy to be useless, it is simply because they've not made use of it themselves.[2] Part of my task here is to help readers to understand why they should use philosophy. Let's just hope that the political ramifications of us doing philosophy are not the same for us as they were for Socrates, who was put to death for it.

2 Right Now

As I write this, poor and dangerous judgments reign supreme in American politics. Anti-intellectualism, financial frustration, fear, and ignorance have fomented an emotionally driven political madhouse. Outside and inside the U.S., and directly influential upon its situation, religious extremism and terrorism is thriving in the world. Diplomacy and dialogue are not only on the decline but, in some circles, are entirely occluded. Emotionally driven language, sometimes even under a rhetorical guise of intelligence, controls so much of the political discourse. Whether one is on the side of those who have absurdly called for the removal of Muslims from the U.S., or on the side of ISIS, there are common truths to both sides—neither understands very much and yet both are certain that they hold the right position on just about everything.

---

1 Plato, 1997, *Apology* 38a5,.
2 Plato, 1997, *Republic* 489b.

The humanities have been under fire for some time for their supposed lack of value. U.S. Senator Marco Rubio's infamous claim that students ought to cease with their studies in philosophy and pursue something more useful, like welding, could just as easily be applied to studies in literature or sociology. These endeavors are seen as high-flown, ethereal musings rather than the machines of critical thought and insight into human being that they are. In a world where "getting something done" is so highly valued, that world has strangely overlooked just what it is that the humanities, and especially philosophy, can do. Philosophy addresses some of the most important issues of our day and yet, it seems, few people listen and many refuse to. Why, for example, would anyone think that because some Muslims espouse extreme and violent views, that all do and that the best course of action is to bar them entrance from the U.S.? Philosophers would call this, among other things, the fallacy of hasty generalization, i.e., concluding something about an entire group based upon an insufficient sample set. Or again, Christians who threaten others with hell, lest they believe, are appealing to fear and force, both fallacies. These are very basic skills that can be learned in an introductory philosophy class to help preempt such bad thinking. Yet, remarkably, few people are listening.

Let's focus on the example of religious extremism, which has long been a problem in some shape or form. In Plato's *Euthyphro*, Socrates catches Euthyphro outside of what was at that time very much like a courthouse. Euthyphro is there to prosecute his father for murder—on questionable grounds—and claims that doing so is pious. Socrates asks Euthyphro what piety is since, if Euthyphro claims that what he's doing is pious, he must know something about piety. Euthyphro makes a number of attempts at defining piety, all of which Socrates seems to refute. As you might imagine, Euthyphro becomes frustrated by his inability to answer adequately Socrates's question, and he blames Socrates for his twisted way of argumentation: "I have no way of telling you what I have in mind, for whatever proposition we put forward goes around and refuses to stay put where we establish it."[3] Euthyphro naturally blames Socrates for this confusion. After all, isn't all of this Socrates's fault to begin with? Shouldn't he have kept his nose out of Euthyphro's affairs? Is he demanding too much from Euthyphro?

I'll leave it to you to judge whether Socrates should have kept to himself. However, I do want to address a possible philosophical criticism of Socrates here. In fairness to Euthyphro, Socrates is asking a lot of him. Specifically, Socrates seems to be asking Euthyphro what he cannot—and maybe no one could—

---

3 Plato, 1997, *Euthyphro* 11b5–7.

do, which is to define a difficult and complex concept. In short, it seems that Socrates is committing a fallacy that some philosophers have named after him, the Socratic Fallacy. When we tell a friend, family member, or lover that we love them, we have a *sense* of what we mean by "love," but if someone were to ask us to define it, we'd likely be at a loss, or else come up against innumerable difficulties in our attempts to define it. It would be unfair, though, to conclude that we then know nothing about love or have no right to use the word. Demanding that someone define love or leave it alone is like asking someone to cease using their body since they know nothing of anatomy or physiology. I think we need to give Socrates more credit. He was not interested in mere schoolyard games.

Socrates has a deeper lesson in mind than besting someone else in argument, and this lesson is revealed by what I see as the philosophical climax—one easily overlooked—of the *Euthyphro*. In his frustration, Euthyphro at one point says "it is a considerable task to acquire any precise knowledge of these things," but then goes on to attempt yet another definition of what piety is.[4] The strange thing is what Socrates says in response: "You could tell me in far fewer words, if you were willing, the sum of what I asked, Euthyphro, but you are not keen to teach me, that is clear. You were on the point of doing so, but you turned away. If you had given that answer, I should now have acquired from you sufficient knowledge of the nature of piety."[5] First, we notice the so-called "Socratic irony" at play. Euthyphro is not keen to teach Socrates? He has dutifully answered every question that Socrates asked! He has even changed his answers, according to Socrates's rebuttals, presumably in an effort to make them better. I suggest, however, that there is more at play here than mere irony (what we might call sarcasm). Hidden in Socrates's irony, and revealed by his following and rather shocking claims, is a deeper message. He is suggesting that Euthyphro does not really have a desire *to teach* Socrates anything at all. Euthyphro is willing to talk, and talk a lot, but not for a second is he willing—or presumably even aware of such a possibility—to challenge his own opinions. He just needs to be comfortable having an opinion. The real teacher has to be a critical thinker. That is, the real teacher must be willing to hold his or her own opinions at bay to deal with the matter at hand. This, though, is uncomfortable—at least at first. The true philosophical spirit always involves this ability and willingness either to refine or abandon one's own beliefs and opinions, or to say that one simply does not know. This is what Socrates asked of Euthyphro. In fact,

---

4 Plato, 1997, *Euthyphro* 14b.
5 Plato, 1997, *Euthyphro* 14c.

this very admission of his own ignorance is apparently what Euthyphro was missing in all of his efforts to say what piety is.

That's it. We're almost at the end of the dialogue, and Socrates says that Euthyphro has breezed past the answer. The answer is that we frail humans don't know what piety is, and the admission of that ignorance *just is* piety. What? Is this not strange to our ears? Piety is *not* a knowledge of what or who the gods (or God) are, what they want, etc. Rather, piety is the recognition that we know next to nothing about the gods. Keep in mind that the stakes are high. Getting Euthyphro to admit his own ignorance might have prevented him from prosecuting his father for murder, who, if convicted, might have been killed for it. What's at stake for us? A religious extremist who doubts the substance of their beliefs will have good reason to doubt that killing or hating others—whether one is hating homosexuals, Muslims, or infidels—in the name of those beliefs is a worthwhile pursuit.

Socrates's epistemological goal is not to strive for ignorance, but simply to admit it when we must and when it is genuinely beneficial for us to do so. We should strive to understand ourselves and our world, and be aware when we have failed to do so. However, our hatred and anger reveal our lack of understanding of our situation. Moreover, we not only lack understanding but also, generally speaking, lack *the desire* to understand the situation. That is, we are not even taking the steps to becoming enlightened about what is really happening because it is uncomfortable to do that. It would require first that we call our own position into question. Yet, it is only through an understanding—understanding the social, psychological, and religious roots of religious fanaticism in all its forms—that we can fight the real battle, which is one of education. When we understand, for example, that "radicalization" often happens to those in fragile or dire circumstances and psychological states, and is often born out of anger and fear rather than reason (much like our response to it often is), we might be better able to address those circumstances before they give rise to such tendencies.

At a deeper and more primary level, I would also suggest that some Socratic admission of our ignorance and the limits of our knowledge would benefit us. When we come to terms with the fact that we do not and cannot know, for example, who or how God is, what God wants or if God wants anything at all, we might be less likely to kill each other—whether psychologically or physically—with our beliefs. To put it more precisely, recognizing our beliefs *as* beliefs and *not* knowledge can help us overcome the urge to epistemic tyranny over ourselves and others. Socrates taught us that there is nothing wrong with ignorance. When, however, we sweep our own ignorance under the rug of false pretenses to knowledge, we harm both ourselves and others. I will go so far as to suggest that one of the greatest influences that has led to our woes is our failure to listen to Socrates's lesson about human wisdom.

3 Reflection and Examination

But before I get carried away and try to solve the world's problems, let's reflect for a moment on why so many of the world's greatest philosophers thought it was proper to talk about ethics before talking about politics. We need first to have considered how to live well individually before we can effectively consider how to live well together. This is perhaps by now a cliché, but it is nevertheless true. While Socrates had conversations about topics ranging from mathematics to epistemology to metaphysics, when it came down to the line—literally, when his life was on the line in his defense of himself against accusations of corruption of the youth and impiety—Socrates claimed that the "unexamined life is not worth living for human beings."[6] "Gravity" is the word that comes to mind when I think of the force of this claim, and it is no less shocking now than when it was uttered nearly 2,500 years ago.

This claim serves as a premise in an argument that Socrates makes in Plato's *Apology*. He argues that discussing virtue and other philosophical matters is of the utmost importance *because* the unexamined life is not worth living. Why is it not worth living? This is a bold and controversial claim. Why not spend our lives on the couch watching television letting "reality TV" become our only reality? Why not blindly believe what we are told? Why not rather seek one bodily pleasure after another rather than pain ourselves with learning? After all, these ways of life seem much more easy and comfortable, and much more akin to the sort of lives we envy in, say, dogs or pigs. But there's the rub, we are not dogs or pigs. Whatever similarities we have with them, and however much those animals have to teach us, the informed intellect tells us to strive for more. Ultimately, I side with both Socrates and John Stuart Mill when they say that the one who has experienced both intellectual and bodily pleasures to a sufficient degree will prefer the life with more intellectual pleasures. Or, more basically, I just *feel* better when I strive to examine both myself and my world. For Socrates, the unexamined life is just not a human life, which is why he says that it's not worth living *for human beings*.

My point here is not to play a game of species centrism or hierarchy, but simply to show that, at a very basic level, we humans want more than just sleep,

---

6 Plato, 1997, *Apology* 38a5.

food, and sex. Take for example even the crudest example of gossip. We gossip because we *want to know*, or at least feel as though we know, what's going on. If some things count as knowledge and some don't, and if we want at some basic level to know, then we ought to seek those things that count as knowledge, or those things that at least come very close to knowledge. We will become better and live more pleasurable lives by seeking to understand the things that matter, and by seeking also to understand when we don't and can't understand. It's difficult to imagine why anyone would want to live in a world that didn't foster mental cultivation, although many in our world do their best, by doing little or nothing, to make this happen. A world of mental cultivation needs examination.

What's the point of this examination? It would be easy to object to Socrates's idea that the unexamined life is not worth living by saying, "it's absurd to think that I'll ever reach some answer for myself or others." Socrates, if you've ever read Plato, almost never claims to have an answer, and I contend that an examination without an answer is not objectionable, but is in fact inherently worth our while. These questions without definite answers allow us to confront our limits as human beings and knowers. Let us revisit Socrates's claim in the *Euthyphro* that he would have had a sufficient understanding of the nature of piety had Euthyphro said that we cannot know exactly what it is. Notice first that this claim comes only after a long and sustained inquiry into the nature of piety. It would be easy in an anti-intellectual culture to say, "See, we don't know what it is, so there's no point in thinking about it." This kind of dismissive answer not only overlooks the point, but it often acts in a psychologically subversive way to lure us back into the comfort of our own delusional, solipsistic, and relativistic beliefs and opinions. "Since none of us can say decisively what's what, there's no point in trying, so I'll continue to believe what I believe, and there's no point in questioning it or any other belief." This is precisely not the sort of admission of ignorance that Socrates has in mind. It's only after careful consideration that he wishes Euthyphro to admit his own ignorance.

To put this argument into our own context, let's suppose that there really is a supremely powerful and perfect God. Let's suppose, too, that God—as many of the world's theistic religions will claim—is beyond the ultimate comprehension of a finite human intellect. Why, then, should we ever suppose that we *know*—or, what amounts to the same thing, believe so strongly that it *feels like* knowing—what this God is, what this God wants for us (if God wants anything at all), that God cares when I score a touchdown, that I live in "God's country," etc. Believers often say that "God works in mysterious ways," but they almost never take this mystery seriously enough to admit that they really know little to nothing about this God. We have an uncanny ability to be seduced into an entrenchment in our own beliefs. We tend to make them static. We want the comfort of knowing what's what, but when it comes to matters of piety and divinity, we know very little. We cannot, however, discover this ignorance until we examine ourselves and what we claim to believe. Moreover, this examination needs to happen often in order to make any difference in our lives. In fact, it seems evident to me that it is the *very activity* of examination, i.e., *doing philosophy*, that is itself beneficial, even when no clear answers appear.

But, wait a second. Isn't Socrates himself stubbornly adhering to his own opinions about the superiority of the examined life, i.e., the life of philosophy? After all, he says in the *Apology* that he refuses to abandon his practice of philosophy, even in the face of his own death: "as long as I draw breath and am able, I shall not cease to practice philosophy."[7] This does seem stubborn, but we need to recall exactly what it is that Socrates is holding onto. He is refusing not to think critically and is ever vigilant about what he claims to know. He refuses to accept without inquiry claims about some of the most important questions. This is important to notice. Socrates is not advocating—as many people seem to believe that philosophers advocate—that we "question everything." We never hear Socrates questioning others about why they part their hair where they do. Socrates thinks critically about the *important* issues, e.g., what virtue or piety is, and refuses to do otherwise. In other words, Socrates will die for his ability to think freely and, therefore, to be free.

Suppose for a moment that Socrates is right that claiming not to know what piety is, just is piety. What would this profession of ignorance entail for us? First, let me begin with a negative answer. It would mean that we are no longer obligated to get red in the face vehemently defending flimsy (or perhaps not so flimsy) beliefs and opinions. That is, we are under no duty to claim to know the nature of the divine or, if atheism suits you, to claim to know that there is no such nature at all. This, as far as I can tell, is freedom from a burden. It's a relief to realize that we don't have to say or think any particular thing about divinity. We are free to withhold judgment and any god that would demand otherwise from us is more a despot than a god.

Positively, it means that every time we carefully consider the nature of piety we come to terms with our finitude. We realize that, despite all we know, there's the ultimate mystery *that* any of this is at all and that whatever is divine is beyond our ability to know. But this takes examination and reflection. Notice that it is the recognition of our ignorance about piety that is itself pious. I contend that this must be a realized—made-real-to-us—recognition. That is, it is

---

7 Plato, 1997, *Apology* 29d.

quite possible to say "I don't know the nature of piety" and not really mean it or realize what it means, just as one might ask another "How are you?" without really meaning it or wanting to know the answer. It is a realization that needs to be revisited and reflected upon. This act of reflection, which is philosophical, allows us to experience all over again our own finitude, the limits of our own being and knowledge. When one has experienced this limitation through philosophical reflection, she will no longer doubt its value, just as one can never genuinely experience a strange, new land and its people and culture until she has been there herself.

To take another example from Socrates, he claims in the *Apology* that fearing death is to claim to know what one does not know.[8] Fearing anything, thinks Socrates, involves some sort of knowledge claim. That is, we fear what we claim to know is bad or evil. Yet, we have no reason to believe that death is bad or evil and, moreover, we might have good reason to believe it is not at all bad or evil. So, we have two distinct but related arguments that lead us to related realizations. When we recognize the limits of our knowledge, we set into relief our own finitude or limitation. Death—the ultimate limit upon our being—is nothing to fear since the most we know about it is that it involves some sort of change in our being. When we realize this, we are able to live more freely. Again, this involves consistent reflection and realization of our own limitations.

Notice, however, that this admission of ignorance and limitation does not preclude beliefs or opinions. Rather, it places them squarely within their proper confines. If we have good reason to believe something, we know that it is still just a belief and that we are not justified into making it anything more.[9] Moreover, if we are consistent and vigilant in our reflections and our criticism of these beliefs—i.e., if we remember to keep them within their proper boundaries as beliefs—we can enjoy them without being seduced into the deception that they are certainties. In Plato's *Phaedo*, the dialogue that recounts Socrates's final day on earth, Socrates relates to his friends a lengthy cosmology and a myth about what happens to souls when the body has died. Remarkably, after this lengthy tale, Socrates says:

> No sensible man would insist that these things are as I have described them, but I think it is fitting for a man to risk the belief—for the risk is a noble [beautiful] one—that this, or something like this, is true about our souls...That is the reason why a man should be of good cheer about his own soul, if during life he has seriously concerned himself with the pleasures of learning, and has adorned his soul not with alien but with its own ornaments,

---

8 Plato, 1997, *Apology* 29a5.
9 This became especially evident to me during a conversation with a student, Kendall Bolin.

namely, moderation, righteousness, courage, freedom and truth, and in that state awaits his journey to the underworld.[10]

Here, after he relays in great detail a cosmology and story of the soul, Socrates admits that it's just a story, but it's one that is beautiful or noble for us to believe. This very recognition, though, places it squarely within the confines of belief and not knowledge. If "no sensible man" would believe that things are exactly as Socrates has said, then that same sensible person would also recognize belief as belief, and be slow to act upon those beliefs where those actions would belie his or her commitment to moderation, righteousness, courage, freedom, and truth.

4 Revisiting Freedom

We should be aware of the vigilance and consistent reflection it takes to recognize and maintain beliefs as beliefs. As I stated above, we have an uncanny tendency to mistake our beliefs for knowledge. We feel as though our beliefs are certainties, and based upon this feeling we sometimes feel compelled to convert others to our "truth." The solution to this is not once and for all to abandon beliefs or one of the great architects of beliefs, imagination. We must rather revisit them regularly, scrutinize them, and remember that, if we are going to hold some particular belief or other, that it is only a belief and not knowledge. Beliefs must, by their very nature, always remain open-ended and mutable. To preserve this mutability, we must allow what I will call here a *restraining idea* to accompany our beliefs. This restraining idea accompanies beliefs to keep them in check. We can ensure this accompaniment by revisiting ourselves and examining consistently, much like Socrates did. We have to remind ourselves that the belief is just a belief and, as such, is much akin to a story that we can revise or relinquish as is appropriate.

Socrates wasn't the only one who put so much stock into the examined life. There were predecessors of his who did the same (Pythagoras, Xenophanes, Heraclitus, etc.) and successors as well. The Cynics, Stoics, Skeptics, and Epicureans each had some sort of philosophical practice. I'd like to bring your attention here to a particular Epicurean practice that illustrates nicely the need to revisit and realize (again) whatever understanding we've gained of ourselves and our world. Epicurus was a hedonist, but of a strange sort. Unlike Socrates, he

---

10 Plato, 1997, *Phaedo* 114d-115a2.

thought that pleasure was the key to happiness or human flourishing, but like Socrates, he de-emphasized bodily pleasure. In fact, he thought that if we accustom ourselves to simple living—bland foods, for example—those simple things will become pleasurable after a time, and we will enjoy richer pleasures all the more when we have them. He emphasized intellectual pleasure. One should learn as much as one can about the physical world (i.e., study physics). Since, according to Epicurus, we are simply physical beings composed of atoms, the more we learn about nature, the more we learn about ourselves. The more we understand, the less we have to fear. This sort of hedonism, thought the Epicureans, leads to *ataraxia*, or the freedom from disturbance.

If, for example, we are just our bodies, then death is literally nothing for us. Fear (and any other emotion that could possibly arise) arises in sentient beings, but in death, we lose all sentience; thus, death is nothing for us (we become nothing) and is therefore not fearsome. Epicurus thought that his followers should memorize basic tenets of his physics and ethics so that they are readily available for contemplation at any time. Why is this important? Since we are changing beings, we cannot merely make one decision to realize the true nature of death, piety, or anything else. We have to revisit these paramount topics in order to realize them all over again. Much as we changing, and changeable, beings cannot simply make a decision to get into good physical condition, but must make it a daily habit or routine, we must also train the mind to habitually realize that which frees us from delusion, falsity, fear, and anxiety. As beings who encounter different situations and events each day—no matter how much like the previous day's events they may seem, they are in fact new and unique, otherwise our lives would be one long day—we must renew our perspective on the world, whether that is renewing the admission of our own ignorance, or remembering what we've learned to apply it to what we are experiencing now.

This is a way of doing philosophy. There are many ways to do philosophy but all of it, if it is true wisdom-loving, must in some way be useful for life, even if it seems only circuitously so. As mentioned above, Socrates says in Plato's *Republic* that the majority thinks philosophers are useless because they do not make use of philosophers. In an analogy discussing who should captain a ship, Socrates says that the majority doesn't:

> ...understand that a true captain must pay attention to the season of the year, the sky, the stars, the winds, and all that pertains to his craft, if he's really to be the ruler of a ship. And they [i.e., the majority] don't believe there is any craft that would enable him to determine how he should steer the ship, whether the others want him to or not, or any possibility of mastering this alleged craft or of practicing it at the same time as the craft of navigation.

> Don't you think that the true captain will be called a real stargazer, a babbler, and a good-for-nothing by those who sail in ships governed in that way...?[11]

It will be easy and common, especially in our hasty and harried age, to see the often slow, ruminating craft of the philosopher as ineffectual babble. Truth be told, many academic and professional philosophers have probably done their part in shaping this image. If, however, we turn away from mind-gymnastics and polemical periodicals towards the big questions, we will see first-hand why they are worth asking. We will, in short, be doing philosophy and we will know its use. We will be freer for it. We will know and live the craft of freedom, while others merely rush after an impoverished, vague mirage of it.

Bibliography

Plato. *Plato: Complete Works*. John M. Cooper (Ed.). Indianapolis: Hackett Publishing, 1997.

---

[11] Plato, 1997, *Republic* 488d-e.

Patrick Stokes
The House Always Wins: Why Philosophy Isn't Optional

Abstract: A prominent strand of criticism of contemporary philosophy comes from high-profile physicists and science communicators. Figures such as Stephen Hawking, Lawrence Krauss and Neil Degrasse Tyson have claimed that philosophy is obsolete, unproductive, and an obstacle to genuine inquiry. Yet all these critiques end up falling into the same trap: they all end up trying to philosophize their way out of doing philosophy. This failure is instructive. It points to the way in which, far from being a relic of an earlier phase of intellectual inquiry we should put aside, philosophy is in fact something we cannot avoid engaging in.

> Philosophy through the millennia is one like one great hymn to reason—though it continually misunderstands itself as finished knowledge, and declines continually into reasonless understanding. As a result, it is always falling into a false contempt of the understanding, and has always been despised as an overbearing demand upon men that permits them no peace.
> Karl Jaspers, *Philosophy of Existence*

1 Introduction

Socrates notoriously said that to philosophize is to practice for death. But philosophers these days get pretty well-practiced in other things too, not least of which is self-justification. To be a professional philosopher is, in large measure, to be continually justifying your existence to people who are surprisingly comfortable dismissing your life's work as a pointless indulgence. Perhaps it's someone at a party who looks at you askance when you tell them what you do. Perhaps it's some random person online who thinks people like you are an unproductive drag on the public purse. Perhaps it's a politician describing your hard-won research funding as "ridiculous" or a "waste."[1]

Or perhaps it's a famous public scientist. Indeed, the "rock star astrophysicist" demographic seems to be uncommonly prone to attacking philosophy. First

---

[1] Bernard Lane, 2013.

Stephen Hawking declared philosophy "dead,"[2] then Lawrence Krauss accused philosophy of offering only "essentially sterile, backward, useless and annoying" answers,[3] and, most recently, Neil deGrasse Tyson dismissed it as unhelpfully "distracting."[4] We can distil most of these criticisms into two main, interconnected claims: philosophy doesn't tell us anything novel, important, or interesting; and it doesn't help us advance our practical interests.

Defending philosophy from these sorts of criticisms can take a variety of forms. Sometimes, we argue for the instrumental value of studying philosophy. We appeal to statistics that show philosophy graduates go on to earn more than their contemporaries (usually without actually stopping to ask *why* that's the case; does philosophy enhance your earning capacity, or do people with high earning capacities gravitate to philosophy?). Or more broadly, we appeal to the value of critical reasoning skills for the workplace. Whenever I'm asked "What job will a philosophy degree get me?" at a university open day, I tend to point out that a student embarking on their first degree today will be in the workforce well into the 2070s, and will likely retire from a job that hasn't been invented yet—but they'll still be benefiting from the generic reasoning skills they've learnt in the philosophy classroom. Admittedly, reminding someone that we're closer in time to the moon landing than we are to their retirement party doesn't always win them over, but it helps get the point across: life is long and vocational skills come and go, but clear thinking is forever.

Alternatively, in our more high-minded moments, we'll appeal to the *intrinsic* value of philosophy. Philosophy isn't worth studying simply because it will give you a better career, but also because it will make you a better person, or will give you a deeper understanding of matters of enduring human interest. This sort of non-instrumental defense of philosophy is vital, but difficult to pull off. Intrinsic value is always hard to talk about; we simply end up pointing furiously at what we value while shouting "don't you see just how *good* that is?" It's a form of argument that largely relies on our listener having the same intuitions as us—and it's far from certain that they do. Even so, simply insisting that there *is* such value, and trying to articulate it as best we can, remains an indispensable task if we're to avoid fighting for philosophy on an instrumentalist battleground of the enemy's choosing.

All of these are important answers to the question, "Why bother with philosophy?" Here, however, I want to take a slightly different approach to meeting

---

2 Stephen Hawking and Leonard Mlodinow, 2010, p. 13.
3 Lawrence M. Krauss, 2012.
4 Katie Levine, 2014.

these challenges. Instead of arguing for philosophy's intrinsic or instrumental value, I want to use its opponents' arguments against themselves, by showing how the very attempt to critique philosophy *itself* depends upon philosophical reasoning. Using Hawking, Krauss, and Tyson as examples, I will try to bring out what we might call the *unavoidability* of doing philosophy. The attempt to bracket philosophical questions is at best only temporarily successful and at worst instantly self-defeating. Philosophy, it turns out, is not optional. We all end up philosophizing, whether we realize it or not; we can simply do it well, or badly.

2 Philosophy Is Dead (Long Live Philosophy?)

There is considerable overlap between Hawking and Krauss, and another overlap between Krauss and Tyson, in their criticisms of philosophy. With respect to the first, here's Hawking and Leonard Mlodinow in their 2010 book *The Grand Design:*

> How can we understand the world in which we find ourselves? How does the universe behave? What is the nature of reality? Where did all this come from? Did the universe need a creator? Most of us do not spend most of our time worrying about these questions, but almost all of us worry about them some of the time. Traditionally, these are questions for philosophy, but philosophy is dead.
>
> Philosophy has not kept up with modern developments in science, particularly physics. Scientists have become the bearers of the torch of discovery in our quest for knowledge.[5]

Philosophy, for Hawking, appears to be a failed competitor to science, or at best an earlier stage in science's development that has continued to lumber away as an increasingly moribund and irrelevant research program. Leave aside, for the moment, the question of just how much philosophy is actually involved in astrophysics, particularly at its more speculative, unfalsifiable end.[6] (Later in the book, for instance, we're told that the Weak Anthropic Principle "may sound like philosophy" but can nonetheless "be used to make scientific predictions"[7] —if generating testable hypotheses is the dividing line between science and philosophy, things don't look so good for string theory, for example.) What should be immediately apparent to even the most generous reader of Hawking is just

---

5 Hawking and Mlodinow, 2013, p. 13.
6 For a response to Hawking on these lines, see Christopher Norris, 2011.
7 Hawking and Mlodinow, 2013, p. 195.

how drastically both "philosophy" and "knowledge" have been gerrymandered here. To declare philosophy dead *tout court* on the grounds that its questions have been answered by science is to ignore a whole range of philosophical questions—not least those of ethics—and to assume that science (and specifically physics) can answer such questions exhaustively. In other words, it's to start from a set of assumptions about the scope of both knowledge and of philosophy that need to be defended. Why should we think that philosophy is *only* concerned with the sorts of questions physics has answered, and why should we think physics' answers satisfactory to philosophers?

Krauss makes much the same move as Hawking, albeit in rather more piquant terms, and in a stronger form; he holds that philosophy has been superseded not simply because it progresses more slowly than science, but because it doesn't progress at all:

> Philosophy used to be a field that had content, but then "natural philosophy" became physics, and physics has only continued to make inroads. Every time there's a leap in physics, it encroaches on these areas that philosophers have carefully sequestered away to themselves, and so then you have this natural resentment on the part of philosophers. [...] Philosophy is a field that, unfortunately, reminds me of that old Woody Allen joke, "those that can't do, teach, and those that can't teach, teach gym." And the worst part of philosophy is the philosophy of science; the only people, as far as I can tell, that read work by philosophers of science are other philosophers of science. It has no impact on physics whatsoever, and I doubt that other philosophers read it because it's fairly technical. And so it's really hard to understand what justifies it. And so I'd say that this tension occurs because people in philosophy feel threatened, and they have every right to feel threatened, because science progresses and philosophy doesn't.[8]

There are legitimate questions to be asked about whether philosophy can, should, or does make progress, and how philosophical progress is to be understood. Krauss, however, seems to be insisting that "progress" is simply coextensive with "answering the questions physicists are interested in." So again, we have a conception of philosophy having been left in the dust by its children, who went after the same goals philosophy was aiming for and got there first. While Krauss has since moderated some of his criticisms of philosophy,[9] he still seems to think that the only philosophical questions are those that "grow up, leave home, and live elsewhere"[10] —that is, become questions for empirical fields. Even the other disciplines within philosophy turn out, according to

---

[8] Ross Andersen, 2012.
[9] Lawrence M. Krauss, 2012, "The Consolation of Philosophy."
[10] Julian Baggini and Lawrence Krauss, 2012.

Krauss, to be largely subsumed within other fields; ethics within political science, for instance. A question that doesn't make that move away from philosophy is not, in the end, an "answerable" question, where "answerable" means "empirically determinable." If Krauss is aware of how many contestable assumptions he's making here, he doesn't seem to be letting on.

3 No Time for Philosophy

Krauss also complains that philosophy of science is of little practical use for scientists. That's a familiar criticism. There's a quote sometimes attributed to the physicist Richard Feynman that sums this attitude up well: "Philosophy of science is about as useful to scientists as ornithology is to birds." In a podcast interview, Neil deGrasse Tyson has also expressed a very similar view:

> My concern here is that the philosophers believe they are actually asking deep questions about nature. And to the scientist it's, what are you doing? Why are you concerning yourself with the meaning of meaning? [...] if you are distracted by your questions so that you can't move forward, you are not being a productive contributor to our understanding of the natural world. And so the scientist knows when the question "what is the sound of one hand clapping?" is a pointless delay in our progress. [...] How do you define clapping? All of a sudden it devolves into a discussion of the definition of words. And I'd rather keep the conversation about ideas. And when you do that don't derail yourself on questions that you think are important because philosophy class tells you this. The scientist says look, I got all this world of unknown out there, I'm moving on, I'm leaving you behind. You can't even cross the street because you are distracted by what you are sure are deep questions you've asked yourself. I don't have the time for that.[11]

There are two criticisms here: that philosophy gets in the way of doing meaningful and productive scientific work, and that it dissolves into mere verbal disagreement. I'll come back to the latter criticism later. As to the former, the first thing to note about this criticism is that it's not entirely false. On a purely pragmatic level, scientists would barely get anything done at all if they were continually wondering whether there was such a thing as a real external world, or whether there are any valid knowledge claims. As Thomas Kuhn noted, scientific paradigms cause a distinctive narrowing in the range of problems and questions available to practitioners working within that paradigm. That narrowing turns out to be essential to scientific progress, because it forces scientists to "investigate some part of nature in a detail and depth that would otherwise be unima-

---

11 Katie Levine, 2014.

ginable."[12] Without this narrowing of focus, such sustained investigation would be impossible. And if this is true on the level of individual scientific paradigms it is surely even more true on the level of the relation of science to philosophical questions about epistemic warrant and ontological status. Indeed, Kuhn notes, in periods of "normal science," when scientific paradigms appear to be working well and the research programs they generate are solving progressively more problems, science "usually holds creative philosophy at arm's length, and probably for good reasons."[13] It's only when scientists enter periods of crisis, with the paradigm no longer functioning as well as it should, that scientists start articulating, in philosophical terms, the tacit rules and assumptions of the paradigm—a process that tends to hasten the paradigm's fragmentation and collapse.

Hence a lack of philosophical engagement arguably helps to sustain the very certainty in the scientific method and its methodological assumptions that keeps scientists going. Yet this can only be achieved at the cost of a certain amnesia. For instance, a core assumption of contemporary science is a commitment to *naturalism*—a term which can be interpreted in various ways, but which very roughly means that supernatural entities can't play any role in scientific explanations.[14] Such a condition seems almost definitional of scientific inquiry, which seems *necessarily* to presuppose a causally closed, uniformly law-governed universe. Yet we only have to go back as far as Newton to see supernatural explanations turning up in physics. Newton's mathematics couldn't quite explain why the orbits of the planets didn't decay over time given their perturbation of each other's orbits. So, he appealed to the ad-hoccest of ad hoc hypotheses: every so often God intervenes to put the planets back into their proper trajectories, like a sort of divine cosmic plate spinner.[15] Yet few scientists would want to claim that Newton therefore wasn't really a scientist, or that Newtonian mechanics are unscientific. Rather, they have to take a curiously ahistorical view of their subject, acknowledging the past as a backdrop (perhaps supplying a grand "emergence from unreason" narrative of the sort Tyson perpetuates in his recent

---

12 Thomas Kuhn, 1970, p. 24.
13 Thomas Kuhn, 1970, p. 88.
14 This is a fairly minimal and methodological construal of naturalism. Stronger (e. g., ontological) versions are also available.
15 See e. g., Isaac Newton, 1718, p. 378. "For while Comets move in very excentrick Orbs in all manner of Positions, blind Fate could never make all the Planets move one and the same way in Orbs concentrick, some inconsiderable irregularities excepted which may have risen from the mutual Actions of Comets and Planets upon one another, and which will be apt to increase, til this System wants a Reformation."

remake of Carl Sagan's TV series, *Cosmos*)[16] while taking its own tacit—and historically contingent and recent—methodological assumptions as timeless and unquestionable truths. The lack of philosophical curiosity that Tyson advocates also cuts the scientist off from the history of their practice—the very history whose progress the scientist takes herself to be contributing to.

4 Stumbling into the Philosophical

I haven't really offered anything like a reply to the specific criticisms Hawking, Krauss, and Tyson make, other than to draw out a couple of questionable implications of their claims. Rather, I want to ask a more general question: what *sort* of critique are they engaged in here?

One thing we can say straight away: it's not a properly *scientific* critique. The claims that philosophy doesn't progress, doesn't trade in "answerable" questions, and distracts scientists from doing their job, are not offered as empirical hypotheses to be tested, let alone as part of any ongoing scientific research program. They are claims *about* science, and to a certain extent they express methodological *presuppositions* of science, but that doesn't make them scientific claims—any more than an ornithological proposition is thereby a bird. Rather, Hawking et al seem to be doing to philosophy what philosophy does to other disciplines. Fields like philosophy of science, philosophy of education, philosophy of art, and so on present themselves as meta-disciplines that interrogate the assumptions and claims of their "target" disciplines. Philosophers of science, for instance, ask questions about the epistemic validity of the scientific method— a question which science itself can't answer, except by the hopelessly circular project of using the scientific method to investigate whether or not the scientific method works! So, in asking whether philosophy produces progressively better

---

16 "Characteristically, textbooks of science contain just a bit of history, either in an introductory chapter or, more often, in scattered references to the great heroes of an earlier age. From such references both students and professionals come to feel like participants in a long-standing historical tradition. Yet the textbook-derived tradition in which scientists come to sense their participation is one that, in fact, never existed. [...] Partly by selection and partly by distortion, the scientists of earlier ages are implicitly represented as having worked upon the same set of fixed problems and in accordance with the same set of fixed canons that the most recent revolution in scientific theory and method has made seem scientific. No wonder that textbooks and the historical tradition they imply have to be rewritten after each scientific revolution." Thomas Kuhn, 1970, pp. 137–8.

knowledge, or any knowledge at all, we might say these critics are simply giving philosophy a taste of its own medicine.

But that medicine tastes decidedly philosophical. As we've already seen, Hawking and Krauss's comments embed a number of claims about what does and does not count as knowledge, and what progress consists in. These aren't delimited to what counts as knowledge or progress *within a particular practice or domain*; to simply say that what scientists mean by "knowledge" and what philosophers mean by "knowledge" are two different things and leave it at that isn't a critique of either philosophy or science, and that's not what Krauss, Hawking, and Tyson are doing either. Krauss, after all, began his critique of philosophy in response to philosophical objections to his use of the term "nothing" compared to how philosophers understand "nothing."[17] But he doesn't simply leave it at noting these divergent uses of the term; instead, he insists that his understanding as a physicist of "nothing" is the superior one, because the more productive.

A defender of Krauss might insist that the term "productive" here is simply being used as shorthand for "scientifically productive," and that when he says philosophy offers answers that are "essentially sterile, backward, useless and annoying,"[18] these terms are likewise indexed to scientific practice. But in that case, there's no critique of philosophy going on here, which Krauss clearly takes himself to be engaged in. He is thus appealing to some set of standards of fecundity, progressiveness, utility, and gratification against which *both* science and philosophy can be judged, and in terms of which philosophy comes out a distant second. But now we're entitled to ask: what *are* these standards? Where do they come from? What makes an answer "useless" or "sterile"? Why should its being "annoying" (or gratifying, or elegant for that matter) count for or against its being true? Likewise, Tyson's complaint that philosophy "devolves into a discussion of the definition of words" where he would "rather keep the conversation about ideas" involves an appeal to standards that need some serious articulation and defense: What, for instance, is the distinction between "words" and "ideas"? What is the substantive difference between these two modes of argument, and why is one superior to the other?

---

17 In Lawrence M. Krauss, 2012, *A Universe From Nothing: Why There Is Something Rather Than Nothing*. Philosophical criticism of Krauss came in the form of David Albert, 2012. Albert admits his critique is "quick, and crude, and concrete," and it certainly pulls few punches. Krauss responded by calling Albert a "moronic philosopher," in Andersen, "Has Physics Made Philosophy and Religion Obsolete?"

18 Lawrence M. Krauss, 2012, "The Consolation of Philosophy."

Phrased thus, it becomes pretty clear that the sort of meta-philosophical discourse that these philosophy refusers are engaged in is recognizably still *philosophical* in character. In seeking to condemn philosophy, Hawking et al have actually ended up engaging in an *implicitly philosophical critique of philosophy*. And in fact, given the nature of philosophy, that is precisely what we should have expected. There's no necessary impediment to there being meta-philosophical disciplines that aren't themselves philosophical (though in practice history of philosophy tends to be philosophical in character, while a sociology of philosophy still seems to be in the process of emerging),[19] but philosophy, due to its conceptually foundational character, tends to encompass discussions *about* philosophy. For instance, philosophy has the somewhat unique property of adjudicating its own boundary disputes, as Wittgenstein notes: "One might think: if philosophy speaks of the use of the word 'philosophy' there must be a second-order philosophy. But it is not so: it is, rather, like the case of orthography, which deals with the word 'orthography' among others without then being second-order."[20]

Just as orthography can spell the word "orthography," or etymology can trace the origin of the word "etymology," without either turning into another, higher-order discipline, so too philosophy deals with the question "What is philosophy?" without stepping outside itself. Likewise, the sort of epistemic critique of philosophy that Krauss and Hawking offer doesn't succeed in reaching philosophical escape velocity. In asking whether philosophy produces genuine knowledge, they're doing epistemology. They're making claims, implicitly or otherwise, about what does and doesn't count as knowledge, and about what sort of standards we should apply in comparing competing knowledge claims. And that is *itself* a task for epistemology.

The same point holds when we shift from questions of knowledge to questions of value. Tyson warns scientists not to mess with philosophy, for fear it will slow them down and distract them from their core task, which is to progress scientific research programs. Charitably, one might say that Tyson is merely saying that *scientifically* it's better to stay away from philosophy (a hypothetical imperative: *if* you want to do science, *then* you should avoid philosophy), which, again, sets up no genuine critique of philosophy as such. And yet this is hard to reconcile with his point about philosophy devolving into semantic quibbling. So, I don't think it's too egregious a violation of the principle of charity to conclude that Tyson is making an implicit value claim: science is a *better* activity to

---

[19] See e.g., Randall Collins, 1988; and Maren Kusch, 2000.
[20] Ludwig Wittgenstein, 1968, 49e.

direct one's energies to. And that, in turn, activates a whole raft of philosophical questions: *Why* is this the better activity? What sort of value is this? How does it stand in relation to other forms of value? What makes it normative? In warning us against entanglement with philosophy, Tyson, like Krauss and Hawking, appeals to crypto-philosophical claims that can then only be defended philosophically. What looked like the path out of philosophy has led them right back into the fly-bottle.

5 Philosophy Cannot Be Stopped

In the epigraph that begins this essay, Jaspers notes that philosophy is often "despised as an overbearing demand upon men that permits them no peace." Such an irritation and impatience with philosophy is operative in the criticisms we've looked at here: philosophy gets in the way of our simply *getting on with it*, by bogging us down in intractable, disorienting questions that admit of no easy or final answers. Something like that is also operative in a great many of the more mundane, everyday dismissals of philosophy one hears in the modern *agora*. What's the point of spending your life engaged in such frivolities? Why should the taxpayer fund people to carry out this sort of research?

In some ways, the response I've offered here to condemnations of the value of philosophy is not dissimilar to a discursive move three-year-olds tend to make: ask a question, then reply to any answer received with "Why?" And, if you've been on the receiving end of those "Why?"s, you know that the answers you're compelled to give get philosophical fairly quickly.[21] The child that does this isn't trying to be annoying so much as she is simply following the inexorable logic of inquiry. That reiterative "Why?" questions lead children into philosophical territory tells us something very important. It tells us precisely what Hawking, Krauss and Tyson's collapse back into philosophy also tells us: like an inquisitive three-year-old, *philosophy cannot be stopped*, except by arbitrary expedients ("Because I said so!") that are a violation rather than a conclusion of that logic of inquiry. The movement of philosophical reflection, as Kierkegaard notes in his unfinished manuscript *Johannes Climacus, or De Omnibus Dubitandum Est*, cannot be brought to a halt by its own internal movement, for that

---

[21] Similarly, if you click on the first hyperlinked word that isn't a proper noun in any Wikipedia entry, then click the first such word in the page that link takes you to, and so on, it's remarkable that you almost inevitably end up back at the entry for 'philosophy' in short order.

movement is precisely one of relentless doubt. Every conclusion reached becomes just another object for its questioning.[22]

That's not to say there aren't sometimes good grounds for temporarily bracketing some questions in order to get started with inquiry. As noted, scientists do have to assume the scientific method and its assumptions to be empirically sound in order to do science at all. And the people Jaspers is describing are right too: philosophy doesn't give us pause, so we have to take our rest breaks from it more or less by force. Even philosophers need a break sometimes, as described in familiar and charming terms by David Hume:

> Where am I, or what? From what causes do I derive my existence, and to what condition shall I return? Whose favour shall I court, and whose anger must I dread? What beings surround me? and on whom have, I any influence, or who have any influence on me? I am confounded with all these questions, and begin to fancy myself in the most deplorable condition imaginable, invironed with the deepest darkness, and utterly deprived of the use of every member and faculty. Most fortunately it happens, that since reason is incapable of dispelling these clouds, nature herself suffices to that purpose, and cures me of this philosophical melancholy and delirium, either by relaxing this bent of mind, or by some avocation, and lively impression of my senses, which obliterate all these chimeras. I dine, I play a game of backgammon, I converse, and am merry with my friends; and when after three or four hours' amusement, I would return to these speculations, they appear so cold, and strained, and ridiculous, that I cannot find in my heart to enter into them any farther.[23]

Things go wrong, however, when we think we can simply leave those questions in stasis forever, or worse, that by ignoring them we've actually disposed of them. As Kuhn's point about philosophy of science reappearing in times of crisis suggests, philosophical questions don't stay buried forever. And, as we've seen, the very attempt to close them off permanently is *itself* a philosophical move, or one that can only be defended philosophically. Moliere famously has a philosophy master explain to the bourgeois M. Jourdain that everything that's not verse is prose, whereupon Jourdain is astonished to realize he's been speaking prose all his life without knowing it. In like fashion, even the opponents of philosophy end up doing philosophy. The very attempt to get out of doing it sucks us back into its orbit—so if we're doomed to philosophize anyway, we might as well do it properly. Hume may have found the backgammon to be the best temporary cure for a philosophical spirit, but philosophy itself is the casino: try and game the system all you want, but the house always wins.

---

22 Søren Kierkegaard, 1985.
23 David Hume, 1826, pp. 340–1.

Bibliography

Albert, David. "On the Origin of Everything." Review of *A Universe From Nothing*, by Lawrence M. Krauss. *The New York Times*, March 23, 2012. http://www.nytimes.com/2012/03/25/books/review/a-universe-from-nothing-by-lawrence-m-krauss.html.

Andersen, Ross. "Has Physics Made Philosophy and Religion Obsolete?" *The Atlantic*, April 23, 2012. http://www.theatlantic.com/technology/archive/2012/04/has-physics-made-philosophy-and-religion-obsolete/256203/.

Baggini, Julian, and Lawrence Krauss. "Philosophy vs. Science: Which Can Answer the Big Questions of Life?" *The Observer*, September 9, 2012. http://www.theguardian.com/science/2012/sep/09/science-philosophy-debate-julian-baggini-lawrence-krauss.

Collins, Randall. *The Sociology of Philosophies: A Global Theory of Intellectual Change*. Cambridge, MA: Harvard University Press, 1988.

Hawking, Stephen, and Leonard Mlodinow. *The Grand Design: New Answers to the Ultimate Questions of Life*. London: Bantam, 2010.

Hume, David. *The Philosophical Works of David Hume*, vol. 1. Edinburgh: Black and Tait, 1826.

Jaspers, Karl. *Philosophy of Existence*. Richard F. Grabau (Trans.). Philadelphia: University of Philadelphia Press, 1971.

Kierkegaard, Søren. *Philosophical Fragments* and *Johannes Climacus, or De Omnibus Dubitandum Est*. Translated by Howard V. Hong and Edna H. Hong. Princeton: Princeton University Press, 1985.

Krauss, Lawrence M. "The Consolation of Philosophy." *Scientific American* 27 (April 2012): http://www.scientificamerican.com/article/the-consolation-of-philos.

Krauss, Lawrence M. *A Universe From Nothing: Why There Is Something Rather Than Nothing*. New York: Free Press, 2012.

Kuhn, Thomas. *The Structure of Scientific Revolutions*. Second Edition. Chicago: University of Chicago Press, 1970.

Kusch, Maren, (Ed.) *The Sociology of Philosophical Knowledge*. Dordrecht: Springer, 2000.

Lane, Bernard. "Coalition Angers Research Community." *The Australian*, September 6, 2013. http://www.theaustralian.com.au/higher-education/coalition-angers-research-community/story-e6frgcjx-1226712215714.

Levine, Katie. "Nerdist Podcast: Neil deGrasse Tyson Returns Again." *Nerdist*, March 7, 2014. https://soundcloud.com/the-nerdist/neil-degrasse-tyson-returns-3.

Newton, Isaac. *Opticks: Or, a Treatise of the Reflections, Refractions, Inflections, and Colours of Light*. 2nd ed. London: W&J Innys, 1718.

Norris, Christopher. "Hawking Contra Philosophy." *Philosophy Now*, no. 82 (January/February 2011). https://philosophynow.org/issues/82/Hawking_contra_Philosophy.

Wittgenstein, Ludwig. *Philosophical Investigations*. G. E. M. Anscombe (Trans.). Oxford: Basil Blackwell, 1968.

Paolo Diego Bubbio
Why We Need Philosophy – and Philosophers

Abstract: The chapter develops the argument that it is impossible to do without philosophy, because philosophy is everywhere, whether one realizes or not. The chapter then advocates for a conception of philosophy as ongoing conversation that is, simultaneously, an interpretation of the world and an attempt to change the world.

1 "Philosophy is that thing…"

When I started to study philosophy, my grandmother used to mock me by repeating an Italian adage: "Philosophy is that thing with or without which everything remains the same" ("*la filosofia è quella cosa con o senza la quale tutto rimane tale e quale*"; in Italian, there is a rhyme in it, which adds a funny effect). At face value, this claim seems to express the thought that the presence of philosophy (and philosophers) has never changed anything in the world, or even that philosophy is structurally incapable of having an actual impact on the world. Moreover, while the claim is descriptive (it purportedly tells us what philosophy is, or what it does—or better, what it does not do), its practical use is clearly meant to express a normative (in this case, quite derogatory) judgment. It is meant to expose the "fact" that philosophy does not change anything—something that, clearly, is regarded as being a "bad" thing. In other words, the claim implies the existence of a goal ("change"), and then it judges philosophy for its lack of capacity to reach such a goal. It judges the *usefulness* of philosophy. Therefore, someone might say that everything comes down to the question, "Is philosophy useful?"[1]

While I maintain that, when we talk about philosophy, there is something correct about the reference to the idea of change (I will come back to this in the second section of this chapter), I think that turning the question into an analysis of the "usefulness" of philosophy is actually a very misleading approach. I could show why it is misleading the long way, by investigating what "useful" precisely means—that is, by using a technique that is almost as old as philoso-

---

[1] Some of the ideas in this chapter were already included in a very short piece published elsewhere: Paolo Diego Bubbio, 2013, pp. 32–33.

phy itself, namely, the Socratic method. Someone might, however, object that this is still a philosophical self-defense "trick." In this instance, therefore, I will refrain from employing such strategy. Rather, let us have a look at the definition of "useful" provided by the Oxford Dictionary: "able to be used for a practical purpose or in several ways." We could concede that philosophy is not, according to this definition, "useful"—but neither are several other human disciplines and activities useful. Think of all the efforts employed (and money spent!) to send a human being to the moon or to run a particle accelerator to look at the subatomic structure of matter. Such endeavors are not "useful" in the sense of any immediate and predictable practical use; and yet they are commonly perceived as worthy of effort. There is, therefore, a sense in which there is a common perception that attempts to increase knowledge about the world are worthy, even if they are not "useful" (according to common standards of "usefulness").

You see that I am developing my argument with a hypothetical interlocutor in mind, someone who is not sympathetic to philosophy and its worthiness (and indeed, there is no shortage of such characters, both in everyday life and in the public debate). For the sake of convenience, let us give a name to such hypothetical interlocutor—Alpha. It is not difficult to imagine, therefore, that Alpha would object that my previous argument does not make a convincing point. Assuming Alpha agrees that there is worth in increasing knowledge per se, regardless of its practical use, Alpha might still object that sending a human to the moon or running a particle accelerator are instances of *scientific* achievements; and science is objective—namely, it tells us how things really are and work. This objection is allegedly justified on the grounds of two (either simultaneous or alternative) implications: first, that a scientific discovery might not have an immediate practical use today, but that one day it might *become* useful (thus bringing the question of worth back to the question of usefulness); second, that a scientific discovery has worth in itself because it contributes to the *progressive* nature of science, which *progressively* builds up on its achievements (and, sometimes, failures). In both cases, the objection relies on a distinction between scientific disciplines, whose main feature is identified in their "objectivity," and those disciplines collectively referred to as "the humanities," that is, disciplines concerned with the study of the various aspects of human cultures.

To answer this objection, one could question the very distinction it relies on, i.e., that of "the sciences" being objective, and "the humanities" being intrinsically "subjective" or, insofar as they are regarded as employing an essentially interpretative methodology, being unable to achieve the same degree of objectivity as the sciences. For instance, one could appeal to the work of Paul Feyerabend (1975) and to his radical assault on the rationality and objectivity of scientific method; but again, our interlocutor could dismiss our rebuttal as a philosophical self-justification—and admittedly, Feyerabend's critique of science is highly disputed within philosophy itself. Rather, let us keep the argument on a more "ordinary" level. The "objectivity" objection is directed towards all the humanities: not only philosophy, but also history, anthropology, religious studies, etc. What is the point, for instance, in investigating the cultural roots of a religious dispute in a country far away from our own? And yet we all know, or have recently become aware of, the importance of such things in a globalized world such as ours, the point being that if something is important for someone somewhere, it might soon become important to us as well. To ignore or underestimate any aspect of human culture means exposing ourselves and our civilization to dangerous risks. As evidence of the seriousness of this risk, consider an article published in the *New York Times* of October 17, 2006. The journalist Jeff Stein asked several Washington counterterrorism officials the following question: "Do you know the difference between a Sunni and a Shiite?" He was not looking for theological explanations, just the basics: Who's on what side today, and what does each want? The outcome of this inquiry was that most American officials he has interviewed did not have a clue. That includes not just intelligence and law enforcement officials, but also members of Congress who have important roles overseeing U.S. intelligence agencies that were (and still are) operating in Iraq and Afghanistan. Clearly, one cannot rely on science and technology alone to understand the cultural implications of such religious dispute. This subject belongs to the humanities. Needless to say, a better knowledge about the difference between a Sunni and a Shiite could have avoided mistakes that had (and still have) very concrete, and serious, consequences. At this point, we can imagine that Alpha might perhaps be willing to concede that the humanities could be useful and/or of worth sometimes. However, Alpha might still want to draw a distinction *within* the humanities. Some of the humanities even won the title of "social *sciences*," because they interpret collectable data: anthropology, sociology, or religious studies could fit this description. Even history could be included in such category (broadly conceived). But, our interlocutor would continue, philosophy cannot: philosophy is the most abstract of the humanities, and it is detached from "concrete reality," is it not?

At that point, I would probably shock Alpha by making a big claim, namely, that everything in the human cultural world is somehow connected with philosophy. Art, music, literature—even science. Without philosophy, we would not have Galileo, or Newton. Galileo was heavily influenced by Neoplatonic philosophy. Newton was, in addition to a scientist, a philosopher, and his idea of God was extremely important in the way he approached (and changed) science. Without philosophy, we would not have poets such as Dante Alighieri (his *Commedia* has a Thomistic structure) or Coleridge (strongly influenced by Schelling and German Idealism). Without philosophy, we would not have artist such as Michelangelo (whose philosophy of art is markedly Neoplatonic).

Once Alpha has overcome any possible shock at my claim that philosophy is connected, and especially *historically* connected (Alpha would probably emphasize this point) with everything in the human cultural world, Alpha could launch his counter-attack: philosophy has been *so far* related to literature, poetry, and art—and so what? Perhaps we can have literature, poetry and art without philosophy now. And even if we cannot (I am pretty sure that I would be able to convince Alpha about this), who says that we need music, poetry—the arts in general? I do not know about Alpha, but a world without music, poetry, and arts seems a sad world to me—one in which I would not like to live. But let us assume for a moment that we are willing to get rid of the arts. Does it mean that we can do without philosophy?

No, even in that case, we could not do without philosophy. Because philosophy is everywhere—whether one realizes it or not. Think of everyday life. We wake up early because we have *responsibilities*—a job, for instance. We spend time with our family because we care about them, or simply because we consider it a *duty*, or because this is what everybody does; we go to church (or we do not) because we think there is a God (or there is not). Usually we don't question these things, but sometimes we might ask questions such as: why did I lose my job? Society is structured in such and such a way; couldn't society be different? I decided to stay home with my kids rather than playing football with my pals, something I really wanted to do—I put my responsibility as a father over my personal desire; was it the right thing to do? And why? The God I am praying to at the Church—is he really up there? What does God look like? Or rather: I do not believe in God—but am I really sure that there is nothing at all beyond this life?

At this point, Alpha might have the image of the philosopher as someone who stops in front his car every morning thinking, "Should I drive my car or walk?"—and questioning every single action. Clearly that is not the way it works. Philosophers are not lost in some kind of navel-gazing activity. We all do things without questioning their meaning, and the philosopher is no exception. The philosopher is just someone who has been trained (and maybe has a natural inclination) to ask relevant questions and to try to answer them in a rational way.

A sort of experiment, which I sometimes use during the first lecture of an Introduction to Philosophy class, can illustrate this point. At the very beginning of the lecture, I ask three students to volunteer, and I invite them to look out the classroom window. I ask them to look at the landscape and to choose one element of it, the one that they think is the most important element of the landscape, or the one that strikes their attention, and to write it on a piece of paper. Then I read what they wrote. Usually each of them choses a different aspect of the landscape: someone choses a building, someone else a tree, someone else a person walking downstairs. If I ask them to justify their choice, they usually provide very good answers: the building is bigger than anything else, the tree is older than anything else, the person is an intelligent entity, etc. This is one of the reasons why philosophy is important—I tell them: each philosophical thought is a world-view, a point of view on reality; and the fact that a philosophical theory emphasizes an aspect of reality more than another does not automatically mean that it is "wrong." Or, that these theories are "useless" or worthless.

At this point, I think our friend Alpha would choose a different strategy. In fact, my line of argument could allow Alpha to object that if, as I argued, philosophy is everywhere, and we all somehow deal with "philosophical thoughts," then everybody is a philosopher. Hence, there is no need for professional philosophers—and even less need to support them in public universities. Isn't it true, Alpha might continue, that I can work in a bank, or as a builder, and then read some books and engage in some philosophical thinking for an hour before going to bed?

Alpha is not completely mistaken here. Of course, Alpha and everybody else can engage in philosophical thinking in their free time. Everyone can philosophize. Everyone can also play soccer. I can play soccer on Saturday afternoon and enjoy myself. But a professional soccer player is obviously more capable than I am at playing soccer. In part this is because he is more talented at soccer than I am. In part, this is because he has spent and he is still spending most of his time training as a soccer player. He has skills that I do not have, and he knows things that I do not know. He can, therefore, achieve goals in his profession that I could never achieve playing soccer as an amateur. The same applies to philosophy (as well as to everything else).

Now Alpha could change his strategy again. He might concede that philosophy is important, and that those who are trained in the discipline develop better philosophizing skills. Fair enough—but what is the benefit of such activity? He might even concede that questioning one's life, actions, and thoughts can be a healthy and useful *individual* activity—but he could still object that philosophy does not make any real impact or provide any benefit on society.

It is not difficult to confute this objection, because one can mention several philosophical ideas that throughout history have drastically changed society and human life as a whole. Here I just mention one of those ideas: human rights. Today, the idea that there are fundamental rights to which a person is entitled simply because she or he is a human being (regardless of color, gender, religion, etc.) is a milestone of our culture, one which is adopted (at least theoretically!) in all Western countries and that nobody would openly dismiss without immediately becoming the subject of collective disdain. However, the idea of "human rights" did not appear out of nowhere. It was the outcome of a complex and long philosophical work. Not the work of a single philosopher, but the result of slow elaboration and different (even contrasting) theorizations that spanned the seventeenth and eighteenth centuries, through the work of philosophers such as John Locke and Francis Hutcheson. And the idea of human rights was not adopted the day after these works were published. Actually, to most people of the time the very idea of human rights probably sounded futile and ridiculous. This did not stop the philosophical work—luckily for us. Finally, the United States Declaration of Independence included the concept of "natural rights," and the French Declaration of the Rights of Man and Citizen featured the definition of some "individual rights." Other philosophers, such as Hegel and J.S. Mill, elaborated on this by emphasizing the aspect of universality. At this point the idea started to look like the one we know and endorse—but we still had to wait several decades before this idea became accepted in constitutions and laws.

Our conversation with Alpha could now take two alternative directions. First, Alpha might want to explore the issue of "change" that I just introduced. In fact, in developing my line of argument, I have often appealed to the value of philosophy insofar as it allows us to understand, or at least to clarify, how the world inside and outside us is organized, how we behave and should behave in it. However, with the last paragraph, I also argued that philosophy is valuable because it produces ideas that can *change* the world. Now, this is a claim on which we are far from having universal consensus—even within philosophy. Like any other discipline, philosophy can employ different methodologies. It can approach questions in terms of discrete problems, capable of being analyzed apart from their historical origins, or it can approach the same questions as determined, at least partially, by factors such as context, language, culture and history, thus researching those factors (and previous philosophical elaborations) as part of the questions being analyzed. Ultimately the goal is the same, or at least similar: understanding or interpreting the world. When it comes to the question of whether philosophy should also change, or try to change, the world, the view is much less unanimous. It is a complex issue, and I will make a few remarks about it in the next section.

A second direction that the conversation could take might concern the type of support that philosophy should receive. In fact, assuming that Alpha now agrees that philosophy is valuable, and that good philosophy requires trained professionals (people who have acquired skills and who spend most of their time doing philosophy), Alpha might ask: Should society subsidize philosophical work? This has increasingly become a subject of public debate in several

Western countries over the past couple of decades. Among those who do not consider philosophy valueless, a common argument against the public subsidy of philosophy is that philosophers of the past did not require it.

This argument is correct and incorrect at the same time. Ancient philosophers often had their schools, with rich students paying to attend them. Ancient economy was based on slavery, so we cannot really compare it to our own. During the Middle Ages, a largely theologically-oriented philosophy was carried on by monks, priests, and bishops. Subsequently, aristocrats hired philosophers as preceptors and tutors for their children, or as counsellors, thus giving those philosophers the required time to think and write. Clearly this model had a significant downside: the dependence of intellectuals on political power. Not all aristocrats were content with the philosophers' dedication on the front page of their books; other wanted to influence, or censor, the ideas of the philosophers who were working for them. This is why the philosophers of the Enlightenment, in the eighteenth century, advanced a different view: the idea that the intellectual should not be a private employee, or someone who can do intellectual work simply because she/he is rich enough not to care about financial support—but a professional who gets her salary from the community because she ultimately works *for* the community. Hence the idea of public, state-funded universities, which use public money, but are not controlled by the political power, so that they guarantee the independence of the scholars—who can also criticize the political power. Thus, we are back to the issue of change. Should philosophy (and philosophers) try to change the world? And if so, how?

2 Between Interpretation and Change: Philosophy as Conversation

In 1845, in his *Theses on Feuerbach*, Karl Marx wrote a claim that was destined to become very popular, and not merely in the context of Marxist philosophy: "The philosophers have only interpreted the world, in various ways; the point is to change it."[2] As we have seen very briefly in the previous section, this claim was not entirely fair towards previous philosophers; albeit indirectly, some of them did change the world. But Marx's claim was meant to have a normative rather than a descriptive value: Marx wanted to express the priority of change over interpretation.

---

2 Karl Marx, 1977, p. 173.

One hundred and twenty-five years later, the philosopher Martin Heidegger allegedly was the protagonist of an interesting event.[3] The celebration of philosopher Hans-Georg Gadamer's seventieth birthday was taking place, and Heidegger, who was Gadamer's mentor and was eighty-one in 1970, was one of the keynote speakers. Heidegger entered the podium and greeted Gadamer and the students. The back of the lecture theater was crowded by radical leftist students showing banners against Heidegger (who had been a member of the Nazi Party in the thirties and forties). Everyone was waiting for the students to start booing Heidegger and everything turning very uncomfortable. There was dead silence in the room. Heidegger took a book from his briefcase: a volume of Marx and Engels. He opened the book effortlessly from the right place, as if that was the only place he had ever opened it at; he cleared his throat, and started reading with his high pitch, tense voice: "Marx says: 'the philosophers have only *interpreted* the world in various ways; the point is to *change* it.' My generation tried to change the world without interpreting it. That was wrong—one should first try to interpret the world adequately, before trying to change it." Heidegger closed the book, put it back into his suitcase, and left the podium. There was movement at the back-row, everyone else was sitting stiff and waiting what happens next. Then the leftist students started moving towards the door, and walked out of the room in a queue, without saying a word.

For the purpose of our argument, and being aware that this is an over-simplification, we can take Marx as advocating for a philosophy that *changes* the world, and Heidegger as advocating for a philosophy that *interprets* the world. Considering such views at face value, and without entering into a discussion of the respective philosophical positions of Marx and Heidegger, we might say that they both seem to have a point. Someone—our friend Alpha, perhaps, assuming that in the previous section we have convinced him that philosophy is a valuable exercise—might ask: what is the point of interpreting the world, if some sort of change does not follow from it? On the other hand, changing the world without interpreting it *first* can have disastrous consequences—those to which Heidegger referred in his talk, for example. But if we wait until we have interpreted the entire world, we might not ever change anything, because interpretation (and any form of understanding) is an endless enterprise. So, change or interpretation?

---

[3] The event was reported to me by my colleague, Heikki Ikaheimo, who heard it being narrated by Manfred Frank, who witnessed the event. Frank maintains he reported this event in a newspaper the next day, but I do not have independent verification.

This is clearly a huge question, and I do not pretend to be able to address it—and especially not with a few paragraphs. However, I would like to advance a few remarks concerning a possible way to respond to this dilemma. The answer might reside, I suggest, in considering philosophy as primarily concerned with *conversation*. Conversation, in my view, comprises both interpretation and change, while avoiding some of the problems that stem from each of the two original horns of the dilemma. By mentioning "conversation," I am referring to the dynamic described by the hermeneutic philosopher Gadamer.

Philosopher Theodore George provided a careful and useful reconstruction of Gadamer's account of conversation in his recent article "Are we a conversation? Hermeneutics, Exteriority, and Transmitability."[4] According to Gadamer,[5] in the *initial* phase of the conversation, the accessibility of a matter is "shaped by the authority of prejudice." Then, "an *intermediary* phase" follows: the authority of prejudice "undergoes a reversal," and we subject our prejudices to a critique. In a *third* phase, we then "work through our prejudices" and "reconsider their appropriateness to the matter under consideration."

As we proceed in the process of understanding, we "always again find that our further efforts to understand are made possible and limited" by still other prejudices. Proper conversation always implies an awareness—or better: a constant process of becoming aware—that nothing in our claims, arguments, or beliefs (including the critique to our preliminary prejudices) is immediate, but everything is always already mediated—an insight which was somehow already present in Hegel's philosophy. Gadamer argues that this "renewed understanding" is "genuinely different from the access granted by our initial prejudices," and it also contributes to a "transformation in our understanding of ourselves."

This account of conversation is consistent with a hermeneutic conception of philosophy, that is—according to Gadamer—philosophy as the attempt "to clarify the conditions in which understanding takes place."[6] As a result, Gadamer continues, "understanding is always interpretation";[7] but interpretation—and here is, I think the most important point—is never merely reproductive, but is rather capable of discovering and producing meanings in the process of its development. Our consciousness is formed by the horizon of our prejudices and fore-

---

4 Theodore George, 2017, pp. 331–350. A draft version of the paper was presented at the 2016 College of Fellows Conference at Western Sydney University. I was fortunate enough to be the respondent to such paper. Most of the reflections that follow originated in dialogue with George's paper.
5 George mainly refers to Hans-Georg Gadamer, 2007, pp. 72–88.
6 Hans-Georg Gadamer, 2004, p. 95.
7 Hans-Georg Gadamer, 2004, p. 306.

meanings; but insofar as the interpretative act is not merely reproductive, but also *productive*, it constantly contributes to the formation of our consciousness and of the world around us.

Let us go back to the process of conversation: an important characteristic of this process is that nothing, including the critique of our initial prejudices, is immune from the experience of hermeneutic displacement, because even our critique is determined by still other prejudices: the failure to acknowledge that aspect would constitute a serious self-delusion for the interpreter. This is the reason why understanding, conceived as interpretation, is a never-ending task —and so is conversation. This is one of the forms that take the hermeneutic circle. Heidegger developed the concept of the hermeneutic circle to refer to the relation between the world (the whole) conceived as something that is always already situated in the experiences of our everyday existence, and to stress that that "whole" has been situated in such experiences by us, that is, by individuals (the parts). Thus, understanding is developed on the grounds of "fore-structures" of understanding, which allow the external world to be interpreted in a preliminary way. Gadamer, then, re-conceptualized the hermeneutic circle as an iterative process through which a new understanding of the whole is developed through the interpretation of the detail of existence. For Gadamer, it is precisely through conversations with others that this "whole" is explored and interpreted—and, if the process is successful, an *agreement* is reached that represents a new understanding. This is, in my view, a *fourth* phase in the process of conversation.

Now, what happens if the process is *not* successful, and an agreement is *not* reached? The first three phases, in fact, can be completed by an individual, or collective, interpretative agent *in isolation*, but the fourth phase—the agreement—requires the successful completion of the process of both the agents involved in the conversation; otherwise we are left with a conversation which is only *asymmetrically* successful, and hence, sadly, ultimately unsuccessful. Like the anti-heroes of Beckett's *Waiting for Godot*, we would be stuck in our hermeneutic self-awareness, hoping for a mutual openness—a shared meaning—that might never actualize.

This is a situation similar to the one French philosopher Paul Ricoeur considers, in a slightly different context, in his work *The Symbolism of Evil*. "How shall we get beyond the 'circle of hermeneutics'?" Ricoeur wonders, and he answers: "By transforming it into a *wager*." And he continues: "That wager then becomes the task of *verifying* my wager and saturating it, so to speak, with intelligibility. In return, the task transforms my wager."[8] It is a three-stage process: wager, verification, and transformation.[9] An interpretative act is always, from its very inception, a wager on meaning; then one must bring about that meaning, one must "make it true" and real (from the Latin *verus-facere*, to make true). If this process is successful, then the world is actually changed, or transformed, as a result of the wager.

Ricoeur's wager can be regarded as complementing Gadamer's account of conversation. As much as—as George points out—Gadamer's resistance to the logics of calculative rationality through a return to conversation "is not a call to retreat from Enlightenment back" to mere tradition,[10] similarly Ricoeur's wager is not a call to retreat into fideism or spontaneism. Rather, Ricoeur's wager is a commitment to a meaning, which affirms itself even against a lack of agreement. This does not mean halting the conversation though, because a wager is always already a call to other interpreters to accept the challenge that such a meaning represents. It is a commitment that, while it remains self-critical in relation to the prejudices that might have determined the wager, also struggles to build a new meaning.

This is consistent with what George claims when he argues that conversation may contribute to our efforts to address the concerns of our times in two manners: by providing a hermeneutical supplement to current debates, including those about the effects of imperialism and colonialism; and by clarifying, and being consistent with, some of the ethical implications of such conversation: "we may if we wish—Theodore George writes—be able to pursue possibilities of shared life even amidst the legacies of the deepest alienations, violence, and subjugation."[11]

I think that an analogy might be drawn here between these two manners and Ricoeur's hermeneutics of suspicion and hermeneutics of reminiscence.[12] Ricoeur uses the term "hermeneutic of suspicion" to refer to the thought of Freud, Marx, and Nietzsche. After the advent of these three thinkers, to seek meaning is no longer to spell out the consciousness of meaning, but to decipher its expressions. However, we also need the hermeneutics of reminiscence—that is, a form of hermeneutics that is based on the restoration of meaning and not on the reduction to illusion.

---

8 Paul Ricoeur, 1967, p. 355.
9 See Sebastian Purcell, 2016, p. 189.
10 Theordore George, 2017, p. 348.
11 Theordore George, 2017, p. 349.
12 Paul Ricoeur, 1970, pp. 32–36.

Conversation, conceived in the way briefly outlined above, is both interpretation and change. It is interpretation of what the other is telling me, and of the world around us; but in a real conversation, everything changes: the other, the world—I, too, change. Conversation is a risky engagement, because it always requires a wager on a meaning. But what is the possible *content* of that wager?

As Heidegger taught us, in order to answer a philosophical question, we should begin by wondering *who* is asking the question. In a recent article, Italian hermeneutic philosopher Gianni Vattimo (who has been strongly influenced by Heidegger in the development of his own hermeneutic theory) wonders what difference is there between the "need for metaphysics" affirmed by the authorities that regret the loss of "truth," and the need for metaphysics "of all those revolutionaries who feel legitimized by universal 'human rights.'" Vattimo's answer is that "Even the action required to make possible a society where different metaphysics may freely confront themselves, negotiating accords that force none of them to annul itself in the name of an absolute truth, demands a 'metaphysical' commitment." And he concludes by suggesting that "a similar commitment has to do with a (not exclusively Christian) precept of charity."[13]

Here, there is a meeting point between Ricoeur's and Vattimo's reflections. What Ricoeur calls "a wager" is, for Vattimo, the choice "of the defeated," or "the oppressed."[14] Such a wager is ethically driven. It is made, as Vattimo would put it, "not in the name of the *veritas*, but in the name of the *caritas*."[15] The reference to Vattimo allows us to go back to Marx's claim about interpretation and change. Vattimo and his co-author Zabala write: "we don't believe he [Marx] was discrediting hermeneutics with this statement but only evoking how, for interpretation to work, a change must occur [...] interpretation must make a new contribution to reality."[16] I think that, here, Vattimo and Zabala are interpreting in a strong sense Gadamer's claim that the act of interpretation is always productive—or, to use a different kind of terminology, that a real interpretation is never a merely epistemological act, but it also has a very practical significance. As such, it should also be able to generate new meanings, and to change the world thanks to such new meanings.

In conversation, we can constantly look for an interpretation that changes our relationships with one another, and with the world; thus, "interpretation" comprises both word *and* action. It is indeed a change. As such, it is something

---

13 Gianni Vattimo, 2014, p. 56.
14 Vattimo and his co-author Zabala borrow this expression from Walter Benjamin, 2003, p. 391.
15 Gianni Vattimo and Santiago Zabala, 2011, p. 4.
16 Gianni Vattimo and Santiago Zabala, 2011, p. 4.

that—philosophers too should remind themselves—cannot be done exclusively from an armchair. But philosophers can, and should, at least try to facilitate this conversation. Ultimately, in fact, conversation is what makes us human. This is why philosophy is, and remains, important.

Despite her rhyming jibe—"Philosophy is that thing with or without which everything remains the same"—I am sure my grandmother somehow realized the importance of philosophy. When she was not busy mocking me, she used to tell anecdotes. One of my favorites was about my grandfather visiting an exhibition and casually encountering Benedetto Croce, the Italian philosopher who was a point of reference for anti-fascist, democratic, and liberal culture during the fascist era. She used to conclude her anecdote by referring to Croce and saying, "You know, at the end of the day, that man really made a difference."

I think my grandma was smart.

Bibliography

Benjamin, Walter. "On the Concept of History." In *Walter Benjamin: Selected Writings, Volume 4, 1938–1940*, H. Eiland and M.W. Jennings (Eds.), pp. 388–400. Cambridge, MA: Belknap Press of Harvard University Press, 2003.
Bubbio, Paolo Diego. "Philosophy is Everywhere, Whether One Realises or Not." *New Philosopher* 2 (November 2013): pp. 32–33.
Feyerabend, Paul. *Against Method*. London: Verso, 1975.
Gadamer, Hans-Georg. *Truth and Method*. J. Weinsheimer and D. G. Marshall (Trans.). London and New York: Continuum, 2004.
Gadamer, Hans-Georg. "The Universality of the Hermeneutic Problem." In *The Gadamer Reader: A Bouquet of Later Writings*, Richard Palmer (Trans. and Ed.), pp. 72–88. Evanston: Northwestern University Press, 2007.
George, Theodore. "Are We a Conversation? Hermeneutics, Exteriority, and Transmittability." *Research in Phenomenology* 47, no. 3 (2017): pp. 331–350.
Marx, Karl. *Selected Writings*. David McLellan (Ed.), Oxford: Oxford University Press, 1977.
Purcell, Sebastian. "Hermeneutics and Truth: From *Aletheia* to Attestation." In *Hermeneutics and Phenomenology in Paul Ricoeur: Between Text and Phenomenon*, Scott Davidson and Marc-Antoine Vallee (Eds.), pp. 175–196. Dordrecht: Springer, 2016.
Ricoeur, Paul. *The Symbolism of Evil*. Emerson Buchanan (Trans.), Boston: Beacon Press, 1967.
Ricoeur, Paul. *Freud and Philosophy*. Denis Savage (Trans.), New Haven and London: Yale University Press, 1970.
Vattimo, Gianni. "What Need, What Metaphysics?" *Parrhesia* 21 (2014): pp. 53–57.
Vattimo, Gianni, and Santiago Zabala. *Hermeneutic Communism: From Heidegger to Marx*. New York: Columbia University Press, 2011.

David Macarthur
Irreverent Thoughts on the Relevance of Philosophy

Abstract: The essay offers an account of philosophy, and then goes on to outline some of the most significant contributions that philosophy has offered, and still offers, in several different areas. It concludes by advocating a view of philosophy as a calling for each of us to free ourselves by having the courage to think for ourselves.

When the ancient Greeks created philosophy some 2000 years ago it was possible to suppose, with Plato and Aristotle, that philosophy is humankind's highest calling, the most exulted use of the powers of reason with which nature has endowed us. Plato even goes so far as to imagine that a truly just society would be one ruled over by none other than philosophers![1] Philosophy was not only relevant to leading what Socrates calls "an examined life" but also to the public good of a well-run society.[2] But when one considers the modern world, the role of philosophy is almost the opposite of that imagined by Plato. To many it has become totally irrelevant; indeed, from a cultural standpoint, almost invisible.[3]

Descartes gave birth to the modern period in philosophy by doubting everything beyond the contents of his own mind. But what on earth do such metaphysical doubts have to do with our everyday lives? The same might be said about pursuing the question how there can be any freedom in a world of physical processes governed by laws of nature; or about the question whether there is a supernatural entity called "God" that falls outside the explanations of natural phenomena offered by the natural sciences. It is characteristic of such *metaphysical* questions, as they are called, that they cannot be answered by appeal to any

---

[1] Plato, 1953, p. 712.
[2] In Plato's *Apology* 37e–38b, Socrates remarks, "the unexamined life is no life for a human being." Plato, 1953, pp. 362.
[3] According to Richard Rorty, literature has taken over the role of being the preeminent defender of nonscientific culture in our age of science. Philosophy is effectively sidelined: "Philosophy, at the moment, is sort of occupying a halfway position between the sciences and literature. But just for that reason, it's tending to fall between two stools and to be ignored by intellectuals… and the reason is that the weight of nonscientific culture has been thrown over to literature." Richard Rorty, 1995, p. 61.

observations or indeed by relying on any of our ordinary methods for settling beliefs in, say, law, medicine or science. Irrelevance to broadly empirical methods for settling beliefs is their defining feature.[4]

But philosophers have always been moved by a deeper sense of the relevance of such questions, that is, of the possibility of reaching *fundamental* answers about how the world *really* is, not just how it appears, that will transform our lives and so *make* themselves relevant. Relevance is a temporal notion and philosophers have from the beginning held out the hope of the *eventual* relevance of their questions even if they are or seem, from the contemporary perspective, irrelevant.[5]

Perhaps this idea of a future relevance is pie-in-the-sky. At least about these and other metaphysical questions—"Do substances exist?" "Do all things of a certain kind have a unique essence?" "Is the world fundamentally physical?", etc.—skepticism is understandable, even reasonable. Fortunately, there is more to philosophy than attempting to answer apparently unanswerable metaphysical questions.

Consider, for example, Alan Turing, the mathematical logician whose theoretical work on computable functions in the 1930s laid the foundations for the development of the modern computer—something without which our contemporary way of living and working would be impossible. Or, consider John Locke's work in establishing the theoretical framework for our modern conception of liberal democracy, including the idea of the social contract and the separation of the powers of government from those of the judiciary—ideas that had a huge influence on modern democracies, e. g., the Constitution of the United States. More recent examples of the relevance of philosophy include John Rawls's work on political justice and Peter Singer's work on the welfare of animals. Such examples can be multiplied. The important point is that each of these thinkers has had profound, and arguably beneficial, effects on the culture and society in which we live. But this is only a partial answer to our question. It is, as we might put it, the *public* face of the question of the relevance of philosophy. But there is also a *private* face.

---

4 A cultural reference to a similar nostalgic attitude towards metaphysics is Giorgio De Chirico's *Piazza D'Italia Metafisica* (1921), a painting that imagines metaphysics as a series of grand but empty and decaying buildings in a deserted piazza as the sun sets. A nice touch is that the long shadow cast by the biggest building in the right foreground seems to spread out to include the viewer.

5 The idea that the traditional (metaphysical) problems of philosophy will eventually be answered definitively seems to me a form of bad faith but I cannot defend that position here.

One way of thinking about this personal sense of relevance is to say that since we are all thinkers, creatures capable of rationally reflecting on themselves, and others, and our place in the world, we will inevitably reflect, sooner or later, on questions of right and wrong, on what our role as father or mother, husband or wife, or friend, lover, citizen, pet owner, or fellow human being, involves. What are our freedoms or lack of them? What do we know, or what don't we, or can't we, know? What do we value and why? And so on without end.

Anyone pursuing these lines of thought will want to draw a distinction between *academic* philosophy, the kind of thing philosophy professors in universities do, and philosophy in a broader sense in which all of us are engaged to a greater or lesser extent simply as a consequence of central features of the human condition. Wilfrid Sellars, a twentieth century American philosopher, famously said: "The aim of philosophy is to understand how things in the broadest possible sense of the term hang together in the broadest possible sense of the term."[6] That is an aspiration that any of us, endowed with reason and the inevitability of being motivated to self-reflection, could gladly subscribe to.

But I'd rather pursue the private face of relevance in another way, by appeal to another more recent American philosopher, Stanley Cavell. His idea is that philosophy is "the education of grownups."[7] Cavell's conception presupposes that one has already been educated in the ordinary sense. The education of children, our first education, occurs by way of parents and teachers and inculcates us into a language and culture and various social and economic roles. Why, then, do we need a *second* education? And who is to teach it?

We can approach these questions by reflecting that we are, each of us, subject to what Henry David Thoreau called "lives of quiet desperation."[8] That is, we tend to be creatures of routine and habit, accustomed to follow others—to quietly accept custom or received wisdom or the status quo. The trouble is that then we can feel that we are not really *living* our own lives but enduring them, letting them pass as if we were mere spectators of ourselves.

To be educated, in Cavell's sense, is to become the individual one is or aspires to be, *against,* or by contesting, an unthinking subjection to the forces of conformity, custom and habit. And this kind of education is precisely what no one can teach you but yourself. No one else can teach you how to choose, hence to value, your own life; in short, we might say that to live deliberately is up to each of us to do for him- or herself. Thoreau, who famously chose to

---

6 Wilfrid Sellars, 1963, p. 1.
7 Stanley Cavell, 1979, p. 125.
8 Henry David Thoreau, 1997, p. 6.

live in seclusion for a two-year period by Walden Pond, Massachusetts, remarked, "I went to the woods because I wished to live deliberately, to front only the essential facts of life, and see if I could not learn what it had to teach, and not, when I came to die, discover that I had not lived."[9]

To educate oneself in this second sense includes making up one's own mind about what one understands by friendship, and love, and citizenship, and duty, and history, and government and so on. In this endless endeavor of making sense of and for oneself (hence for others), philosophy—as exemplified by the great texts of Plato, Aristotle, Aquinas, Leibniz, Kant, Hume, Hegel, Mill, Nietzsche, Frege, Heidegger, Wittgenstein, Anscombe and more—is our best provocation and guide. It can help us to think better about what we cannot avoid thinking about.

Philosophy at its best teaches the enlightenment ideal to think for oneself.[10] But this is paradoxical. Many people are frustrated by the fact that reading philosophy is not like reading the newspaper or a scientific report or a cookbook. It does not provide information, or a set of doctrines established beyond reasonable doubt, nor does it provide a recipe for answering the difficult practical questions that confront us, say, about what work one should do, how to tell true friends from false, whether and who to marry, or to vote for, or to donate to, and so forth. Perhaps this is why philosophy is often felt to be irrelevant, because it does not do what science or religion or Jamie Oliver does. But it cannot be otherwise. Philosophy cannot tell you what to think or do. If it did, your thoughts and deeds would be borrowed, second-hand, not really *yours*.

If philosophy is understood as a set of endlessly fascinating texts, rather than a de-contextualized set of "Big Problems," then the extent to which it has any positive impact it is by way of a different relation between the reader and the text than we are used to—especially in our age of digital information and communications technology. Reading a newspaper, so far as we trust the integrity and veracity of its journalists, is a matter of acquiring knowledge about the matters described, say, about the weather, what our political leaders said, the number of fatalities on Australian roads, the strength of the Australian dollar against the greenback, etc. But philosophy texts are not like that.

It is worth pondering the question why the originating text of modern philosophy, Descartes's *Meditations on First Philosophy* is, as the title suggests, a set of philosophical "meditations" explicitly modeled on religious meditations[11] Just as

---

[9] Henry David Thoreau, 1997, p. 85.
[10] Immanuel Kant, 1989, pp. 54–60.
[11] René Descartes, 1986.

religious texts invite the reader to undergo a process of spiritual transformation so, too, the meditator of Descartes's text is supposed to go through a process of *cognitive* transformation as he progresses through each meditation in the order presented: in the process one is supposed to leave behind the common sense belief that the senses provide our most certain truths and come to endorse the enlightened belief that reason alone provides such truths: for example, that the mind is distinct from the body; or that a good God exists and guarantees the possibility of human knowledge if we use our reason diligently.

Descartes does not suppose that the reader can undergo this transformation him- or herself simply by being told what to think. The meditator's cognitive self-transformation is supposed to be a model of one's own possibility for philosophical transformation. Reading this text will, if it works as intended, motivate you to mediate on your own, following the path laid out by the meditator, in order to arrive at these truths *for yourself*. That is, you are invited to meditate along with the meditator, not to simply accept what he says at face value. By introducing the reader to an intellectual discipline, rather than simply providing arguments or doctrines to passively absorb, a philosophical text (or at least *this* kind of philosophical text) attempts to stimulate one to thoughts of one's own. Of course, Descartes's presumption (or arrogance?) is that you will see your own thoughts reflected in those of the meditator.

Philosophy teaches one to think for oneself to the extent that it is teachable. The Austrian philosopher Ludwig Wittgenstein likens the sort of teaching at issue here to being given, as the occasion demands, "the right *tip*";[12] but there is more to philosophical education than that. It also teaches the importance of self-consistency, or wholeness, which on a practical level involves the ongoing attempt to integrate all the various aspects of our complex, often fragmented, and evolving thoughts and actions into a coherent whole; as well as the importance of self-overcoming or conversion, the struggle to make oneself anew according to one's own self-image. Philosophical education is difficult, perhaps even traumatic, because it is "not natural growth but... conversion... rebirth."[13]

The endless tasks of integration and renewal is part of the reason the ancient Greeks thought of philosophy as a way of living, or better, an *art* of living. Although it can be done better or worse, it cannot be taught in the way one can teach science or mathematics. Kant sagely remarks, "Philosophy can never be learned... we can at most learn to philosophize."[14]

---

12 Ludwig Wittgenstein, 1986, Part ii, sect. 11, p. 227.
13 Stanley Cavell, 1979, p. 125.
14 Immanuel Kant, 2007, A837/B865.

Of course, it is true that academic philosophy seems to be always in danger of discounting or forgetting the ancient mission of philosophy—philosophy, you will recall, meaning "the love of wisdom"—to act as a guide or model for a certain reflective or examined way of life. This is especially so in our current age, in which the sciences and science-inspired technological progress have enormous prestige. Academic philosophy, like many other humanistic disciplines, is (sadly) trying its best to imitate, or situate itself within, the glory that is the natural sciences. So, it is always worth repeating that philosophy is not a body of doctrines. It is an endless enticement to self-knowledge and self-determination where to know oneself is the difficult task of discovering what are one's *genuine* commitments and responsibilities, as well as one's *true* cares and concerns—for oneself, or family, or friends, or strangers, or animals, or for the world—in spite of obstacles to such knowledge in the form of false philosophy (especially metaphysics or skepticism) or the conformist pressures of one's society or a false self-image sustained by self-aggrandizing myths or comforting self-deceptions.

Here it is worth recalling Plato's image of humans as chained together in a cave hopelessly mistaking the shadows cast on a wall for realities.[15] In this image of ourselves as distracted and self-deluded the philosopher is no different from anyone else. She has no special gifts or authority to speak the truth about the world. Like everyone else she tends to take false appearances for realities. What distinguishes her, what earns her the title of "philosopher," is simply that she has the courage and honesty to free herself of illusions—or, as we might put it, to free herself of a life of mere conformity and passive acceptance—by the use of her own powers to come to reasoned judgment, to make up her mind, to think for herself.

In Plato's image, philosophy is a calling for each of us to free ourselves by having the courage to think for ourselves, something that is especially necessary given the inevitability of finding ourselves out of step with others—hence with ourselves—on various personal, moral, social, political or religious matters, to name only the most obvious sources of disagreement and enmity. Perhaps Plato also suggests that when we do use our reason properly we will all arrive at more or less the same views. If so, I'll leave you with this contrary vision of Wittgenstein's: "Working in philosophy… is really more a working on oneself. On one's own interpretation. On one's way of seeing things. (And what one expects of them)."[16]

---

15 Plato, 1953, *Republic* 514a–515c, pp. 747–748.
16 Ludwig Wittgenstein, 1998, p. 24.

Bibliography

Cavell, Stanley. *The Claim of Reason*. Oxford: Oxford University Press, 1979.
Descartes, René. *Meditations on First Philosophy*. J. Cottingham (Trans. and Ed.), Cambridge: Cambridge University Press, 1986.
Kant, Immanuel. *Kant's Political Writings*. H. S. Reiss (Ed.), Cambridge: Cambridge University Press, 1989.
Kant, Immanuel. *Critique of Pure Reason*. N. Kemp Smith (Trans.), New York: Palgrave Macmillan, 2007.
Plato. *The Complete Works of Plato*. Edited by J. Cooper. Oxford: Clarendon Press, 1953.
Rorty, Richard. "Towards a Post-Metaphysical Culture." *The Harvard Review of Philosophy*, Spring 1995, pp. 58–66.
Sellars, Wilfrid. *Science, Perception and Reality*. London: Routledge & Kegan Paul, 1963.
Thoreau, Henry David. *Walden*. 1854. Boston: Beacon Press, 1997.
Wittgenstein, Ludwig. *Philosophical Investigations*. 2nd Edition. G. E. M. Anscombe (Ed.), Oxford: Blackwell, 1986.
Wittgenstein, Ludwig. *Culture and Value*. 2nd Edition. G. H. von Wright (Ed.), London: Blackwell, 1998.

II. What can Philosophy Contribute?

Lisa Bortolotti and Katherine Puddifoot
Philosophy, Bias, and Stigma

Abstract: In this chapter we discuss the impact of philosophical research on our understanding of the world. Considering two examples from our areas of research, we argue that empirically informed philosophy can help us both reduce and control the effects of implicit bias on our behavior, and challenge the stigma associated with the diagnosis of psychiatric disorders. In both cases, knowledge of philosophy and practice of philosophy make a significant contribution to the development of a fairer society.

1 What Philosophy Is and Why It Matters

We take philosophy to be at the same time a practice and a body of knowledge. As a practice, philosophy invites us to adopt a critical attitude towards received opinions and acquire the capacity to assess and develop arguments for or against a certain position. We learn how to spot weaknesses in an argument and build counterexamples to it, but also, more constructively, we learn how to avoid bad reasoning and anticipate objections when we propose an argument for a certain position. Philosophy as a practice is useful in so far as it allows us to think about complex issues avoiding biases and fallacies, to express our thoughts more clearly and persuasively, and to revise our positions in the light of counterevidence or feedback.

As a body of knowledge, philosophy is about gaining an understanding of the issues that matter to us, and to which we apply the analytical and argumentative skills we just described. Do we have an immortal soul? Why is it wrong to have an incestual relationship? Is there anything more to knowledge than a true belief justified by the evidence? These are some of the questions philosophers ask in their daily work. In practical philosophy, we investigate ethical and political issues, and, in theoretical philosophy, we ask questions about the methodology of the sciences, the nature of reality, the complexities of the human mind, and the limitations of our knowledge of the world, among many others. Philosophy as a body of knowledge is more or less useful depending on the issues that

---

The authors acknowledge the support of the European Research Council under the Consolidator grant agreement number 616358 for a project called *Pragmatic and Epistemic Role of Factually Erroneous Cognitions and Thoughts* (PERFECT).

∂ Open Access. © 2019 Lisa Bortolotti, Katherine Puddifoot, published by De Gruyter. [CC BY-NC-ND] This work is licensed under the Creative Commons Attribution-NonCommercial-NoDerivatives 4.0 License.
https://doi.org/10.1515/9783110650990-007

we are planning to investigate and on whether we regard them as central to our understanding of reality and ourselves, or as likely to improve our way of life.

In the rest of the chapter, we would like to focus on two areas in which philosophy has played and continues to play a very important role: (1) our understanding of implicit biases, and the ways in which their effect can be controlled or reduced; and (2) our understanding of mental health, and the ways in which we can challenge the stigma that is usually associated with psychological distress.

2 Implicit Biases: The Phenomenon

Implicit biases are responses to members of social groups (e. g., races, religions, gender, ability groups), associating group members with traits in virtue of their social group membership. They frequently occur unintentionally, seemingly without the believer being aware of their occurrence, and are difficult to control. They can lead to the differential treatment of group members.

For example, in a study of implicit racial bias, Keith Payne presented images of items: either weapons, like a gun, or harmless items, like a tool.[1] But before presenting these pictures, participants were shown a picture of a black or white man's face. Those who were shown the black face were more likely to mistakenly view the image as a weapon than those who were shown the white face. Implicit biases are used to explain this phenomenon: the picture of the black faces primes people to think about violence, because they automatically associate black male faces with violence. That is, they have an implicit bias associating black people with violence. As a result of the implicit association, they are more likely to view the ambiguous picture of the item as violent.

In another set of experimental studies on the effect of implicit bias, undertaken in Sweden, measurements were made of the extent to which certain employers associated Arab-Muslims[2] or obese people[3] with laziness and incompetence. Those employers who strongly associated Arab-Muslims and obese people with these characteristics were less likely than others to invite members of these groups to interview for a job.

By furthering our understanding of these and similar unconscious or unintended forms of bias and prejudice, recent philosophical research on implicit

---

[1] B. Keith Payne, 2001, pp. 181–192.
[2] Dan-Olof Rooth, 2010, pp. 523–534.
[3] Jens Agerström and Dan-Olof Rooth, 2011, pp. 790–805.

bias illustrates the substantial contribution that philosophy can make to understanding the nature of human thought and how it influences interpersonal interactions. In the domain of implicit bias research philosophy is also at its most practical: providing insights about potential ways to reduce the implicit stereotyping involved with implicit bias.

2.1 The Psychology of Implicit Bias

One strand of philosophical research into implicit bias aims to identify the psychological underpinnings of implicit bias. It aims to answer the question, what, precisely, are implicit biases? How do implicit biases relate to better-recognized psychological states? For example, much recent philosophical discussion has aimed to answer the question: "How do implicit biases relate to beliefs?"

For a significant number of the years during which implicit biases have been studied, it has been assumed in the psychological literature that they are merely associations that people make in their thinking—for example, one might associate social groups (e.g., *women*) and their members with concepts (*weakness*) or feelings (*aversion*)—and that they can only be changed via retraining. They have been distinguished from other mental states on the basis that the believer is often unaware of or unable to control the operation of implicit biases. These associations often conflict with our explicit evaluations: we might explicitly endorse egalitarian specific principles (e.g., all races are equal, all genders are equal) while at the same time making associations that do not fit with these principles, (e.g., associating black people with laziness or women with weakness).[4]

On this characterization of implicit biases they seem different to beliefs. Beliefs tend to involve a commitment to a thought, to respond to argument and evidence,[5] while making an unconscious and automatic association does not require commitment and the association is unlikely to respond to argumentation. If someone *believes* that women are weak then one might engage them in a debate or present evidence of strong women. For example, one might say, "Look at me," while flexing one's muscles lifting something heavy, to illustrate that you are a strong woman. In contrast, if someone has an implicit bias associating women with weakness then, according to those who think that implicit biases are mere associations, one should encourage that person to engage in

---

[4] See, e.g., John F. Dovidio and Samuel L. Gaertner, 2004, pp. 1–52.
[5] Tamar Szabó Gendler, "Alief and Belief," 2008, pp. 634–663; Tamar Szabó Gendler, 2008, "Alief in Action (and Reaction)," pp. 552–585.

training to change their habits. In recent philosophical work, however, the idea that implicit biases are distinguishable from beliefs has been challenged.[6] It has been argued that psychological work on implicit bias shows that they are beliefs[7] or belief-like.[8] For example, some psychological findings suggest that implicit biases can be changed via the presentation of evidence.[9] The same findings suggest that implicit biases might not be mere associations; they might have a propositional structure, more like beliefs.[10]

The outcome of debates about the nature of implicit biases could shift our understanding of how we should conceive of thoughts and actions that we engage in, unintentionally and sometimes unknowingly, leading to differential treatment of members of different social groups in virtue of their group membership via the operation of implicit bias. If these responses are the result of beliefs, then there is reason for thinking that we should think and feel the same way towards people displaying these implicit attitudes as we would about people displaying discriminatory beliefs.[11] This discussion could also identify ways to combat implicit bias. If we find that implicit biases are beliefs, then we can aim to combat them via argumentation and evidence.[12]

2.2 The Morality and Epistemology of Implicit Bias

Debates about implicit bias also venture into moral philosophy and epistemology. Implicit biases have moral import because they lead to discrepant behavior, such as members of certain groups being denied interviews for jobs or being given different medical treatment to members of other social groups.[13] This moral import is related to the epistemic import: disparities in treatment often result from biased judgments. For example, a female student's work might be marked harshly because the marker has a negative implicit bias against females, leading them to allow information that should not influence the judgment, i.e., information about gender, to determine the mark awarded.[14] Because of cases

---

6 Eric Mandelbaum, 2016, pp. 629–658.
7 Eric Mandelbaum, 2016, pp. 629–658.
8 Neil Levy, 2015, pp. 800–823.
9 Jan De Houwer, 2014, pp. 342–353; Eric Mandelbaum, 2016, pp. 629–658.
10 De Houwer, 2014, pp. 342–353; Eric Mandelbaum, 2016, pp. 629–658.
11 R. Levy, 2015, pp. 800–823.
12 Alex Madva, 2016, pp. 2659–2684.
13 See, e.g., John F. Dovidio and Susan T. Fiske, 2012, pp. 945–952.
14 Jennifer Saul, 2013, pp. 39–60.

like this, there is reason to doubt both the morality and accuracy of many of our judgments that might be influenced by implicit bias.[15]

However, while behavior performed under the influence of implicit bias is often morally objectionable, there is debate about whether the biased person is morally responsible for the bias and its outcomes. Jennifer Saul,[16] for example, argues that people who act under the influence of implicit bias are not blameworthy for their actions. This is because the actions are not chosen, they are the result of their upbringing; they are not under the control of the thinker; and the believer will not even be aware of the operation of the bias or their discrepant behavior. Jules Holroyd disagrees, arguing, on the basis of psychological evidence, that people can be aware of the operation of implicit bias.[17] While they might not be aware via introspection of the operation of implicit bias, they can have awareness of a body of knowledge about people's tendencies to possess and display implicit bias, or be aware of the manifestation of implicit bias in biased behavior. In addition to this, Holroyd argues that that people *can* control their implicit biases, they can adopt long range strategies to control their implicit biases. For example, if they are employers then they can make sure that when they consider CVs of candidates, the CVs are anonymous, so the employers do not know if candidates are Arab-Muslims or Obese and implicit biases relating to these groups cannot be triggered. Others deny that control is required for responsibility arguing instead, for example, that one is responsible for a mental state if it reflects one's evaluative judgments.[18] For these moral philosophers, whether or not an individual is responsible for their implicit bias depends upon whether the implicit bias is reflective of, or integrated with, their other attitudes.[19]

It is not necessarily the case that either everyone or no-one is responsible for the effects of implicit bias. It might be that only certain individuals are responsible for being aware of implicit biases, that is, persons who act as gatekeepers, like employers.[20] It might be that wider societal change is needed to prevent or mitigate the negative effects of implicit bias, rather than changes to individu-

---

15 See, e.g., Tamar Szabó Gendler, 2011,"On the Epistemic Costs of Implicit Bias," pp. 33–63; Jennifer Saul, 2013, "Implicit Bias," pp. 39–60; Jennifer Saul, 2013, "Skepticism and Implicit Bias," pp. 243–263; Katherine Puddifoot, 2016, pp. 421–434.
16 Jennifer Saul, 2013,"Skepticism and Implicit Bias," pp. 243–263.
17 Jules Holroyd, 2012, pp. 274–306.
18 See, e.g., Angela M. Smith, 2005, pp. 236–271.
19 cf. N. Levy, 2015, pp. 800–823.
20 Natalia Washington and Daniel Kelly, 2016, pp. 12–36.

als.[21] If so, governments and other large institutions, such as media corporations, might be responsible for reducing implicit biases, and be, or stand culpable if they fail to do so. Perhaps each person is potentially responsible for their implicit bias wherever they can reasonably be expected to be aware of the operation of implicit biases and strategies to combat their effects because on such occasions they have a role to play in combating implicit bias and the discriminatory behavior that follows.[22] Some of us are in a better position than others with regards to both the ability to discover the presence of implicit bias and the ability to combat it, due, for example, to our position as academics with access to the psychological literature. For others, though, it would be less reasonable to expect them to be aware of and combat their implicit bias, thus making them less morally irresponsible or blameworthy if they fail to do so.

3 Mental Health and Its Boundaries

Contemporary societies are struggling to counteract mental health stigma and to ensure parity of esteem between physical and mental health. Stigma means that people with a known psychiatric diagnosis are discriminated against, and negative thoughts and actions are being directed at them for the mere reason that they experience mental health issues. Parity of esteem is the view that patients with mental health issues should receive the same level of care and be allocated the same resources as patients with physical health issues. Stigma is very persistent in the area of mental health, and there is a pervasive "them and us" attitude dividing people who experience mental health issues from people who do not. This "them and us" attitude is what needs to change within society for individuals, communities, and institutions to recognize that being unwell should never count as a reason for being ignored, neglected, discriminated, marginalized, or laughed at.

Philosophy can help address these issues by showing that there is no principled reason to prioritize physical health over mental health, and that there is no sharp divide but rather significant continuity between being mentally well and being mentally unwell. Distress can manifest in a variety of ways, ranging from debilitating diseases affecting good functioning for several years, to temporary forms of anxiety or depression that may come to the attention of healthcare professionals but may not have long term consequences and may not need to be

---

[21] Elizabeth Anderson, 2012, pp. 163–173.
[22] N. Washington and D. Kelly, 2016, pp. 11–36.

medically treated. Philosophy can also accelerate and justify the process that leads to breaking the divisive nature of discussions about mental health. Philosophers, often in collaboration with neuroscientists, cognitive psychologists and psychiatrists, study the strengths and limitations of the human mind and are especially interested in those circumstances in which cognitive and affective states do not seem to be shaped or motivated by how things are. False and unsupported beliefs as well as inappropriate emotional reactions are common in clinical and nonclinical contexts alike.

In our own research, we investigate those reports that are often regarded as marks of irrationality and as symptoms of a mental disorder, such as implausible delusional beliefs, distorted autobiographical memories, and attempted explanations of behavior that do not fit the facts. Although such reports can emerge in the context of schizophrenia, dementia, depression, eating disorders, amnesia and other psychiatric conditions, they are not confined to them, and can affect everybody. Research suggests that people routinely ignore evidence when it does not lend support to their often-inflated views of themselves, that they reinterpret memories of failure and overestimate future chances of success, that they see the past as colored by their current beliefs and values, and that they "make up" stories to fill the many gaps in their knowledge of themselves. In the previous section, when discussing sexist attitudes in academia, we saw a common case of imperfect cognitions: vulnerability to implicit biases is very widespread, and it has implications for the rationality of judgments and decisions.

Philosophers ask whether symptoms of mental health issues that are taken to be paradigmatic examples of irrationality differ in kind or just in degree from the common behaviors described above. In collaboration with empirical scientists, we investigate whether the underlying mechanisms responsible for the manifestations of irrationality we find in the clinical population are similar or significantly different from those that we find in the nonclinical population. Cognitions are likely to be less constrained by reality when the person experiences perceptual anomalies, reasoning deficits, memory impairments, and emotional disturbances—so the extent to which symptoms of mental health issues are due to these factors should be taken into account. But the effects of the ensuing loss of contact with reality is made worse by the social isolation people experience when they lack the opportunity to get feedback from others due to the fear of being stigmatized and misunderstood in the home, among friends, and in the workplace.

What the mentally well and the mentally unwell have in common needs to be observed, remarked upon, and studied systematically. Philosophy can help provide an empirically informed perspective on the continuity between irrationality in the clinical and nonclinical contexts. By doing so, it can also help challenge stigma and reject the current "them and us" attitude that characterizes discussions of mental health.

3.1 The Phenomenon of Delusion

The term "delusions" refers to a clinical phenomenon, and in particular to observable symptoms of schizophrenia, delusional disorders, dementia, amnesia, and other psychiatric conditions. In the most recent version of the *Diagnostic and Statistical Manual of Mental Disorders* (DSM-5), delusion is defined as follows:

> A false belief based on incorrect inference about external reality that is firmly held despite what almost everyone else believes and despite what constitutes incontrovertible and obvious proof or evidence to the contrary. The belief is not ordinarily accepted by other members of the person's culture or subculture (i.e., it is not an article of religious faith). When a false belief involves a value judgment, it is regarded as a delusion only when the judgment is so extreme as to defy credibility.[23]

This definition is problematic in many respects, but it remains a useful diagnostic tool. Examples of delusions are *persecution*, where the person reports that other people are hostile and intend to cause her harm, and *jealousy*, where the person reports that her romantic partner is being unfaithful to her. More unusual delusions include *mirrored-self misidentification*, where the person reports that there is a stranger in the mirror, or the *Cotard delusion*, where the person reports that she is dead or disembodied.

Here we focus on delusions as they are often taken to be the mark of madness, an obvious symptom of mental illness and an example of radical irrationality. We suggest that, contrary to what most assume: (a) the irrationality of delusions does not differ in kind from that of superstitious or prejudiced beliefs, and (b) the fact that an action is motivated by a delusion does not necessarily rule out that the person is accountable for that action. If we can make a good case for (a) and (b), then we have a powerful illustration of the thesis that there is significant continuity (and not a categorical difference) between behaviors categorized as manifestations of mental illness and behaviors that do not attract any specific diagnosis.

---

[23] American Psychiatric Association DSM-5 Task Force, 2013, p. 819.

3.2 Epistemic and Ethical Issues Arising from Delusion

Delusions share a form of epistemic irrationality, that is, a failure to meet the standards of rationality for beliefs with respect to the relationship between the content of the belief and the evidence. Delusions are not easily given up in the face of challenges and tend to resist counterevidence.[24] But is the irrationality of delusions different in kind from the irrationality of superstitious or prejudiced beliefs?

The epistemic feature that is considered most distinctive of delusions—resistance to counterevidence—is actually a very common feature of a variety of typical beliefs. Once they adopt a hypothesis, people are very reluctant to abandon it, even when copious and robust evidence against it becomes available. This is true not only of prejudices against racial groups (such as "Blacks are more aggressive") and superstitions that have no scientific foundations (such as "more accident occur in the nights of a full moon"), but also of beliefs in scientific theories, a context in which responsiveness to evidence should be seen as paramount. For instance, Chinn and Brewer found that people discount evidence against a theory they support but do not discount evidence against a rival theory.[25] Self-enhancing beliefs are especially resistant to counterevidence, and people keep believing that they are more skilled, talented, attractive, successful, and moral than average, even when their life experiences repeatedly suggest otherwise. In order to maintain a positive image of themselves, they reinterpret negative feedback and focus on selected evidence that supports their self-enhancing beliefs.[26]

The claim that the epistemic irrationality of delusions is continuous with the epistemic irrationality of nondelusional beliefs has a variety of implications. For instance, it may be an important factor when we want to understand whether a person should be regarded as responsible for those actions that are driven or motivated by her delusional beliefs. There are some legitimate concerns about the connection (either openly acknowledged or implicit in most legal systems) between having psychotic symptoms such as delusions, or having a certain psychiatric diagnosis such as schizophrenia, and being held unaccountable for one's actions. The problem with generalizing from one set of symptoms or one diagnosis to unaccountability is that people with similar symptoms or the same diagno-

---

[24] Lisa Bortolotti, 2016; Lisa Bortolotti and Kengo Miyazono, 2015, pp. 636–645.
[25] Clark A. Chinn and William F. Brewer, 2001, pp. 323–393.
[26] E. Hepper and Constantine Sedikides, 2012, pp. 43–56.

sis may behave in very different ways.[27] This suggests that further information about individual cases is required before making a judgment about accountability: information about how one's symptoms or diagnosis affect decision making, and specifically the making of those decisions which led one to commit the crime.[28]

The presence of delusions is often considered as a key criterion for criminal insanity. In the high-profile case of the mass murderer Breivik, in Norway, the debate about whether he should be regarded accountable for his crime largely depended on whether his anti-Islamic and racist beliefs were regarded as delusional or just prejudiced in the same way as are the beliefs of many extremists. We should take into account two factors before implying that because an action has been motivated by a delusional belief, the person who performed the action should not be held accountable for it.

First, in terms of how delusions motivate criminal action, the role of delusional beliefs does not seem to be different from the role of nondelusional beliefs, unless we assume that the presence of delusions also signals the presence of a specific cognitive deficit that impacts on the decision to commit the crime in question. Second, having beliefs that are epistemically bad and potentially dangerous, such as prejudiced beliefs about the inferiority of a group of people or the legitimacy of using violence towards them, is not always sufficient to give rise to criminal action, whether the beliefs are delusional or not. Having such beliefs may contribute to an explanation for the crime, but does not make criminal action inevitable or excusable.

4 Conclusions and Implications

As we suggested in section 2, discussions of implicit bias in philosophy have the potential to provide a great deal of insight into strategies that can and should be implemented to reduce implicit prejudice. Philosophers discussing implicit bias often focus on this issue. Actions that might ordinarily be used to combat prejudice, such as attempting to adjust one's judgments to make them more fair,[29] are less likely to be successful against implicit bias than explicit prejudice because even where people are aware that they are biased, they are unlikely to be aware of the extent to which they are influenced by bias.[30]

---

27 Richard Bentall, 2006, pp. 220–233.
28 Lisa Bortolotti, Matthew R. Broome, and Matteo Mameli, 2014, pp. 377–382.
29 Miranda Fricker, 2007.
30 Linda Martín Alcoff, 2010, pp. 128–137; Benjamin R Sherman, 2015, pp. 1–22.

Also, implicit biases seem to arise as a result of the fundamental inequalities in our societies,[31] which lead, for example, to young black males as being depicted in the media as more likely to engage in criminal behavior than others.[32] As soon as a social group is associated with a trait, such as being a criminal, others in their society are likely to automatically associate individual members of the social group with crime. Fundamental changes to the structure of society might therefore be required to mitigate the negative effects of implicit bias.[33]

As we suggested in section 3, discussions of mental health in philosophy can help us combat stigma and justify parity of esteem between physical and mental health. Focusing on the phenomenon of delusions, we showed that two common assumptions should be revisited. First, we assume that delusions are irrational in a different, more radical way, than nondelusional beliefs, but their resistance to counterevidence is not a distinctive feature. The emphasis on continuity can shape our attitudes towards people who report delusional beliefs and may also inform the breadth of the treatment options available to people with delusions. Although we tend to think that people cannot be talked out of their delusions, there is some evidence that some forms of therapy are efficacious in reducing the rigidity of delusional states, and the preoccupation of the person with the topic of the delusion.[34]

Second, we assume that the presence of delusions implies criminal insanity, and that people cannot be held responsible for those criminal actions that are driven or motivated by their delusional beliefs. But it is not clear whether the presence of delusions is ever sufficient for criminal action and whether it indicates a more general impairment in people's capacity to make decisions. Thus, a blanket recommendation to consider people with delusions always unaccountable seems to be poorly justified and should be replaced by a more careful consideration of each case history.

Philosophical discussions can contribute to developing practical solutions to the problems raised by implicit bias and the mental health stigma. Philosophy therefore has the potential to fundamentally change interpersonal interactions so that they are no longer underwritten by bias, stigma, and prejudice, which distort judgments and lead to unfair treatment.

---

[31] Tamar Szabó Gendler, 2008, "On the Epistemic Costs of Implicit Bias," pp. 33–63.
[32] Katherine Puddifoot , 2017, pp. 137–156.
[33] E. Anderson, 2012, pp. 163–173.
[34] Max Coltheart, 2005, pp. 72–76; David Kingdon, Katie Ashcroft, and Douglas Turkington, 2008, pp. 393–410.

Bibliography

Agerström, J., and D-O. Rooth. "The Role of Automatic Obesity Stereotypes in Real Hiring Discrimination." *Journal of Applied Psychology* 96, no. 4 (2011): p. 790.
Alcoff, L. "Epistemic identities." *Episteme* 7, no. 2 (2010): pp. 128–37.
American Psychiatric Association DSM-5 Task Force. *Diagnostic and Statistical Manual of Mental Disorders*. 5th ed. Washington, DC: American Psychiatric Association Publishing, 2013.
Anderson, E. "Epistemic Justice as a Virtue of Social Institutions." *Social Epistemology: A Journal of Knowledge, Culture and Policy* 26, no. 2 (2012): pp. 163–173.
Bentall, R. "Madness Explained: Why We Must Reject the Kraepelinian Paradigm and Replace it with a 'Complaint-orientated' Approach to Understanding Mental Illness." *Medical Hypotheses* 66, no. 2 (2006): pp. 220–233.
Bortolotti, L., and K. Miyazono. "Recent Work on the Nature and the Development of Delusions." *Philosophy Compass* 10, no. 9 (2015): pp. 636–645.
Bortolotti, L., M. R. Broome, and M. Mameli. "Delusions and Responsibility for Action: Insights from the Breivik Case." *Neuroethics* 7, no. 3 (2014): pp. 377–382.
Bortolotti, L., "Delusion." In *The Stanford Encyclopedia of Philosophy*, Spring 2016 ed., Edward N. Zalta (Ed.). Stanford: Stanford University, 2016. http://plato.stanford.edu/archives/spr2016/entries/delusion/.
Chinn, Clark A., and William F. Brewer. "Models of Data: A Theory of How People Evaluate Data." *Cognition and Instruction* 19, no. 3 (2001): pp. 323–93.
Coltheart, M. "Delusional Belief." *Australian Journal of Psychology* 57, no. 2 (2005): pp. 72–76.
De Houwer, J. "A Propositional Model of Implicit Evaluation." *Social and Personality Psychology Compass* 8, no. 7 (2014): pp. 342–353.
Dovidio, J. F., and S. T. Fiske. "Under the Radar: How Unexamined Biases in Decision-Making Processes in Clinical Interactions Can Contribute to Health Care Disparities." *American Journal of Public Health* 102, no. 5 (2012): pp. 945–952.
Dovidio, J. F., and S. L. Gaertner. "Aversive Racism." *Advances in Experimental Social Psychology* 36 (2004): pp. 1–52.
Fricker, M. *Epistemic Injustice*. Oxford: Oxford University Press, 2007.
Gendler, T. S. "Alief and Belief." *The Journal of Philosophy* 105, no. 10 (2008): pp. 634–663.
Gendler, T. S. "Alief in Action (and Reaction)." *Mind and Language* 23, no. 5 (2008): pp. 552–585.
Gendler, T. S. "On the Epistemic Costs of Implicit Bias." *Philosophical Studies* 156, no. 1 (2011): pp. 33–63.
Hepper, E.G., and C. Sedikides. "Self-enhancing Feedback." In *Feedback: The Communication of Praise, Criticism, and Advice*, edited by R. Sutton, M. Hornsey, and K. Douglas, pp. 43–56. London: Peter Lang, 2012.
Holroyd, J. "Responsibility for Implicit Bias." *Journal of Social Philosophy* 43, no. 3 (2012): pp. 274–306.
Kingdon, D., K. Ashcroft, and D. Turkington. "Cognitive Behavioural Therapy for Persecutory Delusions: Three Case Examples." In *Persecutory Delusions: Assessment, Theory and Treatment*, edited by D. Freeman, R. Bentall, and P. Garety, 393–410. Oxford: Oxford University Press, 2008.

Levy, N. "Neither Fish nor Fowl: Implicit Attitudes as Patchy Endorsements." *Noûs* 49, no. 4 (2015): pp. 800–823.

Madva, A. "Why Implicit Attitudes are (Probably) Not Beliefs." *Synthese* 193, no. 8 (2016): pp. 2659–2684.

Mandelbaum, E. "Attitude, Inference, Association: On the Propositional Structure of Implicit Bias." *Noûs* 50, no. 3 (2016): pp. 629–658.

Payne, B. K. "Prejudice and Perception: The Role of Automatic and Controlled Processes in Misperceiving a Weapon." *Journal of Personality Social Psychology* 81 (2001): pp. 181–192.

Puddifoot, K. "Stereotyping: The Multifactorial View." *Philosophical Topics* 45, no. 1 (2017): pp. 137–156.

Puddifoot, K. "Accessibilism and the Challenge from Implicit Bias." *Pacific Philosophical Quarterly* 96, no. 3 (2016): pp. 421–434.

Rooth, D-O. "Automatic Associations and Discrimination in Hiring: Real World Evidence." *Labour Economics* 17 (2010): pp. 523–534.

Saul, J. "Implicit Bias, Stereotype Threat, and Women in Philosophy." In *Women in Philosophy: What Needs to Change*, edited by K. Hutcheson and F Jenkins, pp. 39–60. Oxford: Oxford University Press, 2013.

Saul, J. "Skepticism and Implicit Bias." *Disputatio* 5, no. 37, (2013): pp. 243–263.

Sherman, B. "There's No (Testimonial) Justice: Why Pursuit of a Virtue is Not the Solution to Epistemic Injustice." *Social Epistemology* (2015): pp. 1–22. doi: 10.1080/02691728.2015.1031852.

Smith, A. "Responsibility for Attitudes: Activity and Passivity in Mental Life." *Ethics* 115 (2005): pp. 236–71.

Washington, N., and D. Kelly. "Who's Responsible for This? Moral Responsibility, Externalism and Knowledge About Implicit Bias." In vol. 2 of *Implicit Bias and Philosophy*, edited by M. Brownstein and J. Saul, pp. 11–36. Oxford: Oxford University Press, 2016.

Jon Askonas and Katherine Withy
Thinking Failure in the War in Iraq: The Cultural Turn and the Concept of "World"

Abstract: This article demonstrates the power of the phenomenological concept of 'world', and so the importance of philosophical concepts and philosophers, by considering the case of the U.S. Army's 'cultural turn'. After invading Iraq, the U.S. military found that soldiers lacked the training necessary for long-term engagement with a civilian population. Turning to anthropology and sociology, it introduced the concepts of culture, cultural awareness, and cultural sensitivity into its training. We argue that these concepts are crude and inadequate, and that the concept of world does a better job of illuminating the differences and similarities between soldiers' and civilians' respective lived systems of meaning. Through this case, we can see why we need philosophers and philosophy.

1

By 2006, the U.S. Army was in trouble in Iraq. Senior U.S. political and military leaders had intended to conduct an operation that would have a "light footprint," with the majority of troops withdrawn within six months. But the "war in Iraq" became a long-term occupation and counterinsurgency effort. Soldiers who had been trained to invade did not have the skills for post-invasion operations, counterinsurgency, and long-term engagement with a civilian population. To address the latter, the Army turned to cultural training, aiming to foster both "cultural awareness" and "cultural sensitivity" in its soldiers. But the concept of culture did not solve the problem that it was supposed to. Culture might have explained to soldiers why Iraqis acted in some of the ways that they did, but it did not allow soldiers to better interact with Iraqis. For this, the Army would have needed a different concept, which we suggest is the phenomenological concept of world.

"Culture" is an anthropological concept. Anthropologists have widely criticized the U.S. military for working with a concept of culture that is crude and old-fashioned[1] (and which may be so because it was "borrowed" from anthropol-

---

[1] "All of this early material [produced by the military for 'cultural training' between 2003 and 2007] described Iraqi culture with recourse to the national character studies that typified the cul-

ogy and sociology textbooks, as well as The Encyclopedia Britannica[2]). While some of our criticisms of the U.S. military's concept of culture repeat those of anthropologists, our conclusion is different. We conclude that what is needed is not a more sophisticated concept of culture but a different concept entirely. "Culture" is a third-personal concept: it captures something about human life as seen from the outside—from the detached, theoretical stance that an anthropologist traditionally takes up. In contrast, "world" is a first-personal concept. It comes from a sub-discipline of philosophy that emerged in Germany in the early twentieth century called "phenomenology."[3] Phenomenology studies what life is like as it is lived from the "inside," for the person or people experiencing it. To understand a person's world is very different from understanding a person's culture, in ways that we will outline. In particular, the concept of culture highlights the differences between people and implies that their behavior is irrational, whereas the concept of world emphasizes the similarities between people and allows one to grasp the rationality of their actions. In exploring how the concept of culture failed the U.S. Army and how the philosophical concept of world might have better served it, we aim to show—rather than simply tell —why we need philosophy.

---

ture research and cultural anthropology of the 1940s and 1950s. Anthropologists long ago abandoned this approach—which posited that peoples and cultures had a uniform character akin to a set of personality traits—as they found it did not adequately address cultural change over time and was frequently inaccurate." Rochelle Davis, 2010, p. 9. See also Rochelle Davis, Dahlia El Zein and Dena Takruri, 2010. Consider, as well: "[T]he kind of culture the Pentagon wants—a 'product' that can be condensed, objectified, and deployed—is the kind of culture Margaret Mead and Ruth Benedict trafficked in, culture that was—like other enemy communications—a code to be cracked, not the kind of culture generated today by post-Geertzian ethnographers, many of whom are terrified to use the word 'culture' at all." Hugh Gusterson, 2010, p. 289. Gusterson attributes this insight to Robert Albro, who contributed to the Panel on Anthropology, U.S. Intelligence and the U.S. Military, at the Elliott School of International Affairs at George Washington University on April 13, 2007.

2 David Price, 2007.

3 Edmund Husserl discusses the "lifeworld" (*Lebenswelt*) in *The Crisis of European Sciences and Transcendental Phenomenology* (1936), and earlier discussed the "surrounding world" or "environment" (*Umwelt*) in *Ideas II* (1913). Husserl's mentee, Martin Heidegger, introduces the notion of "world" (*Welt*) in his magnum opus, *Being and Time* (1927), and this is taken up by Maurice Merleau-Ponty in his *Phenomenology of Perception* (1945). These concepts have precursors in Dilthey ("life-nexus"), analogues in Wittgenstein ("form of life"), and developments through application in the work of contemporary phenomenologists like Matthew Ratcliffe, 2015. The account of world that we give here is primarily Heideggerian but also incorporates insights from the phenomenological tradition generally.

2

The U.S. military invested significant resources in educating itself about Iraqi culture, starting in a trickle in 2004–2005 and leading to a flood during the years of peak counterinsurgency (COIN) efforts (2006–2010). This "cultural turn" involved educating soldiers, supporting socio-cultural research, and integrating academics from the social sciences into U.S. military operations. To take just one example of each:

a. In 2003, the Pentagon issued the Iraq Culture Smart Card to soldiers in Iraq. The Smart Card was a waterproof, pocket-sized primer containing basic facts about the sociology, religion, history and geography of Iraq, as well as common words and phrases in Arabic, and "cultural" information and tips such as: "Admitting 'I don't know' is shameful for an Iraqi"; "One should not stand close to, stare at, or touch [Iraqi] women"; and "Don't slouch, lean, or appear disinterested when conversing with Iraqi men."[4]
b. In 2008, the Department of Defense launched The Minerva Initiative, which funds academic research in the social sciences in order "to build deeper understanding of the social, cultural, and political dynamics that shape regions of strategic interest around the world."[5]
c. Between 2007 and 2014, the U.S. Army ran the "Human Terrain System" program, which aimed "to: recruit, train, deploy, and support an embedded, operationally focused sociocultural capability; conduct operationally relevant, sociocultural research and analysis; develop and maintain a sociocultural knowledge base to support operational decision making, enhance operational effectiveness, and preserve and share sociocultural institutional knowledge."[6] In practice, this involved employing and deploying academics with social science backgrounds to help military commanders and staff to understand the local "human terrain" (i.e., people).[7]

The biggest and most public event in the "cultural turn" was the release of the Army's new counterinsurgency field manual, FM 3–24: Counterinsurgency, in De-

---

[4] Marine Corps Intelligence Activity (MCIA), 2006.
[5] "The Minerva Initiative," United States Department of Defense, 2016, accessed September 20, 2016, *Internet Archive*. https://web.archive.org/web/20160925172159/http://minerva.dtic.mil/
[6] Colonel Sharon R. Hamilton, 2011, p. 2.
[7] The use of anthropologists in Human Terrain Teams has received much criticism from the anthropology community, including a condemnation of the Human Terrain System project from the American Anthropological Association, 2007.

cember 2006.[8] This signaled a fundamental change in American strategy in favor of counterinsurgency, which involved winning the "hearts and minds" of Iraqis. FM 3–24: Counterinsurgency gives a (bizarrely calculative) definition of winning hearts and minds: "'Hearts' means persuading people that their best interests are served by COIN success. 'Minds' means convincing them that the force can protect them and that resisting it is pointless. [...] Calculated self-interest, not emotion, is what counts."[9] The task is clearly conceived as one of persuasion, and successful persuasion requires attention to "ideas, norms, rituals, codes of behavior"[10]—that is, to the "system of shared beliefs, values, customs, behaviors and artifacts that members of a society use to cope with their world and with one another."[11] It requires, in other words, cultural literacy and sensitivity.

3

As many have noted, there are several problems with the concept of culture adopted by the U.S. Army. An obvious one is that what are presented as cultural accommodations—not staring at women, using female officers to search female civilians, not appearing disinterested during conversation, not discussing sex and religion with people you do not know well—are not special accommodations of a different culture but are instead familiar, polite forms of human interaction. Another obvious problem is the reductive view of culture on which it is a set of simple, bite-sized facts that can easily be taught, memorized, and printed on a pocket card. But the deepest problem, we suggest, is the very conception of culture as something like a quirk that must be acknowledged, understood, and accommodated.

Culture, as the U.S. Army understood it, is much like an accent. An accent is an idiosyncratic, inflected way of speaking a common language, which others who are unlike us have (but we ourselves do not), and which we must learn to understand. Similarly, culture is conceived as an ethnically or nationally idiosyncratic way of going about a human life.[12] It is understood either as:

---

[8] United States Department of the Army and United States Marine Corps, 2006.
[9] United States Department of the Army and United States Marine Corps, 2006, A-26.
[10] United States Department of the Army and United States Marine Corps, 2006, pp. 3–36.
[11] United States Department of the Army and United States Marine Corps, 2006, pp. 3–37. According to David Price ("Pilfered Scholarship") this definition is from Plog and Daniel Bates, 1988, p. 7.
[12] Cuisine is often conceived in a similar way, at least in restaurant guides and grocery stores: *we* eat food but *others* eat "ethnic" food.

a. a style or fashion that a person takes up—a special way of doing something (as opposed to the "normal" or "neutral" way). For example, the Iraq Culture Smart Card suggests that one "[a]llocate plenty of time for refreshments before attempting to engage an Iraqi in business conversation."[13] The assumption is that there is such a thing as a business conversation, and while *we* simply have business conversations, *Iraqis* have a special way of having business conversations—namely, following extensive refreshments. (From the Iraqi perspective, taking refreshments is surely *part* of a business conversation, not a prologue to it);
b. a fixed code or algorithm for behavior that individuals unthinkingly follow and within which they are trapped, and which if soldiers also follow will automatically unlock goodwill and compliance.[14] For example, the ubiquitous advice to soldiers that they should not expose the soles of their feet or shoes to an Iraqi—or that they should not use the "OK" or "thumbs up" signs, which are obscene in Iraq—in effect assumes that such behavior will mechanically cause a negative reaction in an Iraqi, who is in turn unable to make a reciprocal cultural accommodation.[15]

On either approach, culture is understood as a lens that filters or distorts a person's perception of the world.[16] It inflects the otherwise neutral and genuine access to reality that "we"—whether "we Americans," "we Westerners," or "we soldiers"—have. With such access, we are able to act normally and rationally, while those afflicted with a culture act not for reasons but on the basis of tradition, and not spontaneously, but according to an internalized rulebook.

To interact with someone under the influence of such a filter is, first, to acknowledge that it is there, distorting perception and influencing behavior ("the

---

13 MCIA, "Iraq Culture Smart Card."
14 *Counterinsurgency* (United States Department of the Army and United States Marine Corps, 2006) explicitly describes culture as "an 'operational code'" (pp. 3–38) and speaks of "decoding" it (pp. 3–49).
15 Both pieces of advice are given on the "Iraq Culture Smart Card."
16 This conception of culture is explicit in the language of *Counterinsurgency* and in similar texts from "the cultural turn." For example: "A belief system acts as a filter for new information: it is the lens through which people perceive the world." (United States Department of the Army and United States Marine Corps, 2006, pp. 3–47). "Culture conditions the individual's range of actions and ideas" (United States Department of the Army and United States Marine Corps, 2006, pp. 3–38). "Culture influences how people make judgments about what is right and wrong, assess what is important and unimportant" (United States Department of the Army and United States Marine Corps, 2006, pp. 3–38). "[A] culture provides a lens through which its members see and understand the world." Lt. Col. William D. Wunderle, 2006, p. 9.

cultural turn"). Second, one must study the cultural rulebook that the encultured are following ("cultural awareness").[17] Third, one must make allowances for the fact that these others' perceptions and behaviors are subject to cultural influence ("cultural sensitivity"). Persons afflicted with culture must be handled cautiously, as if they are wild, unpredictable animals. Lt. Col. William D. Wunderle uses a different metaphor—one more suited to the concept of "human terrain"—to make the same point: "An American soldier can liken culture to a minefield: dangerous ground that, if not breached, must be navigated with caution, understanding, and respect."[18] Whether an encultured person is an animal or a mine, they are dangerous, unpredictable, and irrational—governed by (cultural) instinct or (cultural) mechanics rather than by reason.

Soldiers on the ground soon found this view of culture to be inadequate. While learning Iraqi norms of interaction was helpful for new encounters, it provided little guidance for long-term relationships. As one marine colonel said: "Don't show them the bottom of your feet, don't eat with your left hand, and I'm left-handed, don't talk about women, sex, religion, politics... and that's all they wanted to talk about once they got to know you!"[19] Or again, soldiers avoiding the "OK" and "thumbs up" signs found within weeks of the invasion that Iraqi children both understood and used these signs in their Western meanings.[20] They found that culture cannot be understood as a rulebook that others slavishly follow and which must be unidirectionally accommodated. Indeed, the very idea that people who have a culture filter reality in a way that "we" do not leads to interactions characterized by condescension and reminiscent of colonial projects. This approach could not help U.S. soldiers to interact more effectively with Iraqi civilians in the long term. What they needed instead was the concept of *world*.

---

17 Wunderle identifies four stages of "culture awareness": acquiring *data*, adding meaning to produce *information*, analyzing that to acquire *knowledge*, and synthesizing that and applying judgement to it in order to *understand*. (William D. Wunderle, 2006, p. 10). Each step advances on the others by virtue of "provid[ing] further meaning" (William D. Wunderle, 2006, p. 10). When cultural understanding is "fused" with cultural intelligence (whatever that is), then we have *cultural competence*, which "implies insight" (William D. Wunderle, 2006, p. 11).
18 William D. Wunderle, 2006, p. 3.
19 Quoted in Davis, El Zein, and Takruri, 2010, p. 307. The same claim was made by "C" (former Marine Corps non-commissioned officer who did a tour of Anbar), in an interview with Jon Askonas, 17 August 2016.
20 "G" (former Army special operations non-commissioned officer who did several tours of Iraq), in an interview with Jon Askonas, August 25, 2016.

Fig. 1: Baghdad Children. Photographer: Klint Janulis. © Klint Janulis

4

A world is a meaningful context in which we dwell. If culture is like a quirky accent with which others speak, world is more like a language.²¹ First, just as a language is not a special way of speaking but what allows one to speak at all, so too a world is not a special way of seeing and acting but is instead what permits one to see and act in the first place. It is not a filter or lens that distorts perception and behavior but the precondition and context for all perception and behavior. Only on the basis of a world can one perceive, experience, or act at all. Because world is the precondition for all human seeing and doing, everyone must have and move within a world, just as everyone who speaks must have and speak with a language.

---

21 This is not just an analogy; language is intimately related to world as a context of meaning. The question of the possible overlap or identity of the two is an important and difficult one.

Because world is the basis on which human experience is possible, *what* one sees and *what* one's actions *count as* depend upon the world that one is in. Just as a language is a context of possible meanings that one might invoke (the semantic) and possible ways of putting them together (the syntactic), so too world is a context of possible ways in which things might be meaningful and possible meaningful relations between things. Thus, in the world of the soldier, the security checkpoint might be meaningful as *a necessary deterrent to violence*, whereas in the world of an Iraqi the same checkpoint might show up meaningfully as *a major inconvenience to be dealt with on the way to work*—or as *presenting a situation in which I and my family might be in danger*. On the basis of these differences in meaning, a behavior like driving through a security checkpoint without stopping is a different sort of action in the different worlds: it is *a threatening provocation* to the soldier, *an expedience* to the irritated Iraqi, or *the surest way to avoid harm* to the fearful head of the family.

Further, such meaningful experiences are our *first* encounter with things, not a result of laying a subsequent interpretation over a neutral encounter. Consider that a particular hand gesture shows up to the U.S. soldier as *an affirmation* whereas it might show up to an Iraqi as *an obscene insult*. Considered first-personally, it is not that we see a particular hand gesture and then interpret it as an affirmation or as an insult. Rather, we simply see *an affirmation* or *an insult*. Try it yourself: it takes a lot of work to perceive the "thumbs up" gesture either as a mere configuration of a human hand or as another culture sees it. Similarly, there is no neutral experience of the *checkpoint* to which interpretations like *necessary deterrent*, *major inconvenience*, or *threat to my family* attach like appendices. Rather, there is just the experience of *(checkpoint-as-)deterrent, (checkpoint-as-)inconvenience*, or *(checkpoint-as-)threat*. No experience is neutral; all experience is always already meaningful in the context of some world. The same is true of speech: we never hear mere noise or sound, but always meaningful speech—even if we do not yet know what it means.

In a language, the range of possible ways in which things can be meaningful is determined by the structure and history of the language, as well as by the ways in which linguistic practice shapes its ongoing development. In contrast, a world is a space of possible meanings that is shaped by *who one is trying to be*. To have a world, I must be trying to be someone in particular—a soldier, a teacher, a civilian under occupation. (Obviously, who I am trying to be is not always something that is entirely up to me to choose). It is on the basis of my project of *trying to be me* that things are meaningful to me as what they are. That is, it is because I am trying to be soldier that a checkpoint shows up as *a necessary deterrent to violence*. And it might be because I am trying to be a teacher—and so, trying to get to class—that the checkpoint shows up as *a major inconvenience*. Who I am trying to be establishes what things are and can be in my world.

Who I am trying to be also makes sense of what I do and determines whether it is rational. To be practically rational is to be able to decide how one should go about achieving one's goals. One must thus first understand what a person's goal is—ultimately, who they are trying to be—in order to determine whether their behavior is rational. Consider this description of appeals to Iraqi honor culture to explain the reactions of Iraqis to house searches:

> A skeptic might ask whether one really needs intermediary concepts of 'honor', 'shame', 'face', or 'fervent religious belief' to understand why a householder might be offended or provoked by having a boot placed on his neck. One effect of introducing such a concept is to portray as alien—read 'culturally driven'—some Iraqi reactions that a soldier or Marine might otherwise find intelligible or normal. And the effect of that, in turn, is to maintain the vision of the U.S. military's own operations—including house searches, detentions, and roadblocks—as tactical imperatives, in and of themselves nonoffensive. Marked as demonstrations of U.S. 'practical reason', they are cast as putatively acultural.[22]

The soldiers view their own actions as rational, and they can do so because they (implicitly) see those actions as instrumental in the project of *trying to be a soldier in a counterinsurgency*. Overlooking another person's project of *trying to be someone* removes the possibility of seeing their actions as practically rational in this way. Their behavior will thus appear irrational. To make sense of it, we attribute it to some irrational feature of the person—in this case, feelings of shame in an honor culture. But simply recognizing that the Iraqi householder is *trying to be a householder* shows his actions to be perfectly rational. Anyone —Iraqi or American—who is *trying to be a householder* would react aggressively to a violent intrusion into their household and would be extremely upset about being physically dominated and incapacitated by a stranger in their own home. When we recognize who the Iraqi is trying to be, his actions manifest as rational —just as it is only when we recognize who the soldier is trying to be that her actions appear rational. Recognizing the concept of world, and how practical rationality is subordinate to it, reveals the same practical rationality shared by members of different worlds.

On the ground, successful soldiers understood this at some level. Our interviews indicated that cultural explanations and verbiage, though often used, were not helpful in helping soldiers decide how to behave. Rather, soldiers found it more helpful to explain Iraqi behavior to each other by way of analogous situations in American society. *Diyah* (blood money/ransom) and *qisas* (equal retali-

---

[22] Keith Brown, 2008, p. 446.

ation) might appear to be foreign concepts to Americans, but the idea that—for example—the head of the family of an elderly woman incapacitated during a hard-knock raid would (a) be extremely angry and (b) want compensation for the harm done is something that any American can grasp as reasonable for someone who is *trying to be a householder*.

5

Recognizing that we each live in some particular world is the first step in successfully interacting with someone who lives in a different world. We live in different worlds because of differences in who we are trying to be, and these differences must be acknowledged and taken account of. Consider that when the U.S. Army's Humvees drove through Iraqi streets in a village outside Baquba, their radio antennas brought down television and electricity cables that had been strung between houses, needlessly causing friction with the local Iraqi population.[23] A "cultural" analysis of the situation might have highlighted the "tribal, favor economy," by which local personages allowed their neighbors to pirate electricity and satellite television from them, and the fact that, in "Iraqi honor culture," the Americans' actions demanded a response. But, as one interviewee (an American veteran with training in anthropology) put it: "It's not that the 'Arab mind' is interested in honor or tribal relationships or that bullshit. The 'Arab mind' is interested in television and air conditioning [in the 50+ degree summer]."[24] The Iraqis were not *trying to save face*, or *trying to sustain a favor economy*, but instead *trying to stay cool and entertained in the middle of summer*. Understanding *this* would have allowed U.S. soldiers to understand the world of meaning that they were disrupting, and to understand why a negative response to that disruption was perfectly rational, understandable, and predictable.

The second step in successfully interacting across different worlds is to find a shared space of meaning. Notice that interacting across worlds is something that we do all the time, usually without any great difficulty. The world of the teacher differs from that of his students, just as the world of the Wall Street executive differs from that of her tailor. But these people manage to communicate and work together nonetheless—because, despite the differences between their worlds, they share some common ground. We inhabit some worlds together: perhaps the world of our neighborhood, our class, our popular culture, our gender

---

[23] "G", 2016.
[24] "G", 2016.

identity, or our nation. We can rely on this shared space of meaning when we interact with others from different worlds. We do the same when we communicate with someone who speaks a different language: we turn to some language that we both share, even if it is just that of simple hand gestures and stick figure drawings.

If two people are to communicate when their primary languages differ, each needs to recognize and make allowances for the difficulty of the interaction. While "cultural sensitivity" is unidirectional—something that "we" do for "them"—interacting across worlds is bidirectional. Through bidirectional accommodation, one can even start to learn the language of the other person, which in this case means: come to inhabit more of the same worlds and so have a more expansive shared space of meaning. We saw that U.S. soldiers found that the Iraq Culture Smart Cards' insistence that the "thumbs up" gesture is obscene in Iraq was overly simplistic, because some Iraqi children used the "thumbs up" gesture in a Western way. These children did so not because they had broken free of a rigid cultural code but because they knew the Western meaning of the gesture and they *wanted to interact with American troops* (if only to get candy). Taking up this new project of *trying to be such a person* brings the Iraqi children into the shared world of Western hand gestures (at least, minimally).

Finally, it is important to recognize differences *within* worlds. We all inhabit multiple, nested and overlapping worlds, since there are multiple, nested and overlapping aspects to *who we are trying to be*. Some of these will be more dominant and organizing than others—more central to our self-identity, and so more constitutive of our world. The centrality of these various identities is constantly negotiated and renegotiated as we live out our lives. Recognizing and exploiting this fact might have helped the U.S. Military to turn Iraq towards a path other than that which led to the violent crisis it is currently experiencing. Consider that in the Arab world prior to 2003, "Sunni" was a vague and dynamic category; most Sunnis experienced their identity un-self-consciously. The exception was the Salafism espoused by the Saudi regime, which sought to reify the gap between "true" Muslims (Sunnis) and the heretic Shia. Such Sunni rejectionism is now at the heart of the Iraqi insurgency and of ISIS, which reject the authority and legitimacy of the Iraqi and Syrian governments. What allowed this shared sense of Sunni identity and grievance to develop and to become such a powerful force? One contributing factor (among many) was the U.S. military's rigid model of Iraqi culture as divided into three primary groups: Sunni, Shia, and Kurd.[25]

---

[25] This parsing was ubiquitous in U.S. training on Iraqi society, as confirmed by both of our

Had the U.S. military been more attentive to the rich variety of identities that all Iraqis were trying to live out, it could have approached its operations in Iraq in a way that fostered and centered identities such as *Iraqi nationalist* rather than *Sunni rejectionist*.

6

For a long time, the U.S. military could avoid making genuine sense of the worlds of Iraqis because of the sheer amount of power it possessed.[26] But as the counterinsurgency efforts continued, understanding and effectively interacting with Iraqis on a person-to-person level became increasingly important—and with it, the need for something like a "cultural turn." We claim that the U.S. military would have been better served by the philosophical concept of world than it was by the old-fashioned anthropological concept of culture. Interacting with others who dwell in a different world requires not learning cultural factoids but finding common ground, not learning the rules of etiquette but learning who people are trying to be and so how their worlds hang together as coherent spaces of meaning. It requires recognizing that we each inhabit spaces of meaning shaped by who we are trying to be, rather than presenting those in different worlds as alien and irrational. It requires a willingness to engage in dialogue and mutual recognition, not unidirectional accommodation and sensitivity to the minefield of culture. It takes, in short, not an etiquette expert but a diplomat.

Can soldiers be expected to be diplomats? We do not pretend to answer that question at the level of policy or strategy. But at the level of tactics, where the philosophers' insights into world need to be operationalized so that they can benefit U.S. soldiers, we see no reason why not. Figuring out how best to present the philosophical concept of world, and the lessons we can draw from it about interacting across worlds, in a way that is both accessible and useful for soldiers

---

interviews and, for a start, by Thomas E. Ricks, 2006, pp. 163,177; and Michael R. Gordon and Bernard E. Trainor, 2012, p. 131.

26 According to David Graeber, the excess of power that occupying militaries and colonial administrations have over local populations leads to inequality in "interpretive labor" and a certain "stupidity" of those in power. Local populations spend significant energy and resources making sense of the occupying administration, adapting where possible to the organizational goals and processes of the occupier rather than pushing back (and, when they do push back, they do so with the knowledge gleaned from their interpretive labor). Because the occupiers do little, if any, interpretive labor, they learn comparatively little but are then baffled as to why the locals seem to make sense of them more readily than they can make sense of local society. David Graeber, 2015, p. 42.

and commanders on the ground will of course be a difficult task. But it is clearly a task for a philosopher.

Philosophical investigation into world can also help us to understand the sort of *world collapse* that Iraqis underwent after the fall of Saddam Hussein and during the U.S. occupation. The spaces of meaning that they previously inhabited changed suddenly and dramatically, because they could no longer in every case *be* the people they were trying to be. In addition, there was something new that they had to try to be: a civilian in an occupied territory (or, an insurgent, a refugee, and so on). What sort of change is this, and what sort of breakdown does it involve? The traditional concept of "culture," with its fixed categories and long-term historical genealogies, is ill-placed to make sense of such rapid change. But if what is at stake in counterinsurgency is precisely how a collapsed world will reconfigure itself into a new, stable world, then answering the philosophical question of how worlds change is crucial to understanding what the goal of counterinsurgency is and how U.S. and international forces can and cannot help Iraqis to rebuild the Iraqi world as a space of meaning.[27]

There is much more theoretical philosophical work to be done to determine what worlds are, how they are structured, how they break down, and how they change over time. That this theoretical work may have a practical payoff for institutions like the U.S. military and societies like Iraq does not validate philosophical investigation (which is valid for other reasons) or reduce its value to utility. But it does give us one reason that we do need philosophy.

Bibliography

American Anthropological Association. "American Anthropological Association's Executive Board Statement on the Human Terrain System Project." Arlington, VA: American Anthropological Association, November 6, 2007. Accessed September 20, 2016. http://s3.amazonaws.com/rdcms-aaa/files/production/public/FileDownloads/pdfs/pdf/EB_Resolution_110807.pdf.

Brown, Keith. "'All They Understand Is Force': Debating Culture in Operation Iraqi Freedom." *American Anthropologist* 110 (2008): pp. 443–453.

"C" (former Marine Corps non-commissioned officer who did a tour of Anbar). Interview with Jon Askonas, August 17, 2016.)

Davis, Rochelle. "Culture as a Weapons System." *Middle East Report* 225 (2010): pp.8–13.

---

[27] This project raises serious concerns about colonialism and imperialism, which must also be addressed by philosophy—specifically, by ethics and by social and political philosophy.

Davis, Rochelle, Dahlia El Zein, and Dena Takruri. "Cultural Sensitivity in a Military Occupation: The U.S. Military in Iraq." In Kelly et al., *Anthropology and Global Counterinsurgency*, Chicago: University of Chicago Press, 2010, pp. 297–310.

"G" (former Army special operations non-commissioned officer who did several tours of Iraq). Interview with Jon Askonas, August 25, 2016.

Gordon, Michael R. and Bernard E. Trainor. *The Endgame*. New York: Pantheon Books, 2012.

Graeber, David. *The Utopia of Rules: On Technology, Stupidity and the Secret Joys of Bureaucracy*. Brooklyn, NY: Melville House, 2015.

Guenther, Lisa. *Solitary Confinement: Social Death and Its Afterlives*. Minneapolis: University of Minnesota Press, 2013.

Gusterson, Hugh. "The Cultural Turn in the War on Terror." In Kelly et al., *Anthropology and Global Counterinsurgency*, 2010, pp. 279–296.

Hamilton, Colonel Sharon R. "HTS Director's Message." *Military Intelligence Professional Bulletin* (October-December 2011): PB34–11–4, Human Terrain System.

Heidegger, Martin. *Being and Time*. J. Macquarrie and E. Robinson (Trans.). San Francisco: HarperCollins Publishers, 1963.

Husserl, Edmund. *The Crisis of the European Sciences and Transcendental Phenomenology: An Introduction to Phenomenological Philosophy*. David Carr (Trans.). Evanston: Northwestern University Press, 1970.

Husserl, Edmund. *Ideas Pertaining to a Pure Phenomenology and to a Phenomenological Philosophy: Second Book Studies in the Phenomenology of Constitution*. R. Rojcewicz and A. Schuwer (Trans.). Dordrecht: Kluwer Academic Publishers, 1989.

Kelley, John D., Beatrice Jauregui, Sean T. Mitchell, and Jeremy Walton (Eds.) *Anthropology and Global Counterinsurgency*. Chicago: University of Chicago Press, 2010.

Marine Corps Intelligence Activity (MCIA). *Iraq Culture Smart Card: Guide for Cultural Awareness GTA 24–01–003*. Quantico, VA: Marine Corps Intelligence Activity, Quality and Dissemination Branch, 2006. Accessed September 20, 2016. https://fas.org/irp/dod dir/usmc/iraqsmart-0506.pdf (via The Federation of American Scientists).

Merleau-Ponty, Maurice. *Phenomenology of Perception*. Donald Landes (Trans.). Oxford: Routledge, 2012.

Price, David. "Pilfered Scholarship Devastates General Petraeus's Counterinsurgency Manual * Core Chapter a Morass of 'Borrowed' Quotes * University of Chicago Press Badly Compromised * Counterinsurgency Anthropologist Montgomery McFate's Role Under Attack." *Counterpunch*, October 30, 2007. Accessed April 7, 2017. https://www.counter punch.org/2007/10/30/pilfered-scholarship-devastates-general-petraeuss-counter insurgency-manual-core-chapter-a-morass-of-borrowed-quotes-university-of-chicago-press-badly-compromised-counterinsurgency/.

Ratcliffe, Matthew. *Experiences of Depression: A Study in Phenomenology*. Oxford: Oxford University Press, 2015.

Ricks, Thomas E. *Fiasco*. New York: Penguin Press, 2006.

United States Department of Defense. "The Minerva Initiative." Washington, DC: United States Department of Defense, 2016. Accessed September 20, 2016.. *Internet Archive*. https://web.archive.org/web/20160925172159/http://minerva.dtic.mil/

United States Department of the Army and United States Marine Corps. FM 3-24 Counterinsurgency, *MCWP3–33.5*. Washington, DC: United States Department of the Army and United States Marine Corps, 2006.

Wunderle, Lieutenant Colonel William D. *Through the Lens of Cultural Awareness: A Primer for US Armed Forces Deploying to Arab and Middle Eastern Countries*. Fort Leavenworth, KS: Combat Studies Institute Press, 2006.

Paul Redding
The Role of Philosophy in "Post-Truth" Times

Abstract: The challenge to the "universal point of view" represented by the election of Donald Trump in 2016 is treated here as a challenge to the conception of "the open society" that many had adopted after the Second World War. Karl Popper's influential modelling of democratic decision making on an idealised conception of the achievement of scientific consensus coincides with the polarisation of the "knowledge classes" from Trump's "forgotten people". A different conception of philosophy and its role in modern society is required as a non-scientistic alternative for reconciling the universal point of view with the views of the broader populace.

Introduction: 2016 and the Retreat from the "Universal Point of View"

In the first weeks of 2017, and the last of his term in office, the outgoing United States president, Barack Obama, published three articles in prestigious refereed academic journals. One assayed the risks accompanying the abandonment of his key policy reform, the Affordable Care Act, or "Obamacare."[1] Another similarly dealt with a topic upon which a president and Harvard-trained lawyer might be expected to have firm opinions, criminal justice reform.[2] The third, addressing the issue of climate change and published in the major journal *Science*,[3] was clearly meant to underline the attitude that Obama had held during his presidency towards the authority of science with regard to policy making, and starkly to contrast it with that manifest by the incoming president elect, Donald Trump.

These publications added to the familiar picture of Obama: an informed, thoughtful and cultivated, reform-oriented politician. In particular, known as

---

I am most grateful to Alex Lefevbre for helpful comments on an earlier version of this essay.

[1] Barack Obama, 2017, "Repealing the Affordable Care Act without a Replacement—The Risks to American Health Care." pp. 277–99.
[2] Barack Obama, 2017, "The President's Role in Advancing Criminal Justice Reform." pp. 816–66.
[3] Barack Obama, 2017, "The Irreversible Momentum of Clean Energy".

https://doi.org/10.1515/9783110650990-009

something of a "science nerd" Obama had, according to his science advisor, taken pride in gathering leading scientists around his dinner table and questioning them on the arcane details of their work.[4] His commitment to the authority of science was in stark contrast to the apparent attitude of Trump, whose communicative skills clearly lay in a form of media strikingly different to that of academic publishing. One of Trump's favored forms of communication was the 140-character-or-less "tweet" of the "information age," and, in November 2012, he had tweeted what might be thought as a preemptory, typically *Trumpian*, rejoinder to the ideas expressed in Obama's later *Science* article. According to Trump, the idea of climate change was a hoax "created by and for the Chinese in order to make U.S. manufacturing non-competitive."[5]

This contrast between the carefully constructed, appropriately footnoted scholarly article, having to face the tests of peer assessment before publication, and the Trumpian "tweet," the contents of which were often radically at variance with informed opinion and delivered with no regard for the provision of evidence, might stand as exemplificatory of a challenge facing the functioning of modern liberal democracies—that of the capacity of democratic governments to formulate and implement policies on the basis of true beliefs about the world. Thus, in the U.S. presidential campaign of 2016, the findings of the army of "fact checkers" employed by the liberal U.S. press to assess the truth or falsity of the claims made by the two leading candidates contributed to the growth of the notion that Western liberal democracies had entered into a new era. Of course, in democracies politicians in general are not thought to be beyond lying or "bending" the truth to attract voters, but Trump had taken the disregard of truth to new levels. Drawing parallels with the campaigns leading up to the "Brexit" referendum in June 2016,[6] commentators announced the transition to "post-truth" or "post-fact" times. Moreover, to liberals in both polities, the success of lying and misinformation came as a shock. With these elections not only had we entered an era of "post-truth," the globalising thrust that had dominated the West since the end of the Cold-War had been replaced by the emergence of a new form of *nationalism*.

The complex causes of this phenomenon will surely be widely debated over the coming years and decades. To what degree should the neglect of the "forgotten people" of the de-industrialized regions by the city-based political classes and "elites" in their pursuit of the benefits of globalization be held accountable?

---

[4] Dave Levitan, 2016.
[5] Donald J. Trump, Twitter Post, November 7, 2012, 6:15 AM.
[6] D. Jackson, E. Thorsen, and D. Wring, (Eds.), 2016.

To what degree should we blame the effect on popular opinion of the rise of "social media" and decline of quality newspapers? Such large and difficult questions, begging the results of diverse empirical research, are well beyond the scope of issues that can be engaged with here. Rather, I want to focus on these events from a distinctly *philosophical* point of view, and regard them as signalling a change in the balance between the terms of a pair of distinctions that have played central roles within *philosophical* thought since the time of the Greeks: those between "the one" and "the many," and "the universal" and "the particular." With these in mind, the apparent flight from issues of "truth," especially from appeals to the authority of *science*, might be seen as having features in common with the rejection of allegiance to *higher-level* political unities, such as the rejection by voting British citizens of the European Union, and the rejection by U.S. voters of "large government," that is, of the type reformist centralized policy agenda associated in the popular mind with reforming presidents like Obama.

Both cases manifest a resistance of voters to adopt a "universal point of view." Politically this is obvious in attitudes towards the universality of rights. In Great Britain, attitudes against immigration, and so against the rights of *non*-UK citizens, clearly fuelled much of the "leave" vote, as it motivated the vote for Trump in the U.S. Seen from the liberal perspective, this is often interpreted as involving a moral incapacity to empathize with the lot of "human beings as such" or to adopt a non-personalized, disinterested, "universal" point of view. In the U.S. Trump similarly appealed to voters resistant to the views of liberals advocating the extension of rights within the community to those traditionally discriminated against. While from the 1950s and 60s, "new social movements" had effectively advocated the extension of those rights *purported* to be universal to those structurally prevented from enjoying them—blacks, women, gays, and so on—this in turn had now come to provoke claims of "reverse discrimination." The male, white, heterosexual *majority*—those whose place in the world had earlier benefited from the restriction of such rights—were now claiming to have *their rights* denied. To appreciate how the rejection of the authority of *science* might be linked to such a retreat from the universal point of view I want to appeal to the ideas of the early American pragmatist, C. S. Peirce, on the "fixation of belief."[7]

In Peirce's "pragmaticist" view, doubt and indecision amount to a problem for action, and thus individuals face a *practical* need to resolve on a set of beliefs on which to act. This *fixation of belief* has throughout history happened in vari-

---

7 Charles Sanders Peirce, 1986, pp. 242–57.

ous ways, and the ways he thought typical of the modern world he regarded as "not so much a natural gift" but as the results of "a long and difficult art."[8] Perhaps the most obvious method for the fixation of belief had always been the "method of tenacity," a simple steadfast holding to one's existing beliefs, yielding the benefits of a "great peace of mind,"[9] a method, of course, that is indifferent to the question of the *truth* of the beliefs involved. Being *social* creatures, however, our beliefs are easily "shaken by the differing beliefs of others," and a more common method will be that of acquiescence to the authority of those others, the authority of one's community. Again, while this method may have the benefits that result from social harmony, that one's community believes such and such is not a measure of its *truth*.[10] The eighteenth century "Enlightenment" might be thought of as the paradigm of a further method in which the harmonizing of beliefs becomes more rational because of the way it is brought about: here "conversing together and regarding matters in different lights, gradually develop beliefs in harmony with different causes."[11] The tradition of *metaphysical* thought, Peirce believed, most reflected *this* method, allowing beliefs to move further in the direction of universality, but here too, criteria that reflected the operations of the human mind as such could still limit the role of truth. Finally, the growth of the *empirical* sciences involved a new notion of having beliefs fixed by something *other* than subjective criteria, "some external permanency," a reality independent of all our ideas of it.[12]

Thus, on Peirce's criteria, philosophy and empirical science represent the most *depersonalized* forms of knowledge, and science in particular was meant to provide a picture of the world that is independent of all the *peculiarities* of human existence and experience. In contrast, the beliefs formed by the earlier "methods" are bound up with the believer's self-conception, either *as* an individual or a member of a group. But on these criteria, it would seem that the experience of 2016 has clearly demonstrated that the methods of "tenacity" and "authority," rather than open dialogue and empirical fixation, had been dominant in the formation of those beliefs determining the outcome of democratic processes, and empirical research seems to confirm this. With respect to the scientific

---

[8] Charles Sanders Peirce, 1986, p. 242.
[9] Charles Sanders Peirce, 1986, pp. 249–50.
[10] Peirce seemed to think of religion as working on the levels of fixation by both tenacity and authority. The "'deep pleasure' of conviction in the afterlife," for example, giving the benefits of tenacity and being reinforced by the authority of group like-mindedness. Charles Sanders Peirce, 1986, pp. 249 and 251.
[11] Charles Sanders Peirce, 1986, pp. 252–3.
[12] Charles Sanders Peirce, 1986, pp. 253–4.

theory of global warming, for example, *political identity* would seem to be the single biggest factor involved in belief fixation, some surveys showing that while around 90 percent of Democrat voters (roughly the same proportion as among the population of scientists) professed belief in anthropogenic climate change, less than a third of Tea Party Republicans did so.[13]

If it is the case that anthropogenic global warming is a reality, as roughly 97 percent of climatologists apparently agree,[14] and that without global actions to reduce carbon emissions we will face consequences of catastrophic proportion, then the events of 2016 signal that our democratic processes are surely failing with regard to the implementation of policies that are in line with the common good. What might philosophy contribute to the array of responses to this extremely worrying situation? In an effort to address this question, I want to start by reflecting on some assumptions about the functioning of knowledge in modern liberal democracies, assumptions that have prevailed since about the middle of the twentieth century and that, I believe, have contributed to the present dilemma. In particular, I want to focus on changing attitudes to the respective roles played in society by philosophy and the empirical sciences —the practices correlating with Peirce's third and fourth "methods" of belief-fixation. The tendency, I suggest, has been to look to the empirical sciences as the *sole* epistemic authority to be called upon to guide our collective action, and to marginalize the role of philosophical reflection. Paradoxically, this has resulted in a threat to the contribution of science itself to the formation and implementation of policy in democratic liberal states, with voters willing to treat a scientific consensus with scepticism.

---

13 Arlie Russell Hochschild, 2016. Of course, this does not imply that individual Democrat voters themselves have formed their beliefs on the basis of rational debate with those of different views or empirical evidence. They *too* might just as easily have had their beliefs formed on the basis of tenacity and authority, identifying with a class they consider rational and that in general accepts the authority of science. That is, we might think of members of *both* groups as expressing an opinion "Around here we don't take kindly to the view that climate change does/does not exist!" Nevertheless, we might still think of liberals' beliefs as in turn resting on a belief or *trust* in a scientific consensus that, on Peircean criteria, had been formed on the basis of a different and distinctive "method."
14 John Cook, et. al., 2016.

1 Philosophy in the Age of Specialist Science

Something obvious but significant about the modern sciences was made apparent to me in the course of a conversation I had with a retired cardiologist in which he offered the following reflection. During his career, he remarked, he often heard individuals lamenting the decline of the generalist physician. A familiar question was: "Who is going to look after the whole patient?" But, he added, the situation was, in fact, much more extreme. Now there aren't any general *cardiologists:* "Now there's no-one to look after the whole *heart!*"

This reflection was hardly reassuring for his philosophical interlocutor: if the existence of general cardiologists, concerned with the *whole heart* has been threatened, what of those meant to be concerned with nothing short of *everything?* In the age of the specialist, what possible role in the "great conversation of humankind" can there be for those concerned, as Wilfrid Sellars expressed it,[15] with understanding "how things in the broadest possible sense of the term hang together in the broadest possible sense of the term"?

It is often said that even by the eighteenth century the amount of specialist scientific knowledge had begun to outstrip the capacity for *any* individual to be adequately informed across the spectrum of the sciences. Given the massive growth of science since that time, how *could* a discipline such as philosophy, which purported to be both scientific *and* necessarily general, constitute a serious undertaking? Doubts of this sort have been a constant even *within* the modern philosophical community itself, and were especially marked within the work of the so-called "Logical Positivists" based in Vienna in the 1930s, who asserted the meaninglessness of claims within "metaphysics"—the sorts of philosophical claims made within Peircean open dialogues but with *no* particular connection to empirical discoveries, claims, we might say, made within dialogues conducted from the armchair rather than across the laboratory bench. The Nazi annexation of Austria dispersed the members of the "Vienna Circle," predominantly to the United States, where they were to have considerable influence upon the development of academic philosophy, and while debates within philosophy have moved on from their views, their "scientism" and distrust of traditional ways of doing philosophy have remained influential. To make a start in attempting to assess some of the more general effects of this annexation of philosophy to the empirical sciences I want to consider the influential work of Karl Popper, a type of "critical fellow-traveler" of the positivists who attempted to overcome some of the

---

[15] Wilfrid Sellars, 1963, p. 1.

limitations of their views, and who, in a widely read work, attempted to apply his views about *science* to the functioning of society more broadly.

Popper, born in Vienna in 1902 and initially formulating his views in the 1930s in the context of the activities of the Vienna Circle, is famous for having criticized his positivist colleagues for their view that the scientific status of theories rested upon their capacity for empirical *verification*. Rather, Popper stressed the importance of inter-subjective *testing* of theories within the community of scientists—good theories were ones that for a time resisted attempts to *falsify* them.[16] Thus he suggested that rather from resulting from attempts to find empirical grounds for a theory that could be known with certainty, science advanced when a provisionally endorsed theory was replaced by the better, *falsifying* one. Accordingly, Popper's epistemology was "fallibilist" and "anti-foundationalist." *No* knowledge was certain: even our *best* scientific theories could be false.

Superficially, this *could* be seen as giving comfort to the *critics* of science: theories, it could be said, are *just* theories, of which we *cannot* be certain. But of course, Popper's theory was more devastating for all *non*-scientific knowledge claims, such as religious ones. As non-falsifiable, they were incapable of rational progress. They did not even have *provisional* legitimacy as worthy of belief. Similarly, Popper's views made problematic the views of common sense. In aligning his views with elements of the critical philosophy of Immanuel Kant, Popper, like Peirce, believed perceptual experience to be always shaped by general concepts or theories. These generalities, of course, could be false, and so seemingly the most obvious perceptual experience as well as experimental evidence could be erroneous. Thus, early advocates of the modern heliocentric view of the universe had to argue against the supposed "facts" of common-sense experience attesting to the sun's movement around a stationary Earth. Rather than focus on the "grounds" or "foundations" of scientific knowledge in the capacities of individuals, Popper effectively combined Peirce's methods of open dialogue and empirical fixation. It did not matter where scientific ideas came from, the crucial thing of science was the *way in which* they could be subjected to rational criticism within the scientific community.

By underlining the *social* nature of science, Popper's approach in turn demonstrated the relevance of specialization. Observations are fallible because they rely on "auxiliary hypotheses" that could turn out to be false. For example, in the

---

[16] Ideas of verification faced the "problem of induction" formulated by Hume: one could never infer to general claims from a finite number of particular ones. For an overview of Popper's philosophy of science, see, for example, Stephen Thornton, 2016.

development of modern cosmology, critics of the heliocentric theory argued that *were* it to be true, the apparent size of other planets in observations made from the earth should vary, given the differences of the solar years involved. But careful observations showed that they remained a constant size. This objection was only overcome much later when it was found that the *appearance* of the constant size of the planets was an artifact of the way the unaided eye responds to light of very low intensities. Thus, specialists working in one area of science rely on the results of those working in very different areas, a feature readily apparent in the complex science of climatology, and unappreciated by many of its non-specialist critics.[17]

Popper's views on science have been influential both inside and outside philosophy, but here I want to turn to the broader effects of his views which combined his ideas about *science* with his ideas about politics. Just as he *socialized* science, Popper might be described as having *scientized society*, and having done so in a way that contributed to a certain conception of politics in which science is treated as the last court of appeal in questions of policy, and issues deemed as not open to empirical falsification, such as *philosophical ones*, are marginalized.

2 Popper and the Excommunication of Philosophy from Politics

Only months after the allies' victory in Europe in May 1945, Popper published a two-volume, popularly written work of political philosophy, *The Open Society and Its Enemies*.[18] While often criticized *within* the academies for many aspects of his analysis and argument, the work quickly broke through the type of reception barrier that usually surrounds the outputs of professional philosophers, and in this regard it soon became a source of ideas for an educated lay audience. Popper set forth the idea of an "open society" that starkly contrasted with "closed" ones. Written during World War II,[19] Nazi Germany was a central target, but, during the following Cold War, the book was seen to apply to the contrast between the West and the Soviet Union. At the time of its publication Popper was relatively unknown, having just taken up a teaching position at the London

---

[17] The tendency of critics of climate change to selectively focus on such apparently refuting empirical findings is popularly referred to as "cherry picking."
[18] Karl Popper, 2011.
[19] While first published in 1945, the book had been substantially completed in the early1940s and Popper had been seeking a publisher since 1942. See: Malachi Haim Hachohen 2000, p.450.

School of Economics (after what he clearly considered a period of *exile* teaching in New Zealand). Popper soon became publically celebrated, however, not so much for his technical work in the philosophy of science, but for this foray into political philosophy.

The Open Society and Its Enemies itself had not so much established Popper's reputation in academia: it was often ignored within academic political science, and criticized by historians of philosophy for what were often taken to be its wildly distorted accounts of classical philosophers. Nevertheless, it was to go through a number of re-editions prior to Popper's death in 1994. Continually remaining in print since its release, the current American edition by Princeton University Press cites its inclusion in an influential list of "100 Best Nonfiction Books of the Twentieth Century."[20] In terms of their practical application, Popper's ideas guided the activities of a former student, the investor and philanthropist George Soros, whose "Open Society Foundation" became involved in the process in "opening" former "closed" societies of eastern Europe after the fall of Communism.[21] In recent years the work seems to have re-emerged into public consciousness in the context of the attacks on our "open society" by the new prototype of a closed one, ISIS.[22] Here I want to consider this influential work as reflecting and even having contributed to the conception of the role of government that emerged after the war.

The repercussions of Popper's theory for claims about the world *other* than scientifically falsifiable ones are obvious. Closed societies such as totalitarian ones provided the most obvious target, and Popper regarded these as built upon the philosophical theories of Hegel and Marx. Such "historicist" theories, he claimed, were based on the unfalsifiable, and so non-scientific, ideas about society developing teleologically in ways predetermined by the *essential nature* of social life itself. In particular, the philosophy of Hegel was behind the historicist, teleological assumptions of both the German Nazis and the Russian Communists, with their beliefs about the destiny of the German *Volk*, on the one hand, and the international working class, on the other.

But Popper's criticism of "historicism" went further than his, textually highly challengeable, attacks on Hegel.[23] Hegel's ideas, he thought, were simply the log-

---

20 See: Princeton University Press (website), http://press.princeton.edu/titles/9984.html.
21 See: Open Society Foundations (website), https://www.opensocietyfoundations.org.
22 In relation to the terrorist attacks in Paris in 2015, see Judy Dempsey, 2015. I suspect that similar circumstances account for the appearance of *The Open Society and Its Enemies* (at number 35) on *The Guardian*'s recent listing of "100 Best Non-Fiction Books." Robert McCrum, 2016.
23 Popper has been much criticized by historians of philosophy for *all* his historical portraits, but especially that of Hegel. His views on Hegel in particular had, on his own admission, relied

ical conclusion of the type of *essentialist* assumptions that had defined ancient Greek philosophies of Plato and Aristotle. Here, like his positivistic Viennese associates, Popper's mistrust of the "oracular" philosophical tradition was deep and comprehensive: effectively *all* forms of philosophy were seen as flawed by Aristotelian assumptions about "essences" of things discoverable by philosophical inquiry.[24] Thus the philosophy of the European phenomenologists, Husserl, Heidegger, Jaspers, and Scheler were included in his critique,[25] as was the work of Ludwig Wittgenstein, early and late, and the type "ordinary language philosophy" emerging in Great Britain at that time.[26] Popper endorsed, but struggled to defend, distinctly "metaphysical" ideas of his own—endorsing a strong form of realism, for example. Effectively, however, his attitude to philosophy *in general* was close to that minimalist approach expressed by another post-positivist philosopher, Willard van Ormond Quine: "philosophy of science is philosophy enough."[27]

At basis, then, Popper's conception of the "open" political community was modelled on the structure and operations of the scientific community as he saw it. Just as it didn't matter *where* scientific ideas came from, analogously, it did not matter *where* particular social policy came from. What was important was that the policies put forward by the rulers could be assessed and rationally criticized *by* citizens. If found wanting, these policies would, like falsified scientific theories, be discarded, the usual mechanism involving the ousting of the policy makers by the ballot box. Thus, Popper's political cosmopolitanism mirrored the international nature of the scientific community, and the technocratic nature of the state as he conceived it mirrored the way scientific knowledge was applied in technology. He promoted "social engineering" as a feature of the Open Society, but of course it could not proceed on *a priori* principles: it had

---

heavily on an earlier book by the Hungarian Aurel Kolnai. Karl Popper, 1945, p. 281. In fact Popper's views here are far more extreme than Kolnai's, who while critical saw Hegel's overall political philosophy as tempered by various liberal elements. Aurel Kolnai, 1938, pp. 127–8.

24 In terms of his anti-Aristotelianism, Popper extended the critique of Aristotle that flowed from the revolution in logic starting in the latter decades of the nineteenth century with the work of Gottlob Frege and developed by Bertrand Russell. Russell had sought to show how almost *all* philosophy up to the turn of the twentieth century had been based on a naïve conception of logic coming from Aristotle, an attitude continued by the Vienna positivists.

25 Karl Popper, 1945, p. 286.

26 Karl Popper, 1945, pp. 226–36. Again, the contrast here with Kolnai is striking. Having studied with Husserl and having been particularly influenced by Scheler, Kolnai endorsed their phenomenological approaches, and his own philosophy had had much in common with the turn to "ordinary language" in British philosophy of the 1950s.

27 Willard Van Orman Quine, 1953, p. 446.

to be "piecemeal" and based on the best scientific theories available at the time.[28] Any effort to think of society as *based on* certain philosophical ideals or assumptions was flawed. In this sense, Popper's views converged with the then popular view of the post-War "end of ideology."[29] However, the events of 2016 have surely brought to the surface contradictions between the technocratic and democratic dimensions of the modern liberal state as conceived since the Second World War.

3 The Tea Party, Trump, and the Knowledge Classes

In a five-year study of Tea Party voters in the U.S. state of Louisiana, many of whom would have later morphed into Trump supporters, sociologist Arlie Russell Hochschild revealed the depth of feeling held against all the Democrat voting big-city "elites" with whom the policies of Obama were identified. Hochschild approached her study as an attempt to understand the "great paradox" manifested in voting patterns that had shown a growing tendency for poor white voters in the poorest states of the U.S. to be attracted to Republican candidates, especially those of its extreme right wing "Tea Party." It might be expected that those *most* in need of and reliant upon help from the federal government would support such government intervention, as had been the case at the time of the Great Depression. Now, however, those seemingly most in need of assistance from the poorest states were attracted to the extreme right, intent on slashing welfare programs. While the livelihoods of many of these people had been destroyed by the financial collapse of 2008, an event clearly brought about by the *non*-regulated activities of Wall Street, they saw such regulation itself as their enemy. Similarly, coming from states that had borne the brunt of environmental degradation due to unregulated industry, they demanded the deregulation of federal environmental policies they saw as *hampering* industry and jobs.

---

28 Popper was not against the idea of the state's intervention into the life of the community and the "open society" was not meant to run on the principles of laissez-faire capitalism. Far from it: as the material conditions of citizens bears on their capacity to be the reflective critics of social policy, government intervention was likely to be needed to keep the open society as an open one. In his early years Popper had flirted with Marxism and then identified as a Social Democrat. Thus, despite their views being often linked, Popper's views diverged from those of his friend, F. A. Hayek, whose *The Road to Serfdom* appeared around the same time. Friedrich A. Hayek,1944.
29 Daniel Bell, 1960.

From a liberal perspective, the beliefs articulating these attitudes seemed easily refutable. Those who had lost jobs through industry closures blamed regulation, but the *wider historical* view, that is, that from the more "universal" point of view, showed diverse causal factors involved here, with blame being misplaced when put at the door of government regulators.[30] But as with the phenomenon of climate change, these refuting views did not penetrate the belief systems of those who found themselves in this dire situation. The views of the "so-called experts" were those of a class of "elites" on the government payroll —inhabitants of the "swamp" that Trump was to promise to "drain."

Hochshild pointed to the depth of emotion and feeling that ran through the self-narratives of these people and that was operative in the ways in which they came to fix on their own beliefs. They felt *let down* by the federal government and the educated elites in its employ. More than that, however, they felt *singled out*, *insulted*, and *persecuted* by the government and its functionaries. As one informant put it, "liberals think that Bible-believing Southerners are ignorant, backward, rednecks, losers. They think we're racist, sexist, homophobic, and maybe fat."[31] Hochschild's studies show the communicative rifts here to be deep. Thus, she underlined that for these people, an account was only believed to be true if was *felt* to be true—if it had what one commentator had earlier labelled, "truthiness."[32] "Truthiness," of course, is not a criterion of rational belief fixation in Peircean or Popperian accounts. Abstract arguments lack truthiness, and besides *this*, their very abstraction is regarded as a source of suspicion. Importantly, arguments advanced by liberals had apparently come to be received by the right-voting poor as foreign to the way *they themselves* spoke—the cold, dispassionate tone of liberal analysis signaling their being the words of someone *not on* one's side. And as many Trump supporters affirmed throughout 2016— "he speaks like us"— signaling that he *was* on their side, despite those obvious features of Trump's biography suggesting something contrary.

Against the background of such perceptions, it is difficult not to see as prophetic, the account put forward by historian Christopher Lasch in the 1990s, who had argued that the universalist aspirations of progressive liberals in America had by-passed the plight of an increasingly impoverished population from "rust bucket" states that had most acutely felt the effects of the decline of Amer-

---

30 For a powerful account of the long-term historical factors leading to job losses in the U.S. see, for example, Richard Baldwin, 2016.
31 Arlie Russell Hochschild, p. 22.
32 Just as "post-truth" would be nominated as "word of the year" in 2016, "truthiness" had been so nominated by the *American Dialect Society* in 2005.

ican manufacturing.[33] Although more from the *left* than the right, many of Lasch's claims read as a variant of those denunciations of Tea Party and Trump Republicans of the "elites" who had become the new "ruling class" in America. Stripped of its moral tone, however, Lasch's analyses are similar to the account of the new class of "symbolic analysts" earlier given by the secretary for labor during Bill Clinton's presidency, Robert Reich.[34]

According to Lasch, the new elites had been brought about by the mobility of capital and the emergence of a global market and constituted its "life-blood." They include "brokers, bankers, real estate promoters and developers, engineers, consultants of all kinds, systems analysts, doctors, publicists, publishers, editors, advertising executives, art directors, moviemakers, entertainers, journalists, television producers and directors, artist, writers, university professors."[35] In line with the views of Hochschild's later informants, the new elites, Lasch claimed were "in revolt against 'Middle America,' as they imagine it: a nation technologically backward, politically reactionary, repressive in its sexual morality, middlebrow in its tastes, smug and complacent, dull and dowdy." As cosmopolitans, "patriotism, certainly, does not rank very high in their hierarchy of virtues. 'Multiculturalism,' on the other hand, suits them to perfection."[36]

Analyses such as Lasch's seem to combine elements of the type of empirical, descriptive and explanatory accounts expected of the members of the "knowledge class" itself, with the type of *particularistic* moral and evaluative reaction to these findings that dominates the "deeply felt" accounts of those protesting *against* the knowledge class.[37] The elements of such accounts reflect a dilemma, well-known in contemporary philosophy, of how to accommodate *moral evaluations* within a world-view that is based on science—the dilemma of the dichotomy between "is" and "ought." It is thus that in much contemporary analysis, such moral dimensions, seeming to float free from the factual, explanatory and generally "scientific" dimensions, quickly degenerate into a type of moralistic hectoring. Thus, from the perspective of the "knowledge class," those who resist the universalizing inclusiveness of society—those against recognizing and responding to the plight of refugees, blacks, women, gays and so on—are denounced as lacking compassion, while their targets denounce the lack of compassion shown by these critics towards *them*.[38] The paradoxes in such situations

---

33 Christopher Lasch, 1996.
34 Robert B. Reich, 1991.
35 Christopher Lasch, 1996, p. 34.
36 Christopher Lasch, 1996, p. 5.
37 Arlie Russell Hochschild, 2016, p. 18.
38 Both Hochshild and Lasch comment extensively on this phenomenon.

are often overt. White heterosexual males are commonly portrayed as having become *disenfranchised*, and as suffering from "reverse discrimination," "political correctness gone mad," and so on, and right-wing critics of reformist legislation against hate-speech, for example, commonly protest this as entailing an infringement of a *right*—the *right to free speech*. That is, they appeal to the same universalistic conception of rights as do the reformers trying to protect the "rights" of individuals to be free from prejudicial actions of others made on the basis of, say, color, gender or religion. "Reverse discrimination" comes to mean discriminating *against* the behavior of the discriminators, but how could this be criticized *as a form of discrimination*, without criticising the discriminatory behavior towards which it is directed?[39]

Conceptual confusions and paradoxes abound here. It is a common view to see the contemporary "backlash" of the "forgotten people" as signalling a *failure* of what, from the time of the civil rights movement on, has come to be called "identity politics":[40] a politics that aims "to secure the political freedom of a specific constituency marginalized within its larger context."[41] So-called identity politics has built on the type of earlier criticism of entirely *abstract* conceptions of rights and freedoms from the point of view of those unable to enjoy those rights and freedoms. In the words of Anatole France, "the majestic quality of the law ... prohibits the wealthy as well as the poor from sleeping under the bridges, from begging in the streets and from stealing bread."[42] Thus, rather than individuals being recognized as abstract "bearers of rights," the argument goes, they need to be recognized *as* members of particular groups that have hitherto, as a group, been denied the conditions which would allow them to exercise those rights. But rather than being *opposed* to identity politics, as such, these analyses advanced by the contemporary right wing seem to be *engaging* in it. The needs of a particular group, those "left behind" by processes such as globalization, should be recognized *as such*, and "the elites," they complain, refuse to do this! A proper understanding of such processes, I suggest, will not be forthcoming within the polarized descriptive–normative discourse that has resulted from the reigning liberal consensus, but clues for a way forward here, I suggest, may come from a reconsideration of a philosophical source that Popper had tried to exclude from the public debate—Hegel. This is because Hegel was alert to both the need to recognize within politics the role played by the *particularity* of indi-

---

39 Thus a conservative Attorney-General in Australia proclaimed the rights of citizens to be "bigots." D. Harrison and J. Swan, 2014.
40 Mark Lilla, 2016.
41 Cressida Hayes, 2016.
42 Anatole France, 1922, p. 62.

vidual "identity," as well as the problems that such particularity posed for a politics conceived, as in liberalism, in "abstractly universal" terms.

4 The Strengths, Limitations, and Paradoxes of the Knowledge Class

Lasch's "knowledge class" might be thought of as a later instantiation of the class making up the civil service in the modern state as described by Hegel in his 1821 work, *Elements of the Philosophy of Right*.[43] This civil service was meant to *mediate* the activities of the various "corporations," guild-like associations within civil society combining individuals with common interests into groups. The demands of these corporations needed mediating because while their administrators had a direct grasp of their needs, they had a "less complete grasp of the connection" between those distinct interests and "the more remote conditions and universal points of view."[44] It was the role of the civil service to bring these interests "back to the universal."

Hegel's executive civil service formed a distinct class or "estate" (*Stand*), the "universal estate," which he clearly conceived of as a Laschian "knowledge class." Thus, the individuals belonging to it could not do so on the basis of considerations of birth or personal nature, but only as *bearers of the requisite knowledge*. It was knowledge that was "the objective moment in their vocation." Thus, entry to this estate was via examination, *formally* guaranteeing every citizen the possibility of service in it. Simply put, this knowledge class represented "the universal point of view," but in calling the civil service a universal *estate*, Hegel was drawing attention to the fact that it was, of course, *not* universal in another sense. It was a *particular* estate, which, in its contrast to the other estates, the agricultural estate and the estate of trade and industry,[45] had its own *particular* self-interests and own distinct "universalizing" way of regarding and thinking about the world.[46] These opposing determinations of universality and particular-

---

43 G. W. F. Hegel, 1991.
44 G. W. F. Hegel, 1991, §289 and remark.
45 G. W. F. Hegel, 1991, §§199–208.
46 In Hegel's logic, such a "universal" is, and is not, *universal*—it is *not* because it always stands in contrast to its contrary, *particularity*. An odd feature of Popper's critique of the philosophy of Wittgenstein, which he decreed not to be *meaningless* (as would follow from the critique of the positivists) but *false*, was that he appealed to a generalization of the mathematically formulated Gödel's Theorem put forward by his friend and former New Zealand colleague, John N. Findlay. Popper, 1945, p. 721, fn 8. Findlay was, in fact, an *Hegelian* and believed that Gödel's

ity introduced a type of structural "contradiction" into the knowledge class, that needed to be somehow *offset* by other factors. When given free-reign, such contradictions became clearly manifest, as in the actions of a structurally similar class that had emerged in relation to the state in eighteenth-century France and that similarly purported to represent the "universal point of view"—the class that gave rise to the revolutionaries who claimed to represent "the people."

In his youth, Hegel had been a keen follower of the progress of the French Revolution and throughout his life continued to identify with its goals. Even then, however, he had been critical of the centralist tendencies of the Jacobins, siding more with the Girondists, whose popular base resided outside the Parisian centre. Hegel's criticism of the Jacobin attempts to impose *reason-based* universal laws on an existing political order, given in both *Elements of the Philosophy of Right* and the *Phenomenology of Spirit*,[47] echoed a similar one articulated earlier by Friedrich Schiller, who linked the terror of the latter years of the Revolution to the influence of an abstractly universalizing moral thought he identified in Kant. Isolated from its substantive relations to other aspects of human life, and in particular, isolated from the forms of feeling that operated in the particularity of lived contexts, this tendency to a one-sided allegiance to abstract principles and rules proved destructive. In Hegel, this idea took the form of a critique of any hypostatizing, over all others, of that particular form of reason as found in modern empirical science as well as in Kant's abstractly universalizing form of morality—a critique that extends to Popper's starting assumptions.[48] This abstractly universal form of thinking was the work of the "understanding" (*der Verstand*). In contrast, "reason" (*die Vernunft*), the type of reasoning found prototypically in *philosophy*, was required to limit the understanding to its proper role, and *mediate* its claims with the equally necessary but equally one-sided claims of common-sense experience with, *one might say*, its features of "truthiness." Only "reason" could capture the dynamics between the universalizing and particularizing forces shaping the lives and thinking of *actual* societies. The one-sided *understanding*, which conflated the real world with the abstractions that

---

theorem showed the relevance of Hegel's *dialectical logic*. Findlay had put forward his Hegel-free version of this argument, in his "Goedelian Sentences: A Non-Numerical Approach," *Mind* 51 (1942): pp. 259–65, but underlined the Hegelian nature of this account in a lecture in 1959, "The Contemporary Relevance of Hegel," in John N. Findlay, 1961, pp. 217–31.

47 G. W. F. Hegel, 1991, §5; and Hegel, 1977, §§582–95.

48 Once more, Kolnai, on whom Popper had drawn, emphasized the ineliminability of the subjective point of view, and the role of emotion, in morality. See, for example, David Wiggins and Bernard Williams, "Aurel Thomas Kolnai (1900–1973)," Aurel Kolnai, 1978, pp. xxiii–xxxix.

thinking subjects formed of it, was structurally inadequate for this role and, when unbalanced, dangerous.

This is not the place to try to assess or defend Hegel's philosophy *in toto*, but perhaps we can extract some rather common-sensical ideas from it in an effort to get purchase on the pressing problems of the current situation. At the heart of Hegel's philosophy was a way of thinking about the dynamic of the "logical" relations between poles of universality and particularity. For Hegel, universals will be employed by *the understanding* in an abstract way so as to "subsume" particulars as in, say, when we explain the behavior of particular elements of the *physical* world. Thus, universal *laws*, such as Newton's laws, will explain, say, the movement of the moon about the earth, by employing concepts of properties—here, "mass," "distance" and so on—the mathematical values of which can be related by the laws. But the way *human beings* are related to their "universals" cannot be understood in the same way. For humans, explanations of their behavior must take account of their own *self*-conceptions, and these are conceptions that, for the most part, they acquire from the particular "universals," the particular societies, to which they belong. The behavior of the moon does not rely on *its* understanding of itself *as* a moon, but the behaviors of, say, a Republican-voting inhabitant of a "red state" or a Democrat-voting member of the international "knowledge class," do rely on their respective conceptions of themselves *as* the *sorts* of people *they* are.

In Hegel's terms, Republican-voting whites in poor southern U.S. states and the members of the "knowledge classes" would be regarded as something like the inhabitants of different "estates": they could be expected to have very differing conceptions of themselves and their relations to society as a whole.[49] Moreover, this difference would *not* to be understood simply in terms of the idea of the presence or absence of *knowledge* or *reason*. In abstracting from the roots of knowledge in human experience, the "knowledge classes" are *just* as prone to one-sided distortion in their thinking as are the classes who *fail* to capture the role of the universal point of view. Accordingly, in his particular conception of the representational mechanisms of the state, not only were the *particular* needs of the estates meant to be represented in the legislative body, the partic-

---

49 Moreover, the concepts or "universals" applied in Hegel's account gain their *own* identities from the relations and oppositions within which they stand. As in the sorts of studies of Lasch and Hochschild, a person may think of themselves as a *Texan*, say, when the contrast is being drawn with the inhabitants of New York or San Francisco, but as an *American*, when the contrast is with Syrian refugees. But all identifications are, by necessity, abstractions from the multiple determinations of our identities. In an important sense, we are *all* "Texans," "Americans," human beings, primates, biological entities, physical systems, etc., etc.

ular *ways* that members of such estates *thought about and understood those needs* were also meant to be so represented. Thus, Hegel sought ways in which the communicative fabric of society might resist fissuring into those between warring factions.

Hegel's conception of the state may or may not have been a viable one in the context of his own time, and it is highly unlikely that its particular suggestions could be transposed to politics in *this* age. But, from the point of view of his philosophy, this is *not* the way to think about what philosophy has to contribute to its age. Philosophy, on his account, was not meant to offer recipes for the solution of practical problems facing human life. Philosophy is *always* retrospective—"the Owl of Minerva spreads its wings at dusk." It can only help us understand where we have come from and how this history has made us the sorts of beings we are. It is not forward looking and does not give us knowledge to be *applied* for particular ends, in the way we expect from the empirical sciences, for example. If it helps to clarify our conception of ourselves and the problematic situations we find ourselves in, it is left up to *us* to come up with solutions. While Hegelian philosophy offers no recipe beyond the problematic nature of what Mark Lilla has described as "identity liberalism,"[50] a better understanding of its problems will surely be a prerequisite to working out a way beyond them.

Popper read Hegel, along with Plato and Aristotle in a very different way. Each is thought of as attempting to provide some metaphysical *foundation* of certainty upon which all other theoretical and practical knowledge can be constructed. On this view philosophy is some super-science constructed by the sheer effort of thinking. Popper, I suggest, was justified in his skepticism regarding the role of such a philosophy in public life. But, at least in Hegel's case, he was fighting a straw man. Hegel, at least as understood by some of his current interpreters, had been just as critical of such an ambition for philosophy as was Popper.[51] Moreover, we might consider Popper's attempt to displace philosophy so-conceived by the empirical sciences as resting on presuppositions about the role of knowledge in human life of which Hegel was an acute critic.

Popper is often thought of as facing a paradoxical situation with regard to his philosophy, i.e. it might be asked: is the view put forward in *The Open Society and Its Enemies* a *falsifiable* one? Given Hegel's criticisms of the "abstract" conception of reason on which it rests, one might think of *his* theory as falsifying in this way. However, if we think of *history* as having to provide a more *empirical*

---

50 Mark Lilla, 2016.
51 For a survey of the ways in which contemporary philosophers approach Hegel, see Paul Redding, 2016.

way of putting Popper's conception to the test, we might think of recent history as having challenged it in its own way as well. To save what has been progressive in liberal politics since the Second World War requires a greater *philosophical* sensitivity to the tensions between "universal" and "particular", as well as "one" and "many", than that allowed by Popper's variant of positivistic anti-philosophy. If there is a conceptual problem with recent "identity liberalism," then it may be because of the incompatibility of the irreducible particularities of "identity" with the abstractly universal thought that is presupposed by Popper and that is still dominant in contemporary liberalism.

Bibliography

Baldwin, Richard. *The Great Convergence: Information Technology and the New Globalization.* Cambridge, MA: Harvard University Press, 2016.

Bell, Daniel. *The End of Ideology: On the Exhaustion of Political Ideas in the Fifties.* New York: The Free Press, 1960.

Cook, J., N. Oreskes, P. T. Doran, W. R. L. Andereg, B. Verheggen, E. W. Maibach, J. Stuart Carlton, et al. "Consensus on Consensus: A Synthesis of Consensus Estimates on Human-caused Global Warming." *Environmental Research Letters* 11 (April 13, 2016). doi:10.1088/1748-9326/11/4/048002.

Dempsey, Judy. "After the Paris Attacks." Judy Dempsey's Strategic Europe. *Carnegie Europe*, November 16, 2015. http://carnegieeurope.eu/strategiceurope/?fa=61980.

Findlay, John N. "Goedelian Sentences: A Non-Numerical Approach." *Mind* 51 (1942): pp. 259–65.

Findlay, John N. "The Contemporary Relevance of Hegel." In *Language, Mind and Value: Philosophical* Essays, pp. 217–31. London: Allen & Unwin, 1963.

France, Anatole. *The Red Lily* (Le Lys Rouge). 1894. Winifred Stephens (Trans.). New York: Dodd, Mead and Co., 1922.

Jackson, D., E. Thorsen, and D. Wring, eds. *EU Referendum Analysis 2016: Early Reflections from Leading UK Academics.* Poole, UK: The Centre for the Study of Journalism, Culture and Community, Bournemouth University, 2016.

Hacohen, Malachi Haim. *Karl Popper: The Formative Years, 1902–1945.* New York: Cambridge University Press, 2000.

Harrison, D. and J. Swan. "Attorney-General George Brandis: 'People do have a right to be bigots.'" *Sydney Morning Herald*, March 24, 2014. http://www.smh.com.au/federal-politics/political-news/attorneygeneral-george-brandis-people-do-have-a-right-to-be-bigots-20140324-35dj3.html.

Hayek, Friedrich A. *The Road to Serfdom.* London: Routledge, 1944.

Hayes, Cressida. "Identity Politics." In *The Stanford Encyclopedia of Philosophy*, Summer 2016 ed., Edward N. Zalta (Ed.). Stanford: Stanford University, 2016. https://plato.stanford.edu/archives/sum2016/entries/identity-politics/.

Hegel, G. W. F. *Phenomenology of Spirit.* A. V. Miller (Trans.), with analysis of the text and Foreword by J. N. Findlay. Oxford: Clarendon Press, 1977.

Hegel, G. W. F. *Elements of the Philosophy of Right*. Allen W. Wood (Ed.). Translated by H. B. Nisbet. Cambridge: Cambridge University Press, 1991.

Hochschild, Arlie Russell. *Strangers in Their Own Land: Anger and Mourning on the American Right*. New York: The New Press, 2016.

Jackson, Daniel, Einar Thorsen and Dominic Wring (eds), *EU Referendum Analysis 2016: Early Reflections from leading UK academics*, Poole: The Centre for the Study of Journalism, Culture and Community, Bournemouth University, 2016.

Kolnai, Aurel. *The War Against the West*. London: Victor Gollancz, 1938.

Lasch, Christopher. *The Revolt of the Elites and the Betrayal of Democracy*. New York: W. W. Norton and Company, 1996.

Levitan, Dave. "Obama's Outgoing Science Advisor Will Keep Watch in 2017." Science. *Wired*, December 16, 2016. https://www.wired.com/2016/12/obamas-outgoing-science-advisor-will-keep-watch-2017/.

Lilla, Mark. "The End of Identity Liberalism." *The New York Times*, November 18, 2016. https://www.nytimes.com/2016/11/20/opinion/sunday/the-end-of-identity-liberalism.html.

McCrum, Robert. "The 100 Best Nonfiction Books: No 35 – The Open Society and Its Enemies by Karl Popper (1945)." *The Guardian* (online), September 26, 2016. https://www.theguardian.com/books/2016/sep/26/100-best-nonfiction-books-karl-popper-open-society-its-enemies.

Obama, Barack. "Repealing the Affordable Care Act without a Replacement—The Risks to American Health Care." *New England Journal of Medicine* 376 (2017): pp. 277–99.

Obama, Barack. "The President's Role in Advancing Criminal Justice Reform." *Harvard Law Review* 130, no. 3 (2017): pp. 816–66.

Obama, Barack. "The Irreversible Momentum of Clean Energy." *Science*, January 9, 2017. doi: 10.1126/science.aam6284.

Open Society Foundation. https://www.opensocietyfoundations.org/.

Peirce, Charles Sanders. "The Fixation of Belief." In *Writings of Charles S. Peirce: A Chronological Edition: Vol. 3, 1872–1878*, Christian J. W. Kloesel (Ed.), pp. 242–57. Bloomington, IN: Indiana University Press, 1986.

Popper, Karl, *The Open Society and Its Enemies*. London: Routledge, 1945. Reissued in one volume. Princeton: Princeton University Press, 2013.

Princeton University Press / The Open Society and Its Enemies. http://press.princeton.edu/titles/9984.html.

Quine, Willard Van Orman. "Mr. Strawson on Logical Theory." *Mind* 62 (1953): pp. 433–451.

Redding, Paul. "Georg Wilhelm Friedrich Hegel." In *The Stanford Encyclopedia of Philosophy*, Spring 2016 ed., Edward N. Zalta (Ed.). Stanford: Stanford University, 2016. https://plato.stanford.edu/archives/spr2016/entries/hegel/.

Reich, Robert B. *The Work of Nations: Preparing Ourselves for 21st-Century Capitalism*. New York: Vintage Press, 1991.

Sellars, Wilfrid. "Philosophy and the Scientific Image of Man." In *Science, Perception and Reality*. Atascadero, CA: Ridgeview Publishing, 1963.

Thornton, Stephen. "Karl Popper." In *The Stanford Encyclopedia of Philosophy*, Winter 2016 ed., Edward N. Zalta (Ed.). Stanford: Stanford University, 2016. https://plato.stanford.edu/archives/win2016/entries/popper/.

Trump, Donald J. Twitter Post. November 7, 2012, 6:15 AM. https://twitter.com/realDonald Trump.

Wiggins, David and Bernard Williams. "Aurel Thomas Kolnai (1900–1973)." In Kolnai, *Ethics, Value and Reality: Selected Papers of Aurel Kolnai*, xxiii–xxxix. Indianapolis: Hackett, 1978.

III. What can Philosophy do?

Robert Frodeman
A Robot Took My Boyfriend and My Job: Positioning Philosophy for a Resurgence

Abstract: Across the 20th and now into the 21st century, philosophy and the humanities have embraced the dogmas of the modern research university – the belief in expertise, the defense of disciplinary peer review, and the billeting of professors within departments. The result has been the marginalization of philosophy. Philosophy can come to play an integral role in 21st century society, but this will require that our field embrace a new epistemic order. Creating a more vital role across society means rethinking of our habits both theoretical and institutional – our self-conception, our place within the university, and in society at large.

> The Lords of the Cloud love to yammer about turning the world into a better place as they churn out new algorithms, apps, and inventions that, it is claimed, will make our lives easier, healthier, funnier, closer, cooler, longer, and kinder to the planet. And yet there's a creepy feeling underneath it all, a sense that we're the mice in their experiments, that they regard us humans as Betamaxes or eight-tracks, old technology that will soon be discarded.
> —Maureen Dowd, "Elon Musk's Billion-Dollar Crusade to Stop the A.I. Apocalypse"

It's the paradox of higher education: while the professorate trends liberal, the institution itself is deeply conservative in nature. The funny hats worn at graduation remind us that the university is a 900-year-old institution, the second oldest in the West, and deeply resistant to change. If liberalism is about challenging the status quo, and conservativism about preserving it, professors are natural liberals: their role is to challenge assumptions. But this critical gaze is rarely directed toward the university's own dogmas—the belief in expertise, the defense of peer review, and the billeting of professors within departments. In all these ways, the professorate is a defender of the status quo.

Raised within disciplinary norms, humanities professors have taken these dogmas for granted. Ironically, tenure seems to have made them less rather than more willing to challenge the status quo. It was thought that by safeguarding jobs, tenure would make professors bolder, giving them the liberty to develop and enact new ideas. Instead, tenure has diminished the incentive for professors to change the system that provides them with job security. On top of that, perennially shrinking budgets encourage conformity and disciplinary orthodoxy rather than daring. And despite the growing tumult outside the ivy-covered walls, academic work still proceeds at a stately pace. As a result, the modern university is increasingly at odds with the rhythms of twenty-first century culture.

Change within higher education, to the degree that it does occur, predominantly comes from the outside. Society makes new demands and alters the conditions under which universities operate. These changes are being driven by three factors: decreased funding, increased oversight, and accelerating technical and scientific invention. Figure 1 charts the first of these in the United States since 2008; but budget cuts have been the norm since the salad days of the 1960s ended. When I was in graduate school in philosophy in the 1980s it was claimed that the academic job market was about to improve, as those hired in the 1950s and 1960s would reach retirement age. Instead, the next two decades saw tenure track positions converted into occasional labor—lecturers and adjuncts, and the peonage of graduate student toil.[1]

The second factor, the rise of the audit culture, today casts a lengthening shadow over academic life. Firms like Academic Analytics are hired by universities to provide quantitative analyses of both programs and individual faculty members; this information, while relying on data that was originally public in nature, is shared with administration officials but typically not faculty. Such information is increasingly used in budgetary allocations and program evaluation. These evaluations are usually less onerous for philosophy and the humanities than the STEM disciplines; the former have so small a footprint that they have not yet been worth coming after. Moreover, the United States has suffered less from such evaluations than other countries: the U.S. has no federal universities, and each of the fifty states set their own budgets and standards for their universities, making it more difficult to exercise control. Now, the audit culture is sure to grow, as the mysticism surrounding expertise fades and bibliometricians and altmetricians find ever more clever ways to measure academic output. But there are probably limits to how intrusive these measures can become in fields that depend on the unchartable workings of the creative mind. Or so we may hope.

The third societal factor putting pressure on universities, and the one of central concern here, is represented by the changes that arise from the effects of technoscientific invention. The next generation of technological advances will have profound effects across the disciplines, but these effects seem likely to be especially portentous for the humanities, as these new technologies profoundly reshape what it means to be human. The principal concern of this essay, then, is to explore the challenges and opportunities that the coming

---

[1] Adam Briggle and Robert Frodeman, 2014.

Total State K-12 Funding Below 2008 Levels in Most States

Percent change in total state funding per student, inflation-adjusted, fiscal years 2008-2014

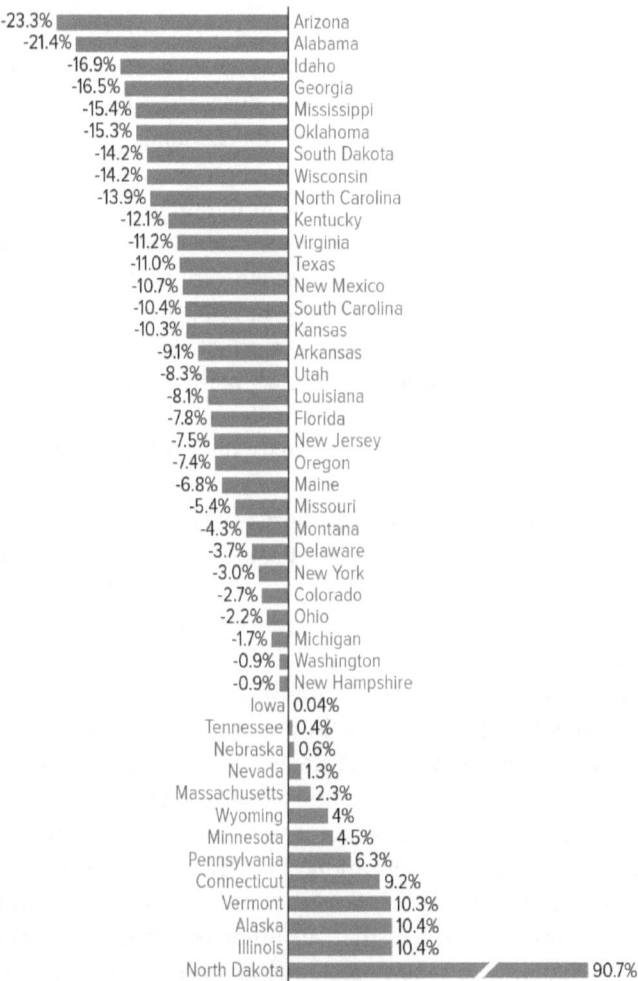

Note: California, Hawaii, Indiana, Maryland, Rhode Island, and West Virginia are excluded because the data necessary to make a valid comparison are not available.
Source: CBPP budget analysis and National Center for Education Statistics enrollment estimates.

Fig. 2: Center on Budget and Policy Priorities, 2016 (http://www.cbpp.org/research/state-budget-and-tax/funding-down-tuition-up)

waves of technoscientific invention will present to philosophy and the humanities.

1

Politicians today make increased demands upon universities, while providing fewer resources. But by focusing on this paradox one misses the larger issue. Recondite knowledge was once the exclusive province of academia. Now knowledge is spread across society in terms of both its production and consumption. Under these conditions, what tasks remain distinctive to the university?

If we seek a historical perspective on our situation, we can attend to a simple but neglected set of facts: the first decade of the twentieth century saw an average of 300 PhDs awarded in the U.S. per year, while in 2014 the number was more than 54,000. In distinction to the earlier era, most of this latter cohort will never work in academia. Today Google employs as many PhDs (2000) as does Stanford. The result of knowledge becoming more central to society is that the university is no longer the only or even primary destination for highly educated people, nor the only or even central source for knowledge production. The sole remaining *exclusive* role of the university consists of the certification of knowledge producers via the awarding of degrees. What, then, are universities for?

Most criticism of the academy comes from conservatives (liberals being more likely to defend the status quo). Conservatives complain of leftwing politics and political correctness, which they associate with the humanities. On their account, business and engineering, the allied health professions, and the STEM disciplines are practical, while most of the social sciences (economics and industrial sociology excepted) and the entirety of the arts and humanities are indulgences, populated by professors whose main effect is to contribute to the undermining of what remains of Western Civilization. For all of the purported irrelevance of the humanities, a more accurate account of the state of things hasn't broken through because of the grip that an outdated philosophy still has upon the cultural imagination. It's a view nicely summarized by the 1935 DuPont advertising slogan (which was used until 1982): "Better Things for Better Living ... Through Chemistry." But this view—that scientific and technological progress is inherently benign—is beginning to change.

There is plenty of evidence of a new epistemic order, one that is largely the result of technological innovation. Globalization has obviously been dependent upon technoscience, whether through the invention of the shipping container,[2] or via advances in information and communication technologies. But what hasn't been adequately accounted for are the effects of serendipity upon the system. When Apple introduced the iPhone in January of 2007, no one could have predicted that it would disrupt both the taxi and hotel industries. Taking the latter, in 2016 Airbnb's market valuation was pegged at $30 billion, more than the Hilton and Hyatt chains combined.[3] But the implications this has for a college education have largely been ignored. What field of study is practical when innovation[4] is so fast and unpredictable that training in any specific skill is in danger of being rendered obsolete?

Obsolescence takes different forms: factories can be moved off shore, and domestically jobs can be replaced by the creation of a robot or an app. But the larger lesson from this is that the most practical skills are those that resist being routinized, and which make it easiest for people to switch fields and directions. Consequently, a general, cultural, humanistic education becomes relevant on the most utilitarian of grounds. It's time to overturn the tired dichotomy between a utilitarian and a liberal education. Reading, writing, and speaking with clarity and insight, having a rich sense of both history and cultural trends, and possessing sensitivity to the opportunities and dangers of our increasingly metaphysical age now become go-to skills.

But while we are in the midst of an epistemic revolution—the HAL 9000 (check that, Google) in our pocket—university life largely goes on as before. Universities are filled with thinkers, but few universities ask their in-house theoreticians to develop a site-specific rethinking of the institution. Take, for instance, the structure of the philosophy major. Approximately 600 colleges in North America offer the major, and all of them teach essentially the same suite of courses. The same is true of the 110 universities that offer the PhD, differences in analytic versus continental philosophy notwithstanding. This is where the conservativism and complacency of the professorate shows itself, for innovation (e. g., having a required course in the philosophy of climate change, or adding a lab component to philosophy courses, as part of the major) would necessitate the breaking of old patterns while at the same time weathering the criticism of skeptical colleagues. Perhaps as a result, few universities ask incoming students to take a course in The Role of the University or The Future of Knowledge. And whatever de facto philosophy of the institution that *is* generated comes from har-

---

2 Barry Levinson, 2008.
3 See Deanna Ting, 2016.
4 The notion of the "disruptive innovation" is discussed in Clayton M. Christensen, 1997.

ried administrators whose disciplinary backgrounds are typically in biology or engineering rather than in, say, history, STS, sociology, or media studies.

What's missing from most attempts to think about the future of knowledge, and of the university, is an appreciation of the Hegelian qualities of our situation. Hegel is perhaps best known for his account of *Aufhebung*, where a concept or a situation reverses itself, both preserving and overcoming its previous condition (in German, *aufheben* means to simultaneously cancel, keep, and pick up). Universities invariably push a STEM agenda as a matter of course, but these fields have now overcome themselves: while still technical, and increasingly so, science and technology are now the site of debates over ethics, politics, and even metaphysics. The 2016 American presidential election offers a case in point: a populist nationalist won the election in large part because people saw globalization as a threat to their livelihood, a process made possible by developments in science and technology.

Granted, the Trump campaign did not criticize the research community or Silicon Valley for paving the way for jobs to be shipped overseas. That argument remains counter-intuitive: people love their iPhones, and scientists still (mostly) have a good reputation. But the view of science and technology as simply consisting of neutral expertise is fading; the politicization of the climate change debate in the U.S. (and similarly the GMO or Vaxxer debates) offers evidence of that. Moreover, the argument against technoscience is there to be made—and has already been made, thirty years ago, by Ted Kaczynski. Kaczynski, aka the Unabomber, is a mathematician by training; he mailed bombs to people like computer scientist David Gelernter because he saw the roots of cultural and environmental disruption as lying in the supposedly neutral activities of technoscience. The day may yet come when Kaczynski will be viewed as prescient, albeit unacceptably vicious in his response. In the future, people may be picketing the bioengineering labs that are creating Humanity 2.0 rather than abortion clinics.

In retrospect, the process by which science and technology became political and philosophical should have been anticipated. If knowledge is power, and power is political, then science and technology were destined to become political. Technoscience is simply too successful not to acquire political and philosophical significance. As is the case with climate change, the effects of science and technology more generally have so far largely been laundered: climate change has expressed itself in more indirect ways such as failed crops or higher utility bills. But the cultural impact of science has become apparent even within the temples of the scientific establishment. The creation (in 1997) and the subsequent steady growth of importance of the broader impacts criterion at the U.S.

National Science Foundation, and similar developments across Europe, underline this point.[5]

2

From the general point about how science and technology have become deeply political and philosophical in nature there is one element that deserves special emphasis. When, prompted by Congress in the mid-1990s, the National Science Foundation decided that the question of the societal effects of science had to be brought within the disciplinary process of peer review, the term of art for these new concerns became "the ethics and values of science." This is a capacious phrase, for values, or in the philosophical lexicon axiology, include aesthetic, epistemic, and metaphysical values in addition to ethical and social-political ones. Nonetheless, it remains a decidedly poor idea to frame your NSF proposal as an investigation into the aesthetic or metaphysical elements of science. On these points, a circumspect silence should reign: one can show that such values are crucial to the concerns of the STEM community without labeling them as such. (More on this below.) Nonetheless, by whatever name they travel under, metaphysical issues seem destined to become a cultural flashpoint. For the STEM disciplines have become metaphysical through their habit of raising prospects that erase the difference between science fiction and technoscientific fact.

I do not mean the metaphysics of contemporary philosophy, which has become scholastic in a way that would make the schoolmen blush. Nor (to state the obvious) is the term being used in its most common cultural parlance, quartz crystals and all that. Rather, I refer to those events within human experience that gave birth to the original impulse toward metaphysics, and which are now being reanimated by technological advance. The problem with what currently passes for metaphysics within philosophy departments does not lie in its categories: being and ontology, identity and change, correlation and causality, determination and free will all remain relevant. But the framing, institutional housing, and above all the rhetoric of these discussions is wrong-headed. Academic metaphysics suffers from the inbreeding of peer-reviewed speculation, rather than having been practiced within the rowdy and undisciplined life of the public square.

---

[5] Robert Frodeman et al., 2013, pp. 153–154.

To be sure, this outbreak of metaphysics is not limited to cutting edge technoscientific research. In 2015, more than 33,000 people died in the United States through the use of opioids like heroin, hydrocodone, oxycodone, and fentanyl. Newspaper accounts and senate hearings now take a sympathetic tone toward addiction since heroin has become a drug of white America. But the crisis still isn't framed as one that is in large part philosophical in nature. This is odd, since addiction involves questions of incontinence and free will, the nature of pleasure and what makes up a good life. The topics of philosophy seminars have now become applicable to matters of public policy—although with rare exceptions, courses are still not structured this way.[6]

What's more, the very distinction between drugs and technology has become problematic. We have long spoken of people being addicted to video games or to pornography, but this now functions less as metaphor and more as a description of the actual state of affairs. Both cocaine and Oculus Rift stimulate the production of brain chemicals, making drugs and "technology" a distinction without a difference. Nor is the issue limited to drugs and technology. Metaphysics (or, if you prefer, epistemology) now pops up everywhere. Governments and media outlets are modern-day versions of Protagoras, rejecting the very idea of a common set of experiences. The disputed nature of reality now shows up in the morning news, as people speak of "alternative facts" and "fake news."

Heidegger once noted that science had become our theory of the real, but the real that technoscience now offers us is not so much enframed as a corporate-enabled expression of our fantasies. People amble down the street, head down, staring at the supercomputer in their hand. The seductions of the virtual world increasingly trump the attractions of the environment that surrounds them. This is especially the case for our less educated fellow citizens—studies show that privileged parents are more likely to restrict their children's media diets. Teen violence is down, but this may be because it has been displaced within video games; sexual promiscuity has declined, but this may simply reflect the onanistic pleasures of the Internet.

Realistic looking, interactive, and fully functional sex robots may lie well in the future, but online pornography already offers a sexual experience that many people (especially men) find adequate: as Ross Douthat notes from a Washington Post article, "Noah Paterson, 18, likes to sit in front of several screens simultaneously… to shut it all down for a date or even a one-night stand seems like a waste."[7] The performers on sites like Pornhub may be real humans, but such

---

6 Robert Frodeman, 2017, pp. 1–6.
7 Matt Douthat, 2016.

sites already have anime characters engaging in sex; and the human performers themselves act robotically, and it does not seem to lessen traffic. Social interaction generally is increasingly constituted by the virtual realities of the Internet. The Japanese Health, Labor and Welfare Ministry claims that there are more than a half million *hikikomori* spread across the country, people, usually young men, who haven't left their homes or physically interacted with others for at least six months.

But while these conditions are already portentous, they pale before the radical possibilities being generated by technoscientific research: increased physical and cognitive powers for those who can afford them, extended life spans, replacing our body parts with better performing synthetic ones, human chimeras, human cloning, human beings by design... the list extends in all directions. Steve Fuller, a philosophical proponent of the transhumanist movement, offers a historical, philosophical, and ultimately theological defense of the development that he calls Humanity 2.0.[8] What's notable, however, is his barely gesturing toward the ethical and political ramifications of transhumanism. This is a telling omission, for the reactions of the left-behind to these transformations may be quite fierce. How will people respond when the rich can buy greater intelligence for their children, or a doubled life span? Or when their children cannot get jobs because the older generation no longer passes on?

But these challenges are not only or even primarily practical in nature; in fact, these challenges upend the very distinction between the practical and the theoretical, as the metaphysical becomes pragmatic. Martin Heidegger's central claim in *Being and Time* is that the meaning of our lives depends upon finitude. It is the preciousness of time, in the face of the inevitability of death, which forces us to make choices and to commit to a course of action. The human condition is ironic, or if you prefer, dialectical: the very limitations we struggle against are also the *sine qua non* of a meaningful life. Human finitude requires that we discipline ourselves if we are to give meaning to our lives. A doubled or tripled lifespan, even one that is healthy, may leave its possessors in a purgatory of ennui.

The traditional dichotomies that have governed our thinking about education—between the pragmatic and the speculative, the STEM disciplines and the humanities—have grown shopworn. It turns out that reality is under assault, politically, economically, socially, and even physiologically. People no longer turn to one another to satisfy their needs; nor, it seems, does the economy need them. Silicon Valley sages, recognizing the direction that technology is tak-

---

[8] Steve Fuller, 2011.

ing us, talk up the virtues of a universal basic income. But they fall silent, or fall back upon clichés, when it is asked what people are to do with all this free time. If there is to be something more than endless amusement, or as Neil Postman puts it, "amusing ourselves to death," we will need a revitalized, practically-oriented humanities.[9] But this will require something more than pouring old wine into new bottles.

3

Philosophy, then, *could* come to play an integral role in society. But the outlook looks grim. Philosophy and the humanities today are blighted: relegated to the university, excessively disciplined and inward-looking, socially marginalized. How many more times must we attend the Eastern Division of the American Philosophical Association and find speakers reading papers to an audience of seven people, three of whom are on the panel and the others checking Facebook on their phone before deciding that things need to change? One hears in reply that people attend such meetings not for the talks but in order to talk to friends and colleagues, to make new connections, or plan new projects over lunch or dinner. But why then isn't the meeting redesigned in order to promote these goals? Nor does this explain why the APA doesn't try to attract a wider audience via local advertising, or develop a public lecture series that's free of charge, or invite panels of scientists or policy makers to come describe the philosophical challenges they face, creating the opportunity for common projects.

Gaining a more vital role across society will require the rethinking of all of our habits, both theoretical and institutional, in terms of our self-conception, and of our place within the university and in society at large. Of course the humanities belong within the university; but not *only* in the university, and not only in the university in the way they currently are. The genteel poverty that has long characterized the humanities needs to end; in its stead we need to generate a Manhattan-project level investigation—which will not cost anywhere near as much as the Manhattan project did—into how to integrate the humanities into societal concerns. The point cannot be said often enough: today we need research *on* as well as in the humanities. For despite the relevance of the humanities to societal concerns, don't expect society to come calling. Humanists must first demonstrate to society that the humanities are relevant.

---

9 Neil Postman, 1985.

Unfortunately, there are few signs that humanists recognize the magnitude of the challenge that they face.[10] These melancholy facts—i.e., the poor track record that philosophy and the humanities have had in their attempts to be relevant, and the lack of awareness that there even is a problem here—is what led us to write *Socrates Tenured: The Institutions of 21st-Century Philosophy*.[11] That book offered an account of the failure of the late twentieth century attempt at societal relevance, which took the form of "applied philosophy." Our central claim was that applied philosophy suffered from disciplinary capture, an undue focus on satisfying the academic standards of the discipline, to the detriment of actually contributing to the mitigation of societal problems. Insecure in its scholarly bona fides, applied philosophy endlessly fretted about its claims to qualify as "real" philosophy. As a result, it ended up embracing the rigor of the academic hothouse rather than focusing on actually being helpful in a wide range of venues. This obsession with disciplinary standards, and the disinclination toward actually participating in inter- and transdisciplinary projects engaged with ongoing societal problems, is what has kept applied philosophy from breaking out of its academic *cul-de-sac*.

Socrates Tenured offers some signposts on the way toward relevance. But its main point was to highlight the fact that we need to treat the question of impact, philosophical or otherwise, as itself a philosophical question. The by-and-large failure of applied philosophy across the twentieth and now twenty-first century suggests that this is far from easy to accomplish. Philosophers have assumed that making philosophy practical consisted of the application of concepts that had already been worked out: the hard work was in the *devising* of the concepts, rather than in the integrating of such perspectives within a particular circumstance. The latter consisted of "outreach" or even "dumbing down" rather than real philosophical work. The error was the failure to treat the question of audience—that is, *rhetoric*—as a serious philosophic issue.

Now, to note that questions of impact and implementation are themselves philosophical in nature, and that this means that philosophical questions of rhetoric need to once again become core to our discipline, is not to claim that philosophers can thereby provide answers to societal challenges. On the contrary, part of the function of a philosophical rhetoric is to confront the fact that the nature of philosophic expertise is fundamentally different from that of the sciences, that philosophers and humanists are experts in a way quite distinct from

---

[10] Yes, there are exceptions, such as the University of Washington Philosophy Department Initiative, *Philosophy Branching Out*, and the meetings of the Public Philosophy Network. But such efforts do not lessen the size of the challenge before us.
[11] Robert Frodeman and Adam Briggle, 2016.

particle physicists and aqueous geochemists. The elision of this point dates to the end of the nineteenth century, at the time of the creation of the modern research university, when philosophy embraced rather than challenged the disciplinary structure of the university. The mistake was twofold: first in making philosophy into another regional field of study like the disciplines of the natural and social sciences, and second in portraying philosophers as specialists who, like those other disciplinarians, as a matter of course mainly talked with one another.

The problem here is that philosophy, and the humanities generally, should *not* be viewed as domains of expertise like those that characterize the sciences. The humanities raise questions that are fundamental rather than regional in nature, concerns that range across all of life, and that can pop up at any point in every discipline or field of endeavor. It is thus impossible for humanists to be experts or to provide answers in the way that those in the sciences can. The "expertise" of philosophy, such as it is, is Socratic and interrogative in nature: while there will be times when philosophy will be able to provide a solution to a particular problem, its main contributions will lie in the expansion of our range of possibilities and the stretching of our moral imaginations. Questions and answers are the yin and yang of thinking; but if the sciences primarily seek to provide answers, and thus knowledge, philosophy and the humanities should be the native home of questions, providing something both less and more than knowledge. To imagine otherwise is to turn philosophers into sophists—knowers—a harsh-sounding but apt critique of what happened to twentieth and now twenty-first century philosophy. To repeat, as will be emphasized below: there will always be a role for philosophy in answering questions. But in the main, philosophy and the humanities are about first and last things, basic orientations and intuitions, issues which are not amenable to demonstration. In the main, then, philosophy consists of the opening up of perspectives and eliciting of the call to conscience.

Today humanists conduct important work on a wide range of topics, research in the intricacies of gender and identity, in political theory and cultural norms. But such work consists of research *in* the humanities rather than research *on* or *about* the humanities. Today such disciplinary work needs to be complemented by a recursive move, where humanists imagine new roles both within and outside the academy. Twentieth century humanists have seen themselves as having two functions within the modern research university, the cultivation of disciplinary expertise, and the handing down of a cultural legacy through teaching. Today, however, we need to pursue a theoretically robust and rhetorically sensitive philosophy of the humanities, where the nature, roles and institutional homes of the humanities are reconceived.

What would such a task consist of? There are a number of possibilities, but high on the list should be the task of identifying instances of success (*and* failure) in bringing humanistic insights to non-philosophic audiences. This should in turn lead to the development of techniques, approaches and perspectives (i.e., "best practices") for better facilitating the transfer of insights to outside audiences—matters that we can teach our undergraduates, graduates, and colleagues. This will also raise questions about whether the humanities should be viewed as disciplines at all, and whether we should explore their dispersal across the university in the seconding of humanities professors to other departments.

4

To codify the point, philosophers and humanists can be seen as having five professional roles to play, three within the university and another two across society. In the university, the first of these roles consists of the type of research that they are already doing within their current disciplinary homes. Specialist research has generated valuable insights across the decades and centuries; this is work that should continue. But this disciplinary role needs to be complemented by a second function, where humanists are horizontally spread across the university, either permanently housed in another department, or seconded there for a two or three-year period, the length of time of a particular project. The STEM disciplines today face questions about the broader impacts of their research, so let us embed humanists in STEM departments on a long-term basis to help them with those broader impacts, at the same time finding interesting new problems to think about.

There is a third role for humanists within the university that operates on the vertical axis: those who devote their energies to the question of the future of the university. Humanists should function in an advisory role, as part of the university's own think tank, to help the university cope with the challenges facing academia today. This role is different from an administrative position (e. g., assistant vice provost of research) as well as from the perspectives offered by current spate of "management consultants" like McKinsey. Rather, humanists would use their training in history, philosophy, sociology, media studies, etc., to help universities respond to the imperatives that they face.

To these three roles two more can be added across society, what we in *Socrates Tenured* called the field philosopher and the philosopher bureaucrat. Field philosophers shuttle between academia and the larger world, while philosopher bureaucrats have "gone native," having a permanent position where they do (somewhat crypto-) philosophical work in the world beyond the academy. Field philosophers remain housed in the university, thereby enjoying the protections of tenure, while doing much of their thinking via case studies where they work with other disciplines or non-academics who are concerned with particular problems and tasks. When a project ends, they return to the department to recharge their disciplinary batteries, sharing the insights they've generated with their students and colleagues. In contrast, the philosopher bureaucrat uses her solid philosophical (or humanistic) training, but has left the academy to permanently work in the public or private sector.

These five roles could constitute the ecosystem of twenty first-century philosophy and humanities. But this is a mere sketch: the larger point is that the status quo ante, where the main responsibilities of the professional humanist have been to teach students and to write books and articles for a cohort of disciplinary professionals, needs to be supplemented by a wider range of roles. The alternative is watch the slow—or perhaps not so slow— diminishing of the humanities through cut-backs and technological replacement.

The point here is that it is time to consider the wisdom and practical efficacy of returning the humanities to their former place as the core function of the university. The STEM disciplines and other so-called "practical" fields get robust support outside as well as within the university. But a healthy society requires a class of thinkers attuned to the humanistic elements of massive technoscientific development—people who, while protected by tenure, recognize their public responsibilities and are resolutely turned outward toward thinking through the problems of society. The answer, then, to the question raised above—What are universities for?—may turn out to be this: they are the place where society thinks through the practical as well as theoretical dimensions of beauty, justice, and the nature of the good life.

There is a last point to add to this outline of the future of philosophy and the humanities: the attention that needs to be paid to the rhetorical elements of working within these different roles. As the melancholy fate of Socrates shows, the rhetorical challenges facing philosophers and humanists can be quite daunting. The sciences are partially protected from the threat of hemlock by the implicit instrumentalism of their practice; the humanities, however, regularly speak of first and last things and challenge people's basic values, a much more dangerous occupation. Kant was alert to the challenges surrounding the speaking of truth to power in *The Conflict of the Faculties* (1798), when he tried to square the circle of the university both serving and criticizing the state. He did so by having the upper faculties of law, medicine, and theology serve the needs of the state, while making the lower faculty of philosophy or the arts autonomous, with the remit to pursue truth wherever it led. Kant mitigated the danger of the latter by emphasizing the theoretical nature of autonomous reason, which would place it at a remove from practical life.

Here, however, I am suggesting a more engaged role for the philosopher and humanist, which calls for an extra element of rhetorical nuance. Those who desire to have influence beyond the academy need to recognize the existence of four distinct roles, which can be called the specialist, the debunker, the worldmaker, and the precautionary.

- By the specialist, I mean the philosopher in their function as an expert. While this should represent the minority of their efforts, there are times when one can contribute in a way similar to any other type of expert by laying out the philosophical elements of an issue in a clear manner. O'Rourke's and Crowley's Toolbox Project,[12] which helps interdisciplinary working groups to become more self-aware of their differing disciplinary assumptions, offers a salient example of this task.
- Perhaps even more than Socrates, Nietzsche provides us with the model for the debunker. Delving beneath the surface of assumptions to reveal new and sometimes uncomfortable perspectives on a problem is a fundamental task of the humanist—albeit one that will often land them in trouble. Churchill's essay on 9/11 is an infamous example of this,[13] but other, less harsh examples can also be found (for instance, in the work of Peter Singer and Stanley Fish).
- The worldmaker is the positive counterpart of the debunker. Worldmakers try to sketch out new possibilities that entail a fundamental reorientation in social, political, or metaphysical norms. Within current political debates the recent series of essays by Ross Douthat, in the *New York Times*,[14] offers a salient example of this. Similarly, a series of publications by Steve Fuller[15] explores new possibilities for human nature in his consideration of questions surrounding transhumanism.
- Finally, in counterpoint to the last, the philosopher should also to keep in mind a point made by Edmund Burke: one should make haste slowly. At times one should have a bias toward the precautionary and the circumspect: social institutions are fragile, and one should exercise caution in terms of what should and should not be publicly stated. Leo Strauss represents the *locus classicus* of this approach.[16]

---

12 See M. O'Rourke, S. Crowley, S.D. Eigenbrode, and J. D. Wulfhorst, 2013.
13 See Ward Churchill, 2001, pp. 1–19.
14 See Matt Douthat, 2017.
15 Steve Fuller, 2011.
16 Leo Strauss, 1952.

The public philosopher or humanist should try to keep all four of these roles in mind. The talents and inclinations of the given individual will vary, and it is only natural that one or another of these perspectives will predominate. But the pursuit of any of these tasks to the exclusion of the others is a dangerous mistake. Exercising concern for the rhetorical context of one's speech is not a call for dissembling. But it is a call for prudence.

Bibliography

Briggle, Adam, and Robert Frodeman. "Wanted: A Future for Philosophy." *Chronicle of Higher Education*, July 16, 2014. http://www.chronicle.com/blogs/conversation/2014/07/16/wanted-a-future-for-philosophy/.

Mitchell, Michael, Michael Leachman, and Kathleen Masterson. "Funding Down, Tuition Up: State Cuts to Higher Education Threaten Quality and Affordability at Public Colleges." *Center on Budget and Policy Priorities* (website). Updated August 15, 2016. http://www.cbpp.org/research/state-budget-and-tax/funding-down-tuition-up.

Christensen, Clayton M., *The Innovator's Dilemma: When New Technologies Cause Great Firms to Fail*. Boston: Harvard Business School Press, 1997.

Churchill, Ward. "'Some People Push Back': On the Justice of Roosting Chickens." *Pockets of Resistance*, no. 11 (September 12, 2001): pp. 1–19.

Douthat, Matt. "The Virtues of Reality." *New York Times*, August 20, 2016.

Douthat, Matt. "A Time for Immodest Proposals." *New York Times*, February 25, 2017.

Dowd, Maureen. "Elon Musk's Billion-Dollar Crusade to Stop the A.I. Apocalypse." *Vanity Fair* (online), April, 2017. http://www.vanityfair.com/news/2017/03/elon-musk-billion-dollar-crusade-to-stop-ai-space-x.

Frodeman, Robert, and Adam Briggle. *Socrates Tenured: The Institutions of 21st-Century Philosophy*. London and New York: Rowman & Littlefield, 2016.

Frodeman, Robert, J. Britt Holbrook, Patricia S. Bourexis, Susan B. Cook, Laura Diederick, and Richard A. Tankersley. "Broader Impacts 2.0: Seeing—and Seizing—the Opportunity." *BioScience* 63, no. 3 (March, 2013): pp. 153–54.

Frodeman, Robert. "The Impact Agenda and the Search for a Good Life." *Palgrave Communications* 3 (February 14, 2017): 1–6. doi: 10.1057/palcomms.2017.3.

Frodeman, Robert. "Imagining the Future of the Humanities." *Inside Higher Education* (February 16, 2017: https://www.insidehighered.com/views/2017/02/02/we-need-systematic-research-about-humanities-not-just-them-essay.

Fuller, Steve. *Humanity 2.0: What it Means to be Human Past, Present and Future*. London: MacMillan Palgrave, 2011.

Guston, David. "Understanding Anticipatory Governance." *Social Studies of Science* 44, no. 2 (2014): pp. 218–242.

Levinson, Barry. *The Box: How the Shipping Container Made the World Smaller and the World Economy Bigger*. Princeton: Princeton University Press, 2008.

O'Rourke, M., S. Crowley, S. D. Eigenbrode, and J. D. Wulfhorst. *Enhancing Communication and Collaboration in Interdisciplinary Research*. Thousand Oaks, CA: Sage Publications, 2013.

Postman, Neil. *Amusing Ourselves to Death: Public Discourse in the Age of Show Business.* New York: Viking Penguin Inc., 1985.
Strauss, Leo. *Persecution and the Art of Writing.* Glencoe, IL: The Free Press, 1952.
Ting, Deanna, 2016. 'Airbnb's Latest Investment Values It as Much as Hilton and Hyatt Combined,' Skift, September 23, 2016, at https://skift.com/2016/09/23/airbnbs-latest-investment-values-it-as-much-as-hilton-and-hyatt-combined/.

Babette Babich
Good for Nothing: On Philosophy and its Discontents

Abstract: In addition to the long-standing divide between so-called 'analytic' and so-called 'continental' philosophy, philosophy is challenged in the political realm and concerns about public spending for philosophy increase. This is matched with a growing effort to popularize philosophy, bringing it into the public sphere. The effort to secure support for philosophy highlights the ambiguity of philosophical demarcation tactics, especially in a post-truth era which tends to underline science and technology education contra philosophy. But as with a concern for the history of science, philosophy's past may yet prove useful in the future. Looking at both hermeneutics and history, inviting more than the usual cast of favorite authors into our intellectual network, it may be possible to bring philosophy into more global and pluralist expressions.

1 After the analytic/continental divide

There are nominally two ways of doing philosophy. The first enjoys near-universal dominance and is typically called "analytic philosophy." There can be ambiguity, inasmuch as, having dominion as it does, this approach is sometimes simply called "philosophy" quite as if it were all there was. The second way of doing philosophy, associated with the "continental" tradition as it, in turn, was once associated with a hermeneutic attention to historical context and language, is increasingly moribund (for reasons of institutional hires), and arguably already extinct (or soon to be so).[1] To this extent, there is only one way of doing philosophy, including analytically-styled versions of 'continental' philosophy. Thus, self-declared versions of 'new' continental philosophy often feature conventionally analytic emphases on (and working definitions of) "ontology" and "methodology." To compound matters, the distinction is, as has been frequently empha-

---

[1] See for a reflective discussion with the author, initiated by the gaming designer and philosopher, Chris Bateman for his blog *Only a Game*, "Babich and Bateman: Last of the Continental Philosophers," http://onlyagame.typepad.com/only_a_game/2016/11/babich-and-bateman-1.html. Accessed: 8 August 2018.

https://doi.org/10.1515/9783110650990-011

sized, not a geographic one.² Further, and increasingly, to the extent that analytic philosophy regards itself as 'continental,' what had been traditional approaches to continental philosophy tend to become invisible.

Both ways of doing philosophy treat of similar problems, the nature of reality, mind or consciousness, self, perception, freedom, ethics, politics, etc., and if philosophy of science is characteristically analytic, continental philosophy of science also exists in hermeneutico-phenomenological variations, beginning with Husserl and Heidegger and Merleau-Ponty themselves, and even Nietzsche.³

Analytic philosophers write on ancient philosophy without reading (too much) past scholarship. So too medieval philosophy, etc. Similarly, today's analytic philosopher who writes on Nietzsche can be inclined not only to ignore past Nietzsche research but much of Nietzsche's own writing, claiming that this or that might be dispensed with, as Nietzsche is said not to have meant it or else to have been "confused."

A little industry has sprung up in the case of recent analytic appropriations of existentialism even if these appropriations clash among themselves.⁴ This works because, like Stoicism also similarly 'co-opted,' existentialism is intrinsically interesting, useful for analytic philosophy which otherwise counts coins in pockets and harbors murderous intentions regarding fat men and trolley tracks.

---

2 Most discussions foreground this point, see David West, Simon Critchley, etc. For one discussion specific to France, Babette Babich, 2012. And see too Paul Alberts, Diego Bubbio, Charles Barbour, and Alex Ling editorial introduction to the 2014 issue of *Parrhesia* on Continental Philosophy in Australasia.

3 See, also for indications of further reading, the contributions to Babich and Ginev (Eds.), 2014 as well as Babich (Ed.), 2017.

4 Analytic encounters with existentialism are represented by a respectably hoary tradition, if one names only Stanley Cavell, 1964 but is now advanced in and on analytic terms, as represented in the contributions to Steven Crowell's collection, *The Cambridge Companion to Existentialism* (Crowell, 2012) which makes everything more accessible for everybody. Thus I refer to David Benatar, 2006 or Skye Cleary, 2015 or Sarah Bakewell, 2016 as well as but also perhaps most significantly and recently, Owen Flanagan's and Gregg Caruso's edited collection *Neuroexistentialism* (Flanagan and Caruso, 2018) which was critically reviewed by the perfectly mainstream or continentally located but respectably analytically formed epistemologist, Markus Gabriel in the Online e-journal, *Notre Dame Philosophical Reviews*. Gabriel himself is author of a new book which may also be counted as a contribution to such an analytic appropriation or revisiting, *Neo-Existentialism* (Gabriel, 2018), as well as *Fields of Sense: A New Realist Ontology* (Gabriel, 2015) would then be characterized in blog posts by the analytically minded, qua analytically trained (Chicago) reader (Eric Schliesser) as a "mediagenic and high profile (non-analytic) philosopher in Germany." Schliesser, 2018. For Schliesser, the contest between analytic and continental philosophy is a done deal as analytic philosophers "had won the fraternal war with continental philosophers over jobs in the discipline."

It also works more pragmatically because if, like reading Nietzsche, all one needs turn out to be the bits that make sense (to analytic or mainstream readers today), existentialism becomes conveniently other than it was for Sartre or Beauvoir, not to mention, as one only rarely mentions, Jaspers, etc.

Where traditional continental philosophical approaches might be inclined to look critically at science and at technology (including today's digital media and such), analytic, mainstream philosophy of science tends to eschew critique, professing unconditional admiration of science provided science does just what philosophy says it *should* do. But science does not (always) do what philosophy says it should not even, to Lakatos's and Popper's professed pain, and on Newton-Smith's historical account of it, what the *philosophy of science* says it should do.[5]

Contra traditional continental readings of science, the physicist Alan Sokal came out in 1996 on the offensive against Derrida and above all, especially in the French press, against Bruno Latour.

In the wake of this journalistically adumbrated fiasco, professional philosophy of science would go on to revive becalmed demarcation debates into conceptual analogues of airport security: screening for 'pseudoscience' claimed to be peddled by scientists: molecular biologists and chemists. Beyond the politically motivated charges of pseudoscience, charges which have now led to a certain blowback regarding social sciences including the recent 'Sokal squared' hoax, similarly involving fake journal submissions),[6] the question remains the relationship between science and philosophy, especially philosophy of science.

For the physicist, Lawrence Krauss, "the only people, as far as I can tell, that read work by philosophers of science are other philosophers of science."[7] When pushed on the matter by his (analytic) philosopher friends, from Churchland and Dennett to Grayling and Singer, Krauss proceeded to make things worse, writing that in his estimation: "philosophical speculations about physics and the nature of science are not particularly useful, and have had little or no impact upon progress in my field. Even in several areas associated with what one can rightfully call the philosophy of science I have found the reflections of physicists to

---

5 See the usefully titled chapter "In Search of the Methodologist's Stone," in William Newton-Smith, 2002, p. 90. The parallel and its related allusions has good scholastic force to it: it is the reason for speaking of philosophy as the queen of the sciences.
6 See the latter sections of Babette Babich, "Hermeneutics and Its Discontents in Philosophy of Science: On Bruno Latour, the 'Science Wars', Mockery, and Immortal Models," in Babich (Ed.), 2017, pp. 163–198.
7 See Ross Andersen's interview with the physicist, Lawrence Krauss in Andersen, 2012.

be more useful."[8] Similarly, pointing to philosophy's failure to keep up "with modern developments in science, particularly physics," the late Stephen Hawking famously declared: "philosophy is dead."[9]

Krauss' claim that the only people reading philosophy of science are philosophers of science seems accurate as scientists read neither *analytic* philosophy of science nor *continental* philosophy of science. Some philosophers have invoked 'scientism' to explain this (from which scientism the analytic philosopher exempts him- or herself). Other studies do not exempt philosophy from the charge of scientism, like Tom Sorrell's *Scientism: Philosophy and the Infatuation with Science*,[10] and more recently, if also more generically, the analytic philosopher, Susan Haack observes in *Scientism and its Discontents*, "Our discipline becomes every day more specialized, more fragmented into cliques, niches, cartels, and fiefdoms, and more determinedly forgetful of its own history."[11]

I have been writing for some time about the distinction between analytic and continental philosophy.[12] I note that there are analytic Husserlians (a lot of them), analytic Heideggerians (likewise increasingly in the majority), analytic Nietzscheans (also lots of these) and so on. Perhaps one index of the distinction is history: continental philosophy takes the historical tradition of philosophy as part of its definition and as opposed to what analytic philosophy names 'history of philosophy.' By the same token, analytic philosophy can tend, as Haack notes above, to dispense with that same historical tradition.

For their part, mainstream or analytic philosophers typically insist that a lack of clarity characterizes continental philosophy. In this spirit, the Toronto

---

8 Lawrence Krauss, 2012. Indeed, even within philosophy of science proper, most philosophers of science have a science background, be they analytic, like Paul Feyerabend or like Peter Galison or, indeed, the continental kind, like Patrick Aidan Heelan (1926–2015): are themselves physicists by training. In my own case, my initial training was in biology.
9 Matt Warman, 2011.
10 An exception is Tom Sorrell, 1991.
11 Susan Haack, 2016, p. 39.
12 Thus, because I write as a philosopher of science concerned with discourse between and across specializations/disciplines (philosophy of science, history of science, and science itself), see an essay that grew out of a conference organized at the last meeting of the interdisciplinary center in Dubrovnik before the siege of 1991–1992, Babich, 1995 in addition, in a gentler mode, to an updated version published in a book collection along with Richard Rorty about a decade or so after this became an issue for the APA, Babich, 2003 in Carlos P. Prado's collection *A House Divided: Comparing Analytic and Continental Philosophy*. Today, the problem has migrated to France, as indeed and of course to Germany and everywhere else. See Babette Babich, 2012, *La fin de la pensée?* as well as a lecture for a 9–10 June 2016 conference on sociolinguistics organized, in part, in response to *La fin de la pensée?* at the University of Tours, France. Some elements of this argument are included in Babich, 2017.

based, Argentinian philosopher of science, Mario Bunge, has recently denounced existentialism, of all things, as "pseudophilosophy."[13] Others, impatient with debate, seek to ban talk of philosophical differences and advocate the simple doing of "good" philosophy.[14] Barring that, there can be name-calling and denigration, hardly limited to Brian Leiter's generic tactics. It seems as if the very act of noting the divide, or else of documenting the analytic-continental "rift" (to use the term Reiner Schürmann used back in the 1980s),[15] or simply highlighting the success of analytic philosophy in taking over the job posts (at most of the universities all over the world), along with the bulk of philosophy journals, philosophical societies and congresses, presses in the case of book publications, including who is (and who is not) cited in philosophical research, i.e., as if adverting to the analytic-continental divide were itself an act of aggression. There is a clear parallel with Kate Manne's notion of 'himpathy' (Manne, 2017, pp. 23, 88, 131 ff.) but that is another story.

2 Is Philosophy Dead?

The same problem emerges with politicians who find philosophers less than useful, pundits who observe that there are no "public philosophers," indicting philosophy with a lack of "impact" (painful in the UK and elsewhere as 'impact' correlates to academic prestige—and funding), where other politicians openly wonder whether philosophical instruction ought to be part of an up-to-date university curriculum at all?

---

13 Mario Bunge to be sure is denouncing 'irrationalism' under which rubric he lists both 'existentialism' and 'phenomenology' as he writes in his philosophical autobiography, *Between Two Worlds*. Bunge, 2016, p. 105.
14 See Babette Babich, 2017.
15 Reiner Schürmann, 1985 and, in English 1994. Cf., in the same spirit, Babette Babich, 2012. See, also, again, the blog posts between England and America (as well as game design and philosophy), detailing a conversation on analytic and continental philosophy, published in weekly intervals beginning at the start of December Bateman and Babich, 2016. The blogs sparked a light flurry of indignation and, among other things, the current author was denounced for intimating that the title of Taylor Carman's *Heidegger's Analytic: Interpretation, Discourse and Authenticity in Being and Time* (Taylor Carman, 2003) matched the conventionally analytic style of his book. But, came the retort, Carman was only writing about Heidegger's use of the term "analytic." This cannot quite be accurate if only because Heidegger is more complex and rather than *Daseinsanalyse*, Carman writes about 'Heidegger's Analytic,' excluding, in the interest of being "jargon free" (so the publisher avers), a number of themes, centering on "some problems at the expense of others, many of them fed by contemporary Anglo-American philosophy." Taylor Carman, 2003, p. 1.

In a banausic age increasingly dedicated to reducing public expenditure wherever possible, these are serious criticisms. What, these political reformers ask, can students *do* with a course in philosophy? Unhelpfully, philosophers confronted with such questions tend to respond in strangely circular ways, arguing that the problem will be solved by adding more philosophy: studying philosophy in primary and secondary schools, having scientists study (analytic) philosophy. Similarly, contemporary academic authors claim that the remedy for any lack of applied impact is to appoint philosophers to advise politicians and include philosophers in policy making.[16]

Yet the failed experiment of philosophy and politics is one that goes back to the beginning of philosophy with Empedocles and Plato, failing, in different ways, for different reasons. The "old saw," as Immanuel Kant reminded his readers, is that what works "in theory" can fail to work in practice.[17]

But what if scientists and politicians and other critics are not wrong when they point to the uselessness of philosophy?

3 Is Philosophy Useless?

My teacher at Boston College, the German hermeneutic philosopher, Hans-Georg Gadamer (1900–2002), would typically intone: "philosophy bakes no bread." His reference was to Plato and to Aristotle and their explications of criticisms lodged against Thales, said to be the first philosopher and famously rebuked for impracticality. The example communicates a morality tale: Thales was celebrated for cornering the market on olive presses as a result of his preoccupation with water, leading him to invent the art of predicting the weather along with speculative capitalism, such that, this is the moral of the story: he could be celebrated for his exemplary practical ingenuity while being reproofed for the uselessness of philosophy. The point is complicated but Nietzsche explains: the nature philosophers of Thales' day were concerned with the nature of the cosmos beyond the here and now. To this extent, philosophic 'wisdom' was contrasted with the "worldly cleverness [*Klugheit*]" that found "its goods within its own circumstances."[18] Thus

---

16 See for discussion, Babette Babich, 2018 as well as the other contributions in the first issue of *Philosophy of the Social Sciences*, organized around Robert Frodeman and Adam Briggle, 2016.
17 Immanuel Kant, 1974.
18 Friedrich Nietzsche, 1921, p. 254.

what Thales and Anaxagoras know would be extraordinary, wonderful miraculous, difficult, divine, yet *of no use* [*unnütz*], because it had for them nothing to do with human goods. Therefore σοφία acquires the character of the *useless* [*Unnützen*].[19]

According to ancient accounts of his achievements, Thales directed feats of geographic river diversion for the sake of military advantage[20] and, using the same ingenuity in the market, effectively invented capitalism or rent-seeking and speculation/monopoly control along with usury (Thales subleased the olive presses he leased), consequently inspiring, so Aristotle informs us, legislation contra the practice from tyrants interested in keeping such market advantages for themselves.[21] At the same time, Thales was regarded as so very *incompetent* in down to earth affairs that he was the object of a joke put into a milkmaid's mouth (a joke compounded in Plato's *Theatetus* by describing her as attractive),[22] whereby Thales, head in the clouds, fell into the well at his feet.

The focus on philosophy *qua* practical, capable of making a killing in the market, baking bread and such like, inspires practical reflection—think of today's popular (and eponymously titled) podcasts as well as a book co-authored by bell hooks and Cornel West.[23] Yet more esoterically on the topic of bread, we may add Heidegger's reflections in poetic constellations inspired by Hölderlin, Trakl, and George. In the technically *poietic* sense, the challenge is less about the factive baking of bread than understanding it, beginning in Heidegger's *Being and Time* with the sheltering of the seed (today we could say everything involved with Monsanto is [not] part of this) and the labor of the farmers,[24] where Heidegger turns to the poet's reflection on the gift of bread to offer a

---

19 Ibid.
20 See for a discussion, Mott Greene's chapter, "Thales and the Halys" in Greene, 1992, a book originally savagely attacked in reviews, so resistant is academia, as Thomas Kuhn once argued, to variation on the standard account which is thus called the 'received' view.
21 Nietzsche is very helpful on just this discussion, including further references, in his *Die vorplatonischen Philosophen*, Nietzsche, 1921, pp. 254 ff.
22 This may also be connected with one of the various accounts of his death as Nietzsche lists one of these as including leaping off a cliff at night, not utterly different from stargazing in the morning and falling into a well. The theme is repeated throughout philosophy, most recently foregrounded with respect to Hannah Arendt, the Thracian milkmaid to Heidegger's Thales, as Jacques Taminiaux reviews this constellation. Jacques Taminiaux, "The History of an Irony" in Taminiaux, 1998, pp. 1–23.
23 See bell hooks and Cornel West, 1991 and Eric Thomas Weber's and Anthony Cashio's popular podcast: *Philosophy Bakes Bread*.
24 See again, if metaphorically to be sure, hooks and West, and more literally: the work of Vandana Shiva. See Shiva, 2010 in addition to other philosophers including Patricia Glazebrook, 2012.

guest, a wanderer, the home, the welcome, the work of hands, the work of the harvest, nature itself.

Is that what we mean by philosophy? Should Heidegger not leave poetry to the poets? And what about real bread? Indeed what about real activities that *do* bake bread? Here we may recall theoretical thinkers of techno-history like the Swiss theorist of interior architecture, Siegfried Giedion[25] who includes a discussion of the difference between European wheat and the kind grown in the new plains of the U.S. in his 1948 book, *Mechanization Takes Command*. Giedion explicates the material differences between the white flour milled to make baguettes for the court of Louis XIV and the flour used to make what is the quintessence of modern white bread that is Wonderbread (the "wonder" being the absence of traditional yeast and/or rising) by contrast with the hard Swiss bread baked to be stored in the rafters, overwintering in alpine huts.

Philosophy, even when it talks about bread, seems to be good for nothing, intruding, in the continental sphere, on the province of poetry, meditation, or prayer. And to keep to Anglophone philosophical reflections on bread, as in the case of David Hume, one can invoke the 'occult' properties of bread as a source of nourishment at one time that can instead turn out to be harmful for one's health,[26] and thus non-nourishing, especially the more you eat of it (as Hume could well attest and which has inspired analytic philosophical discussion of Hume, induction and causality, along with a certain reflection on his diet).[27]

4 Philosophy and Funding

Hume's diet was fabulously non-ketogenic but if we keep to the banausic emphasis of our day, 'bread' has a quaintly metonymic association with money. Concerns with funding (and 'impact') galvanize recent books on philosophy and public, including environmental policy, [28] as one of the meanings of the 'bread' philosophy is meant to be baking. Here there is something of an academic publishing scandal, not limited to philosophy but including the sciences, natural and social as academic authors write for free, articles are vetted and edited for free—therewith the entire debate about open access in a nutshell. Paid content ensures compensation for corporate licensing of such content but not to the

---

25 See here in the section "Mechanization Encounters the Organic," Siegfried Giedion's chapter "Mechanization and Organic Substance: Bread" in Giedion, 1970, pp. 169–208.
26 David Hume, 1956, Section IV, Part II, p. 34.
27 Richard A. Watson, 1985, p. 67. See for discussion, Babich, 2019, specifically, pp. 227–234.
28 See Frodeman and Briggle, 2016. Cf. Roger Kimball, 1990 in addition to Jon Huer, 1991.

benefit of the (academic) content provider or indeed the (academic) content user. Just so 'open access' publishing offers the academic not the option to offer access to potential readers, but rather, as publishers are gatekeepers (hence the language of a 'paywall'), 'open access' translates to the "free" choice to find a sponsor to pay a journal's fee (at the going rate of thousands of dollars).

That academics do not simply post their essays on the internet, that academics respect paywalls for which respect they themselves are not paid, testifies to the supermarket model of ideas: only certain brands are counted as good. Thus one hopes one's philosophical brand will someday be snatched up by a rated publisher capable of delivering one's ideas, at profit, to the world. But popular reception happens rarely, to perhaps one academic author out of hundreds of aspirants, a fact that seemingly deters no one from aspiring to eventual best-seller status.

Other academics likewise call for public relevance, such (if inevitably self-servingly) popular authors such as Alain de Botton but also, himself with considerable "impact," Nigel Warburton's successfully entrepreneurial efforts on behalf, at the very least, of Blackwell's in Oxford.[29] Earlier efforts of note include, in one direction, authors like Suzanne Langer as well as Mortimer Adler, but also Robert Pirsig (and others) and, on the continental side, Karl Jaspers and William Barrett (among others). Today, in addition, we may also count Sarah Bakewell's bestseller, *At the Existentialist Café*, written from a popular albeit analytic orientation,[30] and other re-engagements with Simone de Beauvoir and Sartre, for years disdained by the analytic cohort, now popularly foregrounded in Skye Cleary's *Existentialism and Romantic Love*,[31] or new readings of Nietzsche, some very valuably taking him hiking[32]—better perhaps than the earlier analytically minded readings informing the reader of just *what Nietzsche meant?*[33]— or, again, analytic appropriations of Stoicism, simplified and made digestible.[34] There are others such as Rebecca Newberger Goldstein, with her *Plato at the Googleplex*,[35] and the Warwick sociologist, Steve Fuller joins in with what he names his 'proactionary' ventures and post-truth reflections but also, his earlier, more

---

29 See David Edmonds and Nigel Warburton, 2010.
30 Sarah Bakewell, 2016.
31 Skye Cleary, 2015. Cleary's study outclasses other philosophical studies of love, likewise written from an analytic perspective, like Robert Solomon and Kathleen Higgins, 1991.
32 John Kaag, 2018.
33 Solomon and Higgins, 1991.
34 There are a lot of these, and a distinction from the typically mainstream or analytic orientation is Pierre Hadot, 1995.
35 See Rebecca Goldstein, 2014.

conventionally articulated, *The Sociology of Intellectual Life: The Career of the Mind in and Around the Academy*.[36]

Overall, at issue is the getting of attention, measured by funding and other digital indices, like retweets. Hence, applied philosophy podcasts (some of these, like Jordan Peterson's videos, are on Patreon—the difference between Patreon and YouTube being that the first allows you to pay and the second forces you to watch ads—unless you pay via YouTube Red and suchlike) together with applied philosophy books, resemble "Kickstarter" or go-fund-me campaigns. Lurking behind this may be the urgings of university administrations, as the sciences, both natural and social, do manage to bring in grant monies to the university, at which efforts philosophy tends to lag behind, with the exception, in isolated cases, of exceptionally astonishing grants (say, to Johns Hopkins, and on behalf of analytic philosophy).

5 Markets and Public Intellectuals, Public Spaces

In addition to the securing of funds for the doing of philosophy, other authors foreground philosophy as therapy, elements of the general conundrum of applied ethics (and the oxymoronic challenges endemic to things such as business *ethics* or medical *ethics* or factory farming *ethics*) and with that we are returned to Kant's 'old saw.'

There are a great number of articles and books written on this theme (we can balloon the numbers if we include the curmudgeons, Roger Kimball and Allan Bloom of yesteryear, Roger Scruton today, etc.).[37] Supplementing the effort of philosophers to bring themselves to public attention are the above mentioned "science wars," smoldering ever since the mid-1990s, all of them more scientistic than not, a scientism perhaps especially evident in the recent (including, as mentioned, 'Sokal Squared') variants.[38]

Scholars can suppose the 'science wars' to date back to Galileo and the Church, though Paul Feyerabend puts paid to this (Feyerabend, 1993, pp. 125 f.) and Nietzsche argued trenchantly against this by invoking the genesis

---

36 Steve Fuller, 2009 is concerned with "knowledge management," like Bunge quoted above. Cf., too, Patrick Baert, 2016.
37 I discuss some of the issues in the footnotes to Babette Babich, "Hermeneutic Philosophies of Social Science: Introduction" in: Babich, 2017, pp. 1–21.
38 See, e.g., Alexander Kafka, 2018. See also below, notes 61–64.

of science in ancient Greece and pointing to its utter failure to take off (quite in spite of a lack of a revealed religion to block its doing so) in *The Antichrist*.[39] Seeking a modern evolution, one can suppose the science wars to have begun in 1959 with C.P. Snow's *Two Cultures*.[40] With the question of culture we are back to the issue of public appeal. And authors before Snow, like John Dewey openly ambitioned to take philosophy "public" (to use the language of speculative venture to which it is hoped the enterprise would ultimately correspond).

Departments of philosophy regularly offer detailed explanations of "what philosophy is good for," listing the many professions to which it might lead as post-university career (the law: as we might remember Brian Leiter?, insurance executive, Google analyst, etc.), as a kind of appeal to students, a call for majors, which enrollments in turn support the department's own intra-university funding. The impetus to broaden reflection echoes the American Philosophy Association's own call for philosophers to embrace the role of public intellectual.[41] Further, there has been a political tradition of applied and public philosophical reflection,[42] which is supposed (this is debatable) to have fallen off but which might, it is hoped, be resuscitated.[43]

A persistent problem is the challenge of generating public interest. Attracting interest is the problem of most start-ups, i.e., most entrepreneurial ideas. Here one has a widget, in this case the widget is philosophy (and already defining it would be a problem, hence the silencing of any mention of the analytic-continental divide, which analysts insist is not extant, the better to ignore

---

39 I discuss the details of Nietzsche's argument in Babich, 2014.
40 See Nietzsche's *Untimely Meditations* where his theme is modern science or as reprised in the first two sections of his "Attempt at an Auto-Critique," the preface written in 1886 for the second edition of *The Birth of Tragedy*. See for discussion, Babich, 2010.
41 Thus, the platform of the current American Philosophical Association's Committee on Public Philosophy is stated as founded "on the belief that the broader presence of philosophy in public life is important both to our society and to our profession, the basic charge of the committee will be to find and create opportunities to demonstrate the personal value and social usefulness of philosophy." APA web page, accessed January 8, 2016, http://www.apaonline.org/members/group.aspx?id=110441. But John Lachs is skeptical, attributing the becalmed status of philosophical public presence to, somehow, a "lack of initiative" on the part of said professors of philosophy. See Lachs, 2009.
42 See the contributions to Robert S. Cohen and Marx W. Wartofsky, 1976, as well as the *Philosophical Forum*, which Wartofsky edited until his death. For a version of what such reflections can typically look like today, often lacking a familiarity with the range of such traditions (thus there is a good deal of definition and starting from zero) see Jack Russell Weinstein, 2014.
43 See for a frequently cited example, Richard A. Posner, 2001.

it),⁴⁴ but the widget could be some other thing, maybe a new twist on an old thing, energy drinks and oat or nut milks, and the challenge is to get that putative new thing to the market such that one can find *buyers*, i.e., a public, an audience: consumers.

The problem is the market and the question of market design, interior to a given market includes spatial challenges of placement and the question of stimulating interest is the challenge of desire. But desire is tricky. As the continental philosopher of technology still indispensable for an understanding of digital media, Günther Anders says, today's consumer prays differently than the consumer of olden days. *Give us this day our daily bread* becomes *Give us this day our daily hunger*, becomes *Give us this day our new consumer/digital follower or subscriber*.⁴⁵ Space, literal and metaphorical is part of this. Thus the philosopher and gaming designer, Chris Bateman remarks that both "Shopping malls and videogames: two different market experiences, but both constructing artificial spaces."⁴⁶ At stake is the intersection of design and desire. The notion of an artificial space bears reflection not only with respect to the aesthetic and lived quality of games⁴⁷ but also in terms of Stuart Elden's work on territory (and geography)⁴⁸ and the key hermeneutic and topological arguments that Jeff Malpas gives in his own very different work.⁴⁹

The space metaphor lends itself to a marketing analysis yet at issue is also the question of placement in the academy. And quite in spite of the fact that the *meme du jour* in academia focuses on *digital* humanities, *digital* sociology, *digital* media and all its trends, scholars focused on the sociology of knowledge, seem to be unaware of the digital bubble in which we live and we publish. The meta-

---

44 The game designer and philosopher, Chris Bateman published a series of dialogues on this theme with the author, from December 2016 through to mid-2017. See Bateman and Babich, 2016 and for the first set of dialogues in Bateman and Babich, 2017. The internet activist group, Against Professional Philosophy, reblogged the first set of interviews on continental philosophy and its cooption or appropriation by analytic philosophy.
45 I discuss Anders in this context in Babette Babich, 2018, p. 1110 ff.
46 See Chris Bateman, 4 January 2016. Twitter post. As Bateman immediately explicates for gamers here: "Increasingly apparent that the 'shop' in Dungeons & Dragons was as much of a design innovation as class, level, and experience point."
47 See, for instance, Chris Bateman, 2014, pp. 411–443. See also Bateman, 2011.
48 See Stuart Elden's earlier work on Heidegger as well as his important work on Lefebvre, such as instructively online, his 21 April 2014 publication "Globe World Planet," http://societyandspace.org/2014/04/21/globe-world-planet-stuart-elden/ as well as Elden's *The Birth of Territory*, 2013.
49 See here among his many other studies, Malpas, 2012, especially his central section on topology, too the contributions to Jeff Malpas' edited collection, Malpas, 2011.

phor of the bubble is all about the interface and that, quite by definition, entails exclusion. Not all good things are available in the marketplace and it is only possible to buy/read what is available there. The same is true, arguably more so than in the case of traditional markets, of Amazon and other virtual marketplaces. The same is true of video offerings on cable television and YouTube.[50]

Thus, I began by pointing to the dominant mode (the brand or style) of philosophy on offer, i.e., 'for sale,' in today's university, i.e., analytic, and I highlighted the extent to which analytic philosophers make philosophy an increasingly narrow and consequently boring affair. This is not an accident as analytic or mainstream philosophy as taught at universities today cuts itself off from its own history, thereby creating a separate subdiscipline (of analytic philosophy) which it calls 'history of philosophy.' As a result, 'real' mainstream philosophy can be defined not as what philosophy has traditionally been but just and only as what one finds in tier one journals. Hence, just to continue the metaphor of the market, analytic philosophy took over what had been an abundance of exciting ideas (all historically defined), from the ancient Greek philosophers in all their diversity, to the neo-Platonists, mysticism and aesthetics included, to medieval debates, including questions of realism and idealism, and all the names I am leaving out, with highlights including Kant's *Critique*, Hegel's *Phenomenology*, the massive influence and complexity of Marx, the epistemology and aesthetics of the man who said he was the first to raise the question of science as a question, i.e., Nietzsche, but also the thinkers of existence, including questions concerning absurdity and the "meaning of life." Also excluded would be the complexities of the Heidegger who insisted on questioning (as Heidegger insisted an entire tradition had failed to ask what he called the question of Being). And apart from limited analytic reboots of the above, mainstream analytic philosophy transformed philosophy's traditional concerns into brain-cringing exercises in boredom, fascinating for those interested in solving tinier and tinier puzzles of relevance only to those interested in those same themes à la Quine, who was a tad more interesting than most today, as was his colleague, the late Hilary Putnam, both of whom however played key roles in creating analytic philosophy in their image and likeness.

Here I recall the late Mary Midgley, herself, let it be said, a perfectly analytic philosopher. Midgley argued that the everyday or 'normal' (permitting an analogue to Kuhn's normal science) culture of analytic philosophy is self-perpetuating, in which arguments and 'games,' as she names them, proceed irrespective of

---

50 See my discussion, especially the second section on Adorno, in *The Hallelujah Effect*, Babich, 2016.

anything or anyone else. The culture of analytic philosophy, the circle of this 'normal' process is both masculinized (and aggressive) and incestuous (and boring). To quote Midgely:

> What is wrong is a particular style of philosophising that results from encouraging a lot of clever young men to compete in winning arguments. These people then quickly build up a set of games out of simple oppositions and elaborate them until, in the end, nobody else can see what they are talking about. All this can go on until somebody from outside the circle finally explodes it by moving the conversation onto a quite different topic, after which the games are forgotten.[51]

If Midgely's reading is a sympathetic (i.e., indulgent) one, the Kuhnian assessment is essential. The stakes increase as time goes on as analytic philosophy has succeeded in being (to use the filmic language of the John Ford Western) the only game in town. To this extent, analytic philosophy paints itself into irrelevance because analytic philosophy has so succeeded that even the continental voices we have are, as noted at the outset, analytically conceived.

Above I suggested that part of the problem is the 'becoming boring' of philosophy (for an older account, see Babich, 1995). The assumption—there is no argument offered as to why it is not 'bad' philosophy—is that analytic philosophy is, in the words of *1066 and all That*, a 'Good Thing' (Yeatman and Sellar, 1930).

The foregoing circularity, continuing from Midgely's observation above, is worth mentioning as it illuminates the conviction for many who have surrendered to the academic rule of analytic philosophy that all one requires for "impact" is that *philosophers* assume the role of public intellectuals whereupon everything will change. Embedded is the assumption that the only thing our world needs today is public intellectuals (presumably one can smuggle in the sorts one prefers) given the only thing those intellectuals require, no labs but and just a public forum: hence the UK festival *How the Light Gets In*, featuring nearly uniformly analytic philosophers primed to entertain, along with other academics from many other disciplines, including the sociologist Steve Fuller and his reflections 'post-truth,' etc., all together for the same reason of entertainment, along with "long nights" of (analytic) philosophy in Paris, Brooklyn etc. wherein the philosophers compete for the recognition that is their due, complete with adequate airtime, preferably on evening talk shows, day-time if need be. Get philosophy out of the ivory tower, it is imagined, and everything will be great.

---

51 Mary Midgley, 2013.

The empirical fact that such events/popularizations have been going on for some time, just to mention Mortimer Adler's television efforts in the 1960s, along with Bryan Magee's interviews and the BBC efforts that continue to the present day, all of these for decades without noticeable 'impact,' seems scarcely noted. Likewise the even older tradition of philosophy cafés – or shall we call them salons? – yet if one points this out, one can expect to be referred, once again, to *Philosophy Bites* (Edmonds and Warburton, 2010) or more generically to primetime popularizations (shades of *Welcome Back, Kotter*) like the likewise analytically conceived TV sitcom, *The Good Place*.

What is for sale when it comes to media exposure is the viewer's attention (I argue, along with Adorno and Anders, that this has always been the case with radio and so on).[52] It is this attention (consciousness) that is caught and controlled by mainstream media (to the surprise of some commentators, this is rather more a matter of Facebook and Twitter and whatever else than Fox News or the BBC) and a few alternative outlets to the same (soon to be more controlled as the obviously named "information bubble" is drawn tighter and tighter).

Today, academics increasingly clamor for the right to be judged by their presence in the marketplace of ideas: which "right" subsequently translates less to giving credit to those who manage to have had some supposed "impact" (think Judy Butler, think Slavoj Žižek) than, and this should get our attention, imposing upon *all colleagues*, especially graduate students and new recruits, the task of coming up with some way to do so and using the failure or success in the same, this is the REF, as an evaluative scale. Here I refer to rankings, tiers as we speak of them, including measures to hire, to tenure or retain or else, more grievously, to dismiss colleagues deemed 'sub par.'

6 Demarcation and Today's Philosophy: Good and Bad, Facts and Post-Truth

Part of the problem concerns the analytic-continental divide, by which I do not mean the distinction concerning the difference mainstream philosophy is fond of denying but the equivocation with (and in) philosophy that results. Thus mainstream philosophers deny that there is an analytic-continental distinction, insisting instead on speaking only of "good" philosophy, meaning what they do as well as what they recognize as good by contrast with "bad" philosophy, by which is commonly meant whatever they don't recognize, haven't read, and per-

---

52 See for a discussion and further literature, Babette Babich, 2015.

haps most importantly: have no wish to read. This assertion can all-too-routinely extend to a desire to have the offending others eliminated from philosophy departments and, this is part of the Brexit-effect, in an age of new jingoism, this can go very far indeed.

Discussion of philosophy in the public sphere benefits from both the silencing of the analytic-continental divide and the above equivocation. Advocating for "philosophy," more and more of it, what one means to promote varies depending upon what one takes philosophy to be. Here hermeneutic reflection comes in handy just to parse the equivocation in play. Nevertheless, and this is my point in the final third of this essay, academic colleagues outside philosophy, including those in the public sphere, assume philosophy to be a vastly more traditional thing than it is today. That is the reason it was essential to begin by invoking the analytic-continental divide.

Philosophy today is *not* what your father learned in his college philosophy class nor is it what university administrators (or even presidents of entire countries like Ireland) might remember having once studied. Thus, a leading journal announces a new article on "Type-Ambiguous Names" (a real title of real article though there are others I could give). Most folks in and out of the academy would have little idea what such a technical title might be about or why it might count not as linguistics but as philosophy, given philosophy's traditional definition, literally, as 'love of wisdom.'

The presence of philosophy in the university curriculum, this is a matter of market placement—sometimes, if increasingly rarely, a *required* presence[53]—benefits from this equivocation. But philosophy has not been what it used to be for years now. If university philosophy departments predate the divide, course titles and descriptions in sundry college catalogues can bear no relation to the actual content of courses taught. This is not news to philosophy faculty. The equivocation comes in for fellow faculty in other university disciplines who can be inclined to assume that their colleagues in philosophy teach the kind of philosophy they remember from their own studies. Some may even assume scholasticism to be on offer in philosophy. Otherwise one can assume, if not the Thales mentioned above than at least Plato or Aristotle, including more facility with Ancient Greek than has ever been on offer among the M&E contingent. In general, facility in language, not just Greek but also German and French is lacking. Among analytic approaches to the "history of philosophy" there are

---

[53] Philosophy is currently a required course at religious universities like Fordham, the Jesuit university at which I have taught for almost three decades, but also (I know this because I have lectured at) the United States Military Academy at West Point but in general it is not a required university course.

those who write on Aristotle or Plato without knowing Greek just as analytic Nietzscheans write on Nietzsche (ditto Heidegger) without the bother of knowing German.[54] The logical problem exceeds issues of translation as terms vary, affecting nuances and coherence in framing arguments.

I have not sought to argue that philosophy is a waste of time and that philosophy should not be required but rather that if one wishes, as analytic philosophy effectively proposes, to require everyone to take courses in (analytic) philosophy, one should identify it as such and offer an argument for this requirement that does not insult other the humanities and the sciences, natural and social, by claiming that only (analytic) philosophy teaches reasoning and/or critical thinking.

7 English as Lingua Franca or Citation Technique

Even as analytic philosophy means to aspire to the status of a science, philosophy as a field is distinguished by its lack of scholarly citation practice in philosophy journals and philosophy books. Compared to other human sciences like sociology or psychology, philosophers, analytic and continental (parsed in whatever variety one pleases), cite *other* philosophers only sparingly. And we have graphs, tacked as these are through sociology, to prove that.[55] Such is the visualization prized by our academic culture (as the late art historian John Berger analyzes this throughout his career). This is also what Ivan Illich called the "age of the show,"[56] it is central to what Guy Debord called the "spectacle" and Jean Baudrillard analyses as the monological character, i.e., essentially *non-reciprocable* essence of the "virtual,"[57] i.e., digital media).[58] This visual fetishism is part of the reason that studies of citation frequency are not about the need for more footnotes (I argue for this below) but network analysis in philosophy.

Still: citation *is* scholarship and scholars can (and should) be expected to take at least the fact of the work of their colleagues into account: certainly,

---

54 This is a complicated issue and I have found that learning a language is not a remedy as some may suppose and analytic scholars can know German without letting it affect their reading.
55 See Dan Wang, 2012, Neil Caren, 2012 Moody, Kieran Healy, 2013, and Marcus Arvan, 2014.
56 See Babette Babich, 2018.
57 See, the general discussion in Jean Baudrillard, 1970, 1981, and 2005. Cf., for a different assessment, Noam Chomsky and Edward S. Herman, 1988.
58 This monological character is also the reason scholars to this day protest against Baudrillard, on the model of: No way! The Gulf War did take place! I saw it! On TV! Googled it! etc.

one cannot get a book published without mentioning "competing" titles—if only in one's prospectus submitted to a possible press. At the same time, and now we are back to the notion of 'himpathy,' the analytic culture of philosophy exemplifies a practice of systemic non-reading and systematic non-mention. Why, so goes the sentiment, talk about what is "bad"? Should one not much rather pretend it does not exist? Non-mention is damnation: scholarly death. So revolutions turn, according to Thomas Kuhn, and it is how what is called good gets to be so named, and what is deemed bad gets dismissed into non-existence.

Marcus Arvan observes and correctly characterizes I believe (and note that his comment highlights the moraline tendency that would seem to animate the practice of non-citation): "To fail to cite a paper simply because you think it is 'bad work' or not worth paying attention to is not the function of citations—for it simply misleads the reader into thinking that work on the subject has not appeared when in fact it has. A more fundamental problem with the practice of citing 'only things you find relevant' is that it invites bias, exclusion, institutional capture (i.e., 'publication rings' of people just citing their friends' work), etc."[59] Part of this scholarly obliviousness may operate in simple "bad faith," i.e., in all "good conscience," owing to the analytic orientation that justifies excluding past names and concerns as so much "history of philosophy."

In a separate discussion of the theme of citation practice, I pay attention to the frustration of German scholars who lament the lack of citation of their work by their Anglophone counterparts.[60] *Anglophone* authors limit citation to *Anglophone* authors (friends cite friends).

The reigning explanation for such limited citation practice overlooks the fact that analytic philosophical modalities are disinclined to cite. Instead it is (charitably) assumed that lack of citation results from linguistic obstacles: German scholarship being published in German. The solution (since adopted by German and French and Italian universities, beginning with the sciences) remedies the ghettoization of language by writing and lecturing in English. To date this new practice has yielded few non-Anglophone names in philosophical citation and limited citation continues to remain a problem.

---

[59] Marcus Arvan, 2014.
[60] Babette Babich, 2017.

8 On the Science Wars

One French author who has long published in English is Bruno Latour who remains a kind of "canary in the mine" suffused by the residual vapors of Sokal's "Science Wars."[61] These days, Latour is featured as having duly recanted all of his past transgressions, and returned to the fold of the science he himself has (repeatedly) told us he never abandoned (Ava Kofman, 2018 but cf. Latour 2013). In 1996, as noted above, Sokal, an NYU physicist, was sufficiently agitated by literary theory/philosophy that he was driven, on his own account of it, to pen his infamous "parody."[62] Subsequently, Sokal authored a series of attacks on the person of Latour, efforts he took care to publish in French.[63]

---

[61] Thus, in Jennifer Ruark, 2017, readers are reminded of the right side to come down on in the so-called wars, still "Sokaled," to give the late Ellyn Willis credit for a light joke on his name, after all these years. Ruark's Chronicle "oral history" article needed as many words in its title as it includes because most of the clever titles are long since taken. The article reviewing the literature—Steven Corneliussen, 2017—is more balanced, pointing to John Bohannon's "sting operation" in the journal *Nature* [John Bohannon, 2013, pp. 60–65], which saw more than 150 "fakes" accepted by science journals and a report in the Physics section of *The Guardian*. See further, Elle Hunt, 2016, which concerns an autocomplete paper written—or generated—by Christopher Bartneck of the Human Interface Technology laboratory at the University of Canterbury in New Zealand as a joke or a hoax, or else in Sokal's parlance, a "parody"—*Physics Today* is careful to give Sokal his own description of his achievement—accepted for presentation at an Atlanta conference on nuclear physics. Apart from Bohannon's more earnestly self-reflective experiment (an editorial in the *Lancet* emphasizes the problems with replicability even in cases that are not, as such self-described "parodies" or fakes), the hoaxes tend to be perpetrated across the disciplines and it is not as if IT scholars are off the hook. Thus, Hunt's article concluded, as one can hardly resist concluding, by noting that a "bogus research paper reading only 'Get me off Your Fucking Mailing List' repeated over and over again was accepted by the *International Journal of Advanced Computer Technology*, an open-access academic journal, in November 2014." Hunt cites Michael Safi's report of the hoax: "Journal Accepts Bogus Paper Requesting Removal from Mailing List: Australian Computer Scientist Dr. Peter Vamplew Submitted Emphatically Titled Paper to 'Predatory' Journal and 'Nearly Fell off Chair' When it was Accepted." Michael Safi, 2014. Cf., for the most recent instauration, Kafka 2018.

[62] As early as 1996, the current author had pointed out that Sokal's 'parody' was at best flat-footed. If you need to call something a parody, it is not (quite). See, for the argument published in *Common Knowledge* in a section *Science in Question*, organized around my essay and including a contribution by Paul Feyerabend, Babich, 1997, pp. 23–33. John Guillory repeats this distinguishing point in Guillory, 2002, pp. 470–508. I am grateful to the historian, Greg Afinogenov for bringing Guillory's essay to my attention via a recent Twitter exchange.

[63] Sokal's "Les mystifications philosophiques du professeur Latour" ["The philosophical mystifications of professor Latour"] was published as: Sokal, "Pourquoi j'ai écrit ma parodie", *Le Monde*, January 31, 1997. I published an essay on Sokal's hoax in the 1996 issue of *Telos* in ad-

At stake are issues that should concern us whatever our formation in our deepest prejudices as academics, that is *the life of the mind*, to use Hannah Arendt's formulation for what she conveyed as politically as she did. Thus, to note a sociolinguistic hermeneutic assumption, we remain convinced that if only our discourse were clear enough, if only our style were rightly framed, with just the right words, the right punctuation, we might have success in our grasp. It is this conviction that preserves the power of those in power. Thus we pretend style has no play (i.e., anything can be said clearly) and influential scholars declare there is no distinction between analytic and continental philosophy (this is what has been learned by most younger scholars and indeed it has verisimilitude inasmuch as the only philosophical kind left standing is analytic), and that the only thing that decides a grant application, publication success, a university post is *quality*, a conviction enthusiastically repeated by those with grants, regular publications, job security, etc.

However, in a "post-truth" era, in these days of so-called "fake news," it is sobering to note as the historian Ellen Schrecker observes of the fallout from Sokal's hoax: "Today is the culmination of 40 years of attacks on academic expertise. It's fine if you want to make fun of deconstruction, but it's not fine if you make fun of climate change."[64] To this extent, faults one may wish to lay to the account of so-called "deconstructionists" and "postmodernists" haunt more respectable scientists in an era of generic denial of expertise, extending as Schrecker emphasizes, to the science authority we wish to claim on climate change and so on. And science itself can be minded to police its more speculative voices, especially when it comes to controversial topics including not only vaccines and homeopathy (on which the consensus is that no research is needed because there we have the truth)[65] but more problematic claims including the industry standard assertion that cell phone radiation (4G or 5G), presents no health issues and that GMOs drenched in herbicide (much of the point of GMO crops is to make them herbicide resistant such that such herbicides may be used without further precaution) are just fine for consumption and planting everywhere. In the case of post-truth attacks on journalism, it can be hard not to wonder if, like Sokal's hoax, the language of "post-truth" itself might not be a bullying tactic deployed by a regime nostalgic for a single media voice and even more eager to silence different voices?

---

dition to a web publication for University of Chicago "Focusing" conference organized in 1996 by the late Gene Gendlin, and again, in 1997, in *Common Knowledge*. I included a review summary of the hoax in Babette Babich, 2002, pp. 67–78. See Babich, 2017.
64 Schrecker's quote is highlighted in both Ruark, 2017, and Steven T. Corneliussen, 2017.
65 See further, Babette Babich, 2015, pp. 1–39.

9 What is to be done?

I cannot resolve the troubles of the analytic-continental dispute save to note that analytic philosophy won the game cuckoo style, displacing continental voices, replacing their specialties with analytic versions of the same, including what was once 'continental.' If today's Stoics experts are analytic, so too are Husserlians and existentialists. It's a done deal. At best we might familiarize ourselves with the literature of what was once philosophy. I do not believe we can simply halt the culture of insult that can be part of the university culture of analytic philosophy[66] as this also characterizes the interactive modes of digital media (especially, as noted above, given the anonymity that guides the thoughtless exposition of power claims—there are corollaries that follow for peer review, making appointments, tenuring, and so on in this regard). Nevertheless, my suggestion of reading and citation, i.e., "acknowledgement," is modest enough. No one need buy anything, no foundations need make donations, no one needs to place philosophers on the roster of think tanks or on community planning boards. I do realize that the last list is what constitutes "impact," but that is not what I am talking about.

Reading and citing is the practice of scholarship (which is also what we should, as scholars, be doing in any case). To do this, more broadly, we need to begin by reading (this is not a plea for 're-reading' as if one had already read) the old texts themselves. We need continental philosophy as traditionally defined, meaning that we need history and to this end, we need hermeneutics, as we need to learn (and to relearn) to read. This hermeneutics of texts is key and perhaps patent if we consider ancient Greek or Latin but also French or German or Italian texts. Nietzsche and Heidegger are notoriously hard cases but if we read Hume, mentioned above, or even Locke or certainly Emerson and surely if we read Peirce, we will need a hermeneutics of English style (across the Atlantic but also north and south, to include Australia, New Zealand, and South Africa) and its complexities.

I argue that such broadening of reading/attention can also work on an introductory basis (required classes and the like), if only because it feeds into a range of other disciplines, and this last is one of the key reasons philosophy has always been part of the university curriculum, as it also the reason the highest degree in any discipline, the Ph.D., is named via philosophy and the reason physics for years up to and including Isaac Newton's day was called *natural philosophy*.

---

[66] See Sally Haslanger, 2008, pp. 210–223. Cf., too, Kate Manne, 2017.

This too can run the risk of equivocation but is drawn from broad and sensitive applicability.

Thus, rather than insisting that natural scientists be compelled to read philosophy or requiring philosophy at all levels of education, primary, secondary, university, we might, to counter our increasing narrowness and, again, to recall Mary Midgley's exclusive (and exclusionary) puzzles, read philosophy more broadly: widely, truly, deeply, madly—that is, with abandon—and that also means—back to the above comments on citation and non-citation—that we must engage one another.

This is part and parcel of Gadamerian (not the same as Rorty style) conversation: a matter of recognizing those marginalized in our profession, including those invisible others we do not take to be marginalized. Further, as we turn to broaden philosophy from its current very Western confines to include other world traditions, it matters to change the defining climate of philosophy so that we do not simply replicate the defining of other traditions as analytic philosophy has defined (and limited) these. To this end, history and hermeneutics, the mainstays of traditional continental philosophy can help.

Rather than declare (as more than a truism) that one cannot read everything (or proceed swiftly to conclude that one ought not bother), we might expand the conversation at every level: students and contingent faculty, as is increasingly emphasized but also the invisible midcareer professors, and 'senior' scholars who have left or else are on the edge of leaving the field.

Nietzsche suggested that one needed to direct criticism against oneself—a hermeneutic rule I have argued that he learned from his own teacher, Friedrich Ritschl—arguing that one ought to set a question mark after oneself, multiple question marks indeed. One of the best ways to question oneself and one's "convictions" as Nietzsche liked to speak of these, is to read others who write on similar even more than those who write on dissimilar things. To do so opens our own thinking to the public of other philosophers, which is itself a step on the way to the public as such.

I am not forgetful of the fact that we read our (junior) colleagues all the time, we do this for appointments, we do this for renewals. Yet we do not read our 'invisible' colleagues, including peers and senior colleagues, not least because we cannot see them. I also know that reading can tend, more often than not, to "confirm one's prejudices."[67] Yet it is reading that remains the heartblood of scholarship and if one simply undertook to cite more work than we typically

---

[67] For the formula, as for its insight, I am indebted to Holger Schmid.

do, if this undertaking did not automatically benefit one's thinking, the citations themselves, only provided they are there, might benefit others.[68]

Thales, the first philosopher, left no text; Anaximander, the first who did, offered an 'ethical' thinking that is also a physics: the origin of cosmology (Kahn, 1960). From its inception, philosophy has been concerned with matters above and beyond the practical: good for nothing and good beyond ourselves, good, that is, beyond our traditional limitations, above and beyond our prejudices.

It is because philosophy is good for nothing that it is also, as Heidegger emphasized, recalling Parmenides—and upsetting Carnap—ideal for thinking about *nothing*. And this is not unrelated to the nothing physicists (like Krauss) are still trying to think about.

And when it comes to thinking, as Heidegger also reminded us, science may not be left to its own devices.

Bibliography

Alberts, Paul, Diego Bubbio, Charles Barbour, and Alex Ling. "Continental Philosophy in Australasia." *Parrhesia*. no.21/1–2. (2014): pp. i-iii.
Andersen, Ross. "Has Physics Made Philosophy and Religion Obsolete?" *The Atlantic*, 23 April 2012.
Arvan, Marcus. "A Campaign for Better Philosophy Citation Practices?" *The Philosophers' Cocoon* (blog), April 24, 2014. http://philosopherscocoon.typepad.com/blog/2014/04/a-campaign-for-better-philosophy-citation-practices.html. Online.
Babich, Babette. "Against Analysis, Beyond Postmodernism." In: *Continental and Postmodern Perspectives in the Philosophy of Science*. Babette Babich, Debra Bergoffen and Simon Glynn (Eds.), pp. 31–54. Aldershot: Avebury, 1995.
Babich, Babette. "The Hermeneutics of a Hoax: On the Mismatch of Physics and Cultural Criticism." *Common Knowledge* 6, no.2 (September 1997): pp. 23–33.
Babich, Babette. "On the Analytic-Continental Divide in Philosophy: Nietzsche's Lying Truth, Heidegger's Speaking Language, and Philosophy." In *A House Divided: Comparing Analytic and Continental Philosophy*, C.G. Prado (Ed.), pp. 63–103. Amherst, NY: Humanity Books, 2003.
Babich, Babette. "Sokal's Hermeneutic Hoax: Physics and the New Inquisition." In *Hermeneutic Philosophy of Science Van Gogh's Eyes, and God*, Babette Babich (Ed.), pp. 67–78. Dordrecht: Kluwer. 2002.
Babich, Babette. "Towards a Critical Philosophy of Science: Continental Beginnings and Bugbears, Whigs and Waterbears." *International Journal of the Philosophy of Science* 24, no. 4 (2010): pp. 343–391.

---

[68] Citations exist for this reason as Pierre Hadot taught Michel Foucault and the rest of us; see Hadot, 1995 and see too Anthony Grafton, 1994.

Babich, Babette. "On Mitchell and on Glazebrook on βίος." In *Proceedings of the Heidegger Circle: Supplement*, Pol van de Velde (Ed.), pp. 3–14. Milwaukee, WI: Marquette University Press, 2011.

Babich, Babette. *La fin de la pensée? Philosophie analytique contre philosophie continentale*. Paris: L'Harmattan, 2012.

Babich, Babette. "Calling Science Pseudoscience: Fleck's Archaeologies, Latour's Biography, and Demarcation or AIDS Denialism, Homeopathy, and Syphilis." *International Studies in the Philosophy of Science* 29, no. 1 (2015): pp. 1–39.

Babich, Babette. "On The Hallelujah Effect: Priming Consumers, Recording Music, and The Spirit of Tragedy." In *Proceedings of the Society for Phenomenology and Media*, pp. 1–12. San Diego: National University Press, 2015.

Babich, Babette. *The Hallelujah Effect: Reflections on Music, Performance Practice, Technology*. London: Routledge, 2016. First published in 2013.

Babich, Babette and Dimitri Ginev, eds. *The Multidimensionality of Hermeneutic Phenomenology*. Frankfurt am Main: Springer, 2014.

Babich, Babette. "Nietzsche's Philology and the Science of Antiquity: On the Genealogies of Ancient Science." In *Nietzsche's Value as a Scholar of Antiquity*. Helmut Heit and Anthony Jensen (Eds.), pp. 233–262. London: Broadview, 2014.

Babich, Babette. "Are They Good? Are They Bad? Double Hermeneutics and Citation in Philosophy, Asphodel and Alan Rickman, Bruno Latour and the 'Science Wars.'" In *Das Interpretative Universum*, Paula Angelova, Jaassen Andreev, and Emil Lessky (Eds.), pp. 259–290. Würzburg: Königshausen & Neumann, 2017.

Babich, Babette. "Between Heidegger and Adorno: Airplanes, Radios, and Sloterdijk's Atmoterrorism." *Kronos Philosophical Journal*. Vol. VI (2017): pp. 133–158.

Babich, Babette. "On Heidegger on Education and Questioning." In *Encyclopedia of Educational Philosophy and Theory*, Michael A. Peters (Ed.), pp. 1–10. Singapore: Springer, 2017.

Babich, Babette, ed. *Hermeneutic Philosophies of Social Science*. Berlin: de Gruyter, 2017.

Babich, Babette. "Ivan Illich's *Medical Nemesis* and the 'Age of the Show.'" *Journal of Nursing Philosophy*. 19/1 (2018): pp. 1–13.

Babich, Babette. "Philosophy Bakes No Bread." *Philosophy of the Social Sciences*. 48/1 (2018): pp. 47–55.

Babich, Babette. "On Günther Anders, Political Media Theory, and Nuclear Violence." *Philosophy & Social Criticism*. 44/10 (2018): pp. 1110–1126.

Babich, Babette. "Nietzsche's Aesthetic Science and Hume's Standard of Taste." In *Reading of David Hume's Standard of Taste*, pp. 213–246. Berlin: de Gruyter, 2019.

Baert, Patrick. "The Philosopher as Public Intellectual." In *Public Intellectuals in the Global Arena: Professors or Pundits*, M. Desch (Ed.), pp. 163–181. Notre Dame, IN: University of Notre Dame Press, 2016.

Bateman, Christ. January 4, 2016, https://twitter.com/SpiralChris. Online.

Bateman, Chris. "Empirical Game Aesthetics." In *IEEE Handbook of Digital Games*, Marios C. Angelides and Harry Agius (Eds.), pp. 411–443. Oxford: Wiley-IEEE Press, 2014.

Bateman, Chris. *Imaginary Games*. Chicago, IL and Winchester, UK: Zero Books, 2011.

Bateman, Chris, and Babette Babich. "The Last of the Continental Philosophers: A Dialogue." *Only a Game* (blog), December 21, 2016. http://onlyagame.typepad.com/only_a_game/2016/12/the-last-of-the-continental-philosophers-a-dialogue.html. Online.

Bateman, Chris and Babette Babich. "Living with Machines: A Dialogue." http://onlyagame.typepad.com/only_a_game/2017/03/living-with-machines-a-dialogue.html. Online.
Baudrillard, Jean. *For a Critique of the Political Economy of the Sign*. St Louis: Telos Press, 1981.
Baudrillard, Jean. *La Société de Consommation*. Paris: Editions Denoël, 1970.
Baudrillard, Jean. *Intelligence of Evil: or the Lucidity Pact*. Chris Turner (Trans.). London: Bloomsbury, 2005.
Benatar, David. *Never to Have Been*. Oxford: Oxford University Press, 2006.
Bakewell, Sarah. *At the Existentialist Café*. New York: Other Press, 2016.
Bohannon, John. "Who's Afraid of Peer Review?" *Science* 342, no. 6154 (October 4, 2013): pp. 60–65.
Bunge, Mario. *Between Two Worlds: Memoirs of a Philosopher-Scientist*. Dordrecht: Springer, 2016.
Carman, Taylor. *Heidegger's Analytic: Interpretation, Discourse and Authenticity in Being and Time*. Cambridge: Cambridge University Press, 2003.
Caren, Neal. "A Sociology Citation Network." *Neal Caren* (website post, May 18, 2012). http://nealcaren.web.unc.edu/a-sociology-citation-network/.
Cavell, Stanley. "Existentialism and Analytic Philosophy." *Daedalus* 93, no. 3 (Summer, 1964): 946–974.
Chomsky, Noam and Edward S. Herman. *Manufacturing Consent: The Political Economy of the Mass Media*. New York: Pantheon Books, 1988.
Cleary, Skye. *Existentialism and Romantic Love*. London: Palgrave Macmillan, 2015.
Cohen, Robert S., and Marx W. Wartofsky, (Eds.) *Science and Its Public: The Changing Relationship*. Boston Studies in the Philosophy of Science, Vol. 33. Dordrecht: Reidel, 1976.
Corneliussen, Steven T. "Commentators Reexamine Physicist Alan Sokal's Purposeful 1996 Parody Paper: 'Transgressing the Boundaries: Towards a Transformative Hermeneutics of Quantum Gravity' Still Packs a Sly Punch." Commentary and Reviews. *Physics Today*, January 26, 2017.
Crowell, Steven, ed. *The Cambridge Companion to Existentialism*. Cambridge: Cambridge University Press, 2012.
Elden, Elden "Globe World Planet." http://societyandspace.org/2014/04/21/globe-world-planet-stuart-elden/. Online.
Elden, Stuart. *The Birth of Territory*. Chicago: University of Chicago Press, 2013.
Edmonds, David and Nigel Warburton. *Philosophy Bites*. Oxford: Oxford University Press, 2010.
Flanagan, Owen and Gregg Caruso, eds., *Neuroexistentialism: Meaning, Morals, and Purpose in the Age of Neuroscience*. Oxford: Oxford University Press, 2018.
Frodeman, Robert and Adam Briggle. *Socrates Tenured: The Institutions of 21st Century Philosophy*. Lanham, MD: Rowman and Littlefield, 2016.
Fuller, Steve. "Science Has Always Been a Bit 'Post-truth.'" *The Guardian*, December 15, 2016.
Fuller, Steve. *The Sociology of Intellectual Life: The Career of the Mind in and Around the Academy*. London: Sage, 2009.
Feyerabend, Paul. *Against Method*. London: Verso, 1993. First published in 1975.
Gabriel, Markus. *Neo-Existentialism*. London: Polity, 2018.

Gabriel, Markus. "Review of Owen Flanagan and Gregg Caruso, eds., *Neuroexistentialism: Meaning, Morals, and Purpose in the Age of Neuroscience*." *Notre Dame Philosophical Reviews*. 2018.11.25. https://ndpr.nd.edu/news/neuroexistentialism-meaning-morals-and-purpose-in-the-age-of-neuroscience/. Online.

Gabriel, Markus. *Fields of Sense: A New Realist Ontology*. Edinburgh University Press, Edinburgh 2015.

Gideion, Siegfried. "Mechanization and Organic Substance: Bread." In *Mechanization Takes Command: A Contribution to Anonymous History*, pp. 169–208. Oxford: Oxford University Press, 1970. First published in 1948.

Glazebrook, Patricia. "The Agrarian Vision: Sustainability and Environmental Ethics." *Journal of Peasant Studies* 39 (January 1, 2012): pp. 206–210.

Goldstein, Rebecca. *Plato at the Googleplex: Why Philosophy Won't Go Away*. New York: Pantheon, 2014.

Grafton, Anthony. "The Footnote from De Thou to Ranke." *History and Theory: Proof and Persuasion in History*, Vol. 33, No. 4 (December 1994): pp. 53–76.

Greene, Mott. *Natural Knowledge and Preclassical Antiquity*. Baltimore: Johns Hopkins University Press, 1992.

Guillory, John. "The Sokal Affair and the History of Criticism." *Critical Inquiry* 28, no. 2 (Winter 2002): pp. 470–508.

Haack, Susan. *Scientism and its Discontents*. London: Rounded Globe Publishers, 2016.

Hadot, Pierre. *Philosophy as a Way of Life: Spiritual Exercises from Socrates to Foucault*. Oxford: Basil Blackwell, 1995.

Haslanger, Sally. "Changing the Ideology and Culture of Philosophy: Not by Reason (Alone)." *Hypatia* 23, no.2 (2008): pp. 210–223.

Healy, Kieran. "A Co-Citation Network for Philosophy." https://kieranhealy.org/philcites/. Accessed 10.1.2019. Online.

Holland, Nancy J. *Ontological Humility: Lord Voldemort and the Philosophers*. Albany: State University of New York Press, 2013.

hooks, bell and Cornel West. *Baking Bread: Insurgent Black Intellectual Life*. Boston: South End Press, 1991.

Huer, Jon. *Tenure for Socrates: A Study in the Betrayal of the American Professor*. Guilford, CT: Greenwood, 1991.

Hume, David. *An Enquiry Concerning Human Understanding* La Salle, IN: Open Court, 1956.

Hunt, Elle. "Nonsense Paper Written by iOS Autocomplete Accepted for Conference. New Zealand Professor Asked to Present His Work at US Event on Nuclear Physics Despite It Containing Gibberish All Through the Copy." *The Guardian*, October 21, 2016.

Illich, Ivan. *In the Vineyard of the Text: A Commentary on Hugh of St Victor's* Didascalicon. Chicago: University of Chicago Press, 1993.

Kaag, John. *Hiking with Nietzsche: On Becoming Who You Are*. New York: Farrar, Straus and Giroux, 2018.

Kafka, Alexander. "'Sokal Squared': Is Huge Publishing Hoax 'Hilarious and Delightful' or an Ugly Example of Dishonesty and Bad Faith?" *Chronicle of Higher Education*, 3 October, 2018.

Kahn, Charles. *Anaximander and the Origins of Cosmology*. New York: Columbia University Press, 1960.

Kant, Immanuel. *Critique of Pure Reason.* Norman Kemp Smith (Trans.). New York: St. Martin's Press, 1965. First published in 1929.
Kant, Immanuel. *On the Old Saw: That May be Right in Theory But It Won't Work in Practice.* Translated by E. B. Ashton. Philadelphia: University of Pennsylvania Press, 1974.
Kimball, Roger. *Tenured Radicals: How Politics Has Corrupted Our Higher Education.* New York: Harper Collins, 1990.
Kleinman, Daniel Lee. "Democratizations of Science and Technology." In *Science, Technology, and Democracy*, Daniel Lee Kleinman (Ed.), 139–166. Albany: State University of New York Press, 2000.
Kleinman, Daniel Lee, with Sainath Suryanarayanan. "Be(e)coming Experts: The Controversy over Insecticides in the Honey Bee Colony Collapse Disorder." *Social Studies of Science* 43, no. 2 (April 2013): pp. 215–240.
Kofman, Ava. "Bruno Latour, the Post-Truth Philosopher, Mounts a Defense of Science." *The New York Times Magazine.* 25 October 2018. https://www.nytimes.com/2018/10/25/magazine/bruno-latour-post-truth-philosopher-science.html Online.
Krauss, Lawrence. "The Consolation of Philosophy." *Scientific American.* 27 April 2012.
Lachs, John. "Can Philosophy Still Produce Public Intellectuals?" *Philosophy Now* 75 (2009): 24–27.
Latour, Bruno. *An Inquiry into Modes of Existence: Anthropology of the Moderns.* Cambridge, MA: Harvard University Press, 2013.
Latour, Bruno. *We Have Never Been Modern.* New York: Harvester Wheatsheaf, 1991.
Manne, Kate. *Down Girl: The Logic of Misogyny.* Oxford: Oxford University Press, 2017.
Malpas, Jeff. *The Place of Landscape: Concepts, Contexts, Studies.* Cambridge, MA: MIT Press, 2011.
Malpas, Jeff. *Heidegger and the Thinking of Place: Explorations in the Topology of Being.* Cambridge: MIT Press, 2012.
Malpas, Jeff, (Ed.) *The Intelligence of Place.* London: Bloomsbury, 2015.
Midgley, Mary. Letter to *The Guardian.* Thursday, 28 November, 2013. https://www.theguardian.com/world/2013/nov/28/golden-age-female-philosophy-mary-midgley. Online.
Moody, James, Daniel McFarland, and Skye Bender-deMoll. "Dynamic Network Visualization." *American Journal of Sociology* 110, no. 4 (January 2005): pp. 1206–1241.
Newton-Smith, William. *The Rationality of Science.* London: Routledge, 2002.
Nietzsche, Friedrich. *Die vorplatonischen Philosophen, Gesammelte Werke. Vierter Band, Vorträge, Schriften und Vorlesungen 1871–1876.* Munich: Musarion, 1921.
Posner, Richard A. *Public Intellectuals: A Study of Decline.* Cambridge, MA: Harvard University Press, 2001.
Rorty, Richard. "Phony Science Wars." *The Atlantic* (November1999): pp. 120–122.
Ruark, Jennifer. "Anatomy of a Hoax: Bait and Switch. How the Physicist Alan Sokal Hoodwinked a Group of Humanists and Why, 20 Years Later, It Still Matters. An Oral History." *Chronicle of Higher Education*, January 1, 2017.
Safi, Michael. "Journal Accepts Bogus Paper Requesting Removal from Mailing List: Australian Computer Scientist Dr. Peter Vamplew Submitted Emphatically Titled Paper to 'Predatory' Journal and 'Nearly Fell off Chair' When it was Accepted." *The Guardian*, November 25, 2014: https://www.theguardian.com/australia-news/2014/nov/25/journal-accepts-paper-requesting-removal-from-mailing-list. Online.

Schliesser, Eric. "When a Continental Philosopher Hasn't Heard the News that The War is Over." https://digressionsnimpressions.typepad.com/digressionsimpressions/2018/11/when-a-continental-philosopher-hasnt-heard-the-news-that-the-war-is-over.html. 29 November 2018. Online.

Schoubye, Anders J. "Type-Ambiguous Names." *Mind* 126, Issue 503 (1 July 2017): 715–76.

Schürmann, Reiner. "De la philosophie aux Etats-Unis." *Le temps de la réflexion* 6 (1985): pp. 303–321.

Schürmann, Reiner. "Concerning Philosophy in the United States." *Social Research* 61, no. 1 (Spring 1994): pp. 89–113.

Shiva, Vandana. *Staying Alive: Women, Ecology and Development.* Brooklyn: South End Press, 2010.

Sokal, Alan. "Pourquoi j'ai écrit ma parodie". *Le Monde*, January 31, 1997.

Solomon, Robert and Kathleen Higgins. *The Philosophy of (Erotic) Love.* Topeka: University of Kansas Press, 1991.

Sorrell, Tom. *Scientism. Philosophy and the Infatuation with Science.* London: Routledge, 1991.

Taminiaux, Jacques. *The Thracian Maid and the Professional Thinker: Arendt and Heidegger.* Albany: State University of New York Press, 1998.

Wang, Dan. "Is There a Canon in Economic Sociology?" *Accounts* 2, no. 2 (2012): pp. 1–8.

Warman, Matt. "Stephen Hawking Tells Google 'Philosophy is Dead.'" *Telegraph*, May 17, 2011.

Watson, Richard A. *The Philosopher's Diet: How to Lose Weight & Change the World.* London: Atlantic, 1985.

Weinstein, Jack Russell. "What Does Public Philosophy Do? (Hint: It Does Not Make Better Citizens)." *Essays Philos* 15 (2014): pp. 33–57.

Yeatman, R.J. and W. Sellar. *1066 and All That: A Memorable History of England.* London: Methuen, 1930.

Jeff Malpas
On Thinking in a Thoughtless Time

Abstract: This essay explores the contemporary relevance of philosophy through a consideration of philosophy as it stands in relation to thinking, and through a consideration of thinking itself. It argues is that the thoughtlessness that underlies so much of what we see around us in the contemporary world is a forgetting or refusal of what thinking itself is, and that this forgetting or refusal is essentially a forgetting or refusal of limit or of bound, and a forgetting or refusal of truth. In this, it involves a forgetting or refusal, not only of philosophy, but also of what is essential to the human.

> If you want a picture of the future, imagine a
> boot stamping on a human face—for ever.
> —George Orwell, *1984*

1 The Flight from Thinking

"Thoughtlessness is an uncanny visitor who comes and goes everywhere in today's world," declared Martin Heidegger in 1955, "For nowadays we take in everything in the quickest and cheapest way, only to forget it just as quickly, instantly... Man today is *in flight from thinking*."[1] At the end of 2018, and after more than two years of Donald Trump as President of the United States, Heidegger's comments seem especially apt. Trump seems to epitomize a mode of celebrity culture and populist politics that substitutes the slogan for the idea, braggadocio for strength, and impact for truth—to symbolize a time in which politics has become a reality TV show, and public discussion is conducted by Twitter feed and Facebook post.

In such a time, and in the midst of the larger state of world affairs in which deceit seems more prevalent than truth, violence and threat are more often employed than persuasion or reason, and in which poverty, oppression, and violence continue to dominate the lives of many, questions about the contemporary relevance of *philosophy* might seem almost beside the point. Yet, if the present ills of the world can indeed be seen as symptomatic of a refusal of thinking, which surely implies a refusal of genuine feeling also (especially of the felt

---

1 Martin Heidegger, 1966, p. 45.

https://doi.org/10.1515/9783110650990-012

thoughtfulness that is manifest in compassion), then philosophy must indeed come directly into the picture, since, no matter how it is institutionalized, the real character of philosophy is surely to be found in its own character as a mode of thinking.

In this essay, my aim is to explore the relevance of philosophy through a consideration of philosophy as it stands in relation to thinking, and through a consideration also of thinking itself. Part of what I shall argue is that the thoughtlessness that underlies so much of what we see around us in the contemporary world (a thoughtlessness that may well be inextricably bound up with the very character of that world) is a forgetting or refusal of what thinking itself is, and that this forgetting or refusal is essentially a forgetting or refusal of limit or of bound, and a forgetting or refusal of truth. In this, it involves a forgetting or refusal, not only of philosophy, but also of what is essential to the human.

2 From Value-in-Itself to Value-for-Money

If philosophy is indeed a mode of thinking, and a particularly important mode at that, then to ask for a reason why philosophy might be relevant today—why it might be relevant even in its institutionalized forms in universities and our schools—is partly to ask after the relevance of thinking itself. This is all the more so when one recognizes that philosophy is not just *one* kind of thinking among others, but rather it is that specific *kind* of thinking that also takes thinking (whether the thinking that is philosophy itself or thinking of any other kind) as its object. Philosophy is thus essentially reflective, essentially a form of self-questioning or self-exploration. And this is so even when philosophy looks to understand the world, since such world-exploration is undertaken by philosophy in a way that aims to address both the world and the nature of our exploration of it, and it is precisely this that makes such exploration philosophical. On this basis, to ask after the reason why philosophy might be relevant today is itself to ask an essentially philosophical question—it is to ask the sort of question that already belongs to philosophy.

The way the question concerning the relevance or value of philosophy is taken up in most contemporary public discourse, however, usually pays little or no attention to the philosophical nature of the question. Instead it typically assumes a view of philosophy as more or else identical with a supposedly narrow and esoteric academic thinking that can be held to account, and should be so held, by what are seen as the practical demands and concerns of everyday life. The critique of philosophy is thus something that is supposed to be possible from a place assumed to lie outside of and apart from philosophy, and that also has priority over it in virtue of its practical origin and embeddedness, unlike philosophy, in the "real" world. What is assumed here is essentially the priority of the practical and more specifically, the instrumental—the idea that something is valuable, not in itself, but because of what it brings about. Value is essentially, then, a matter of usefulness. The result, almost inevitably, is that philosophy comes to be viewed as lacking in value or relevance precisely because, as a mode of thinking that takes thinking as its primary concern, it remains to some extent apart from any specific practical application or activity.

Yet inasmuch as the questioning of philosophy is taken to involve a questioning *of thinking*, then the idea that philosophy might need to justify or account for itself in instrumental terms should already appear as a strange and peculiar demand. This is not merely because the questioning of philosophy already moves within the domain of that which it questions—so to question philosophy is already to participate in philosophy—but because the idea that thinking itself needs justification, and especially that thinking requires instrumental justification, is itself strange, if not incoherent. Justification arises only as a form of thinking, and depends for its value and significance on the significance already given to thinking.

Even were one to argue that thinking is best understood as an evolved capacity, and so as a capacity that we come to possess because of the instrumental advantages that it has brought in evolutionary terms, still this would not legitimate the idea that the value or significance of thinking is to be assessed primarily instrumentally. To suppose that it was would simply be to confuse the *causal grounds* of thinking with its own *rational* structure—which includes the structure of justification. It would also be to confuse thinking understood purely as a biological and evolutionary phenomenon, alongside many other such phenomena, with thinking as that which enables the inquiry into any and all phenomena. More generally, to suppose that thinking is valuable because of what it is useful for is to misunderstand the way all assessments of value and of use are possible only from *within thinking*. The value and significance of thinking thus has to stand outside of any merely instrumental understanding, since such instrumentalism already presupposes thinking. The value of thinking is a value thinking has *in itself*.

The attempt to construe thinking in instrumental terms readily leads, not merely to misunderstanding, but also to distortion. The way this occurs is partly through the way instrumental desire affects judgment. As various forms of cognitive dissonance show, we are highly prone to favor judgments that are consistent with existing desires, interests, and prejudices. When we frame our thinking in strongly instrumentalist terms, then we also give added strength to such prior desires, interests, and prejudices. Effectively, we reinforce the already present instrumentalist tendencies that are there in thinking anyway. The result is that we tend to value particular outcomes, not on the basis of whether they accord with the demands of thinking, but on the basis of whether they fit with a set of, often short-term, instrumentalist concerns.

The tendency for instrumentalism to distort thinking turns out to be instrumentally misguided (or can be construed as such), but this is simply a reflection of a more fundamental deficit in thinking that arises from the imposition of external considerations on the process of thinking. This point cannot be evaded or avoided by declaring that instrumentalism is not so much about *how* we think, but rather concerns that *to which* our thinking is directed. Such a distinction is not only false in itself, but also begs the question in its treatment of thinking as if it were indeed an instrument that could simply be directed to different objects. Moreover, although it is true that all thinking is influenced by prior desires and interests (and one might even say, from a hermeneutic perspective, that this is essential to the very possibility of thinking), such influence operates within a larger structure that demands that we attend also to the structure of thought—to considerations of reason, evidence, integration, and coherence. The prioritization of the instrumental, however, all too readily leads to that larger framework, and the considerations that it brings with it, being over-ridden or ignored, and so diminishing the extent to which it can operate to mitigate the influence of those prior desires and interests.

It is nevertheless the prioritization of the instrumental, and of an instrumental view even of thinking, that is at the root of the antagonism that is nowadays often expressed towards philosophy. Moreover, it is not just that the instrumentalism at stake here is one that prefers the "practical" over the "theoretical" or "academic." It is a much more specific form of instrumentalism than just that—an instrumentalism that operates in a way determined by a narrowly business and commercial orientation (essentially an orientation derived from modern capitalism), that looks to render all value in terms of the common currency of quantity and number, and that in fact assumes, if we are blunt about it, the *monetization* even of utility: the only real "value" is effectively taken to be monetary value and "value-for-money" replaces any sort of "value-in-itself."

In the context of the contemporary university, in which philosophy, and so also thinking, appears in its institutionalized form, this sort of monetized instrumentalism[2] is evident in the transformation of research and teaching into forms

---

[2] Elsewhere, I have referred to it as "economism." See Jeff Malpas, 2016, pp. 11–23. One might also take it to be closely related to what is commonly referred to as "neo-liberalism," although the latter has a more specific usage at the same time as it is often used quite indiscriminately.

of economic production. In the case of research, the commoditized outputs of such production include publications and grants, both of which are valued in terms of their direct or indirect contribution to income, along with consultancy advice, patents, and other saleable ideas and expertise, but reputation has also become one of the things research "produces," since it is reputation as measured in university rating and ranking exercises that itself serves indirectly to generate further institutional income (and so also often contributes to the financial betterment of those who occupy the leading managerial positions within universities[3]). In the case of teaching, it is individuals, trained to meet the needs of industry, who are the primary product, although what the university sells to the individual is a vocational ticket to, supposedly, greater financial wealth and security. The university, once the place where the value of thinking was itself enshrined in the institutionalized commitment to knowledge and education as valuable, not for any instrumental purpose, but in themselves—an idea most famously given articulation in Newman's *The Idea of a University*[4]—now itself appears as the embodiment of the instrumental transformation of thinking.

The instrumentalist orientation that is evident in the contemporary university is not restricted to the university alone—indeed, its presence even within the university is indicative of how strongly it is present in contemporary society and in its central institutions. The idea of thinking as having a value that belongs to thinking *in its own terms* is almost everywhere, in public and corporate discourse, overridden by the idea that there can be only one way of understanding or measuring value, and that the value of anything and everything must therefore be convertible into this single currency. Thinking appears either as mere "calculation," or as one of the means by which things can be produced for calculation—the contemporary emphasis on "creativity," "design thinking," and "innovation" are themselves examples of this transformation of thinking into a mode of commercial production.

Thinking is not alone in being threatened in this way—all of human life is threatened with such conversion and reduction. In the case of thinking, however, it is especially problematic, since it threatens our very capacity even to see or to analyze what is happening here. In a world in which everything is understood in quantized and monetized terms, how are we to find terms in which to consider alternative positions let alone engage in any effective critique of such quantification and monetization? How is genuine public discussion and decision-making possible when such discussion and decision-making has itself become nothing

---

[3] See Michael Burawoy, 2016, pp. 941–942.
[4] See John Henry Newman, 1927.

more than an instrumentalist process geared to certain monetized ends (and so has ceased to concern itself with the real questions of truth and evidence that are otherwise the concerns of thinking)? Is it any wonder, then, that in the face of the dominance of mere "calculation" over genuine thoughtfulness, any resistance to such calculation or to its effects either lacks a space to voice its arguments or else becomes manifest in popular form as anger, disillusionment, and alienation?

3 Money's Boundlessness and Thinking's Limit

It is often argued that the prioritization of the monetary, the commercial, and the financial is itself instrumentally grounded in the fact that, especially in modern societies, all other forms of well-being depend on financial and economic well-being. Ensuring sound monetary and financial management is thus presented as simply prudent, and to do anything else as foolish and irresponsible. Yet this is to overlook or ignore the point already made above: *that it is only on the basis of what we already value that we can determine what is prudent or useful—prudence and utility are both relative to a prior evaluative framework.*[5]

The prioritization of the monetary and the financial not only leaves this point out of account, but it also obscures it, since that very prioritization often brings with it a tendency to treat money as itself the primary locus of value, and similarly, for all forms of well-being to indeed be seen as derivative of and secondary to financial or economic well-being.[6] When monetary and financial considerations become primary in this way, when what is not properly a value comes effectively to function as one, then other values are either lost or else, if they continue to function, do so in ways that are often hidden. Frequently this means that those values are not subject to broader societal scrutiny or moderation. Self-interest, for instance, is more likely to flourish in a context in which monetary and financial considerations are prioritized, since not only does such prioritization itself tend to reinforce forms of self-interested behavior, but it can

---

[5] This does not mean that we can simply assume our values, since they themselves can and ought to be subject to scrutiny, but rather concerns the fundamental point that the question of the end is always prior to the question of the means.

[6] So, for instance, inequality of distribution is often justified on the grounds that it nevertheless enables increases in wealth overall or for a significant part of the population. Whether this is factually correct can be disputed, but more problematic is the underlying assumption that it is wealth as measured in monetized terms that is important, and the tendency to ignore other effects besides those that relate simply to monetized wealth or income.

itself allow such behavior to appear as if it were simply another aspect of the sort of sound monetary and financial decision-making that supposedly benefits all. Self-interest thus becomes covertly—and sometimes, it has to be said, *overtly*—legitimized.

There is a long history that opposes *thinking*, especially in the form of philosophy, and *money* and the pursuit of money, especially in the form of business and commerce.[7] One finds this in Socrates's refusal to take payment from his students[8] and in Adam Smith's warning against the class of "merchants and master manufacturers" whose interests are only their own and who seek "to deceive and oppress the public."[9] One might argue that the contemporary suspicion of philosophy is, in some respects, simply, the reverse side of this long-standing antagonism between philosophy and the monetary or commercial—and in a world in which the monetary and the commercial rule, it is perhaps unsurprising to find philosophy so much under threat. Yet what is different about the contemporary situation is the extent to which the monetary and commercial now dominate even the institutional framework within which philosophy itself is situated as well as the larger framework of public discourse and debate. Indeed, the dominance of monetized instrumentalism threatens the very idea of any form of thinking, whether philosophical or otherwise, that does not take the instrumental and the monetized as primary.

Undoubtedly, instrumentalist thinking constitutes *a kind* of thinking—indeed, as noted above, thinking often has an instrumentalist character, even though such instrumentalism cannot be taken as lying at the heart of thinking. Where such thinking operates in recognition of its character as instrumentalist (which includes some awareness of its own desires and interests), and so in acknowledgment of the prior determination of the ends to which it looks to find the means, then instrumentalism does not present itself as especially problematic. Yet in the form in which instrumentalism is today so widespread—the form in which instrumental thinking, and especially monetized instrumental thinking, is taken to be primary, and in which the only end is the furtherance of monetized instrumentality as such—then it becomes unclear even what sense can be attached anymore to the idea of the instrumental.

Instrumentality depends on ends that lie outside of the instrumental system. As things stand in the contemporary world, however, it is increasingly harder to identify such non-instrumental ends, since properly understood, money is itself

---

7 See Marcel Hénaff, 2010, for an account of some of this history.
8 See D. C. Schindler, 2009, pp. 394–426.
9 Adam Smith, 1980, p. 359.

valuable solely in its own character as instrumental (in terms of what it enables one *to buy*), and inasmuch money comes to function *as if it were an end*, then so there is no end to be found other than in the instrumentality of money. The very act of monetizing what is valuable thus translates such value into a pure system of instrumentality alone, which is to say, a system in which there are no ends but *only* means, but in doing so the system properly ceases to be even instrumental, since the distinction of means from end, of instrument from purpose, is lost. The way this happens mirrors the loss of value that also occurs when financial and monetary consideration are similarly prioritized.

What we lose touch with when think purely instrumentally—or purely calculatively—is precisely the idea of *distinction*, but so also of *limit* or *bound*. This is evident in the very fact that an orientation towards the instrumental or calculative alone itself involves a forgetting or ignoring of the particular character of the instrumental and the calculative, which is to say, a forgetting or ignoring of their own bounds and limits. The tendency towards just such forgetting and ignoring of distinction, of bound, and of limit has been one of the main criticisms that philosophers, from Plato onwards, have made against money and the dominance of the commercial. The way money operates in this way is itself at the heart of money's often remarked-upon tendency to corrupt, which is not simply a matter of money having a tendency to encourage greed or avarice, but rather concerns the way in which it tends to distort and obscure the real character of things (including its own character as instrumental).

The latter point appears in the work of Georg Simmel in his claim that money, through its transformation of everything into a system of pure number and quantity, effectively destroys the very possibility of differentiation.[10] The problem at issue here arises because of the way number and quantity lack any basis in themselves for limit or bound—and it is limit or bound that are the basis for differentiation and distinction. This lack of limit or bound can be seen, in the case of money, in the way in which, unlike most other things, money offers neither an upper limit to its accumulation nor any lower limit that would constrain its loss (there is thus neither an upper limit to monetized wealth nor a lower limit to monetized debt[11]) and this lack of limit is made all

---

10 Georg Simmel, 1978, p. 272.
11 This lack of limit is particular to monetary wealth—it does not apply in the same way to forms of wealth that are based in commodities, not only because supplies of commodities are always limited, but also because, land aside, most commodities need to be stored, and so there are spatial constraints on the capacity for commodity accumulation, and because some commodities cannot be stored beyond a certain point without spoilage or loss. This can present problems when commodity wealth is understood only in monetized terms, since such monetiza-

the more evident in contemporary societies in which money has become almost entirely abstract—credit cards replace cash, payments are made electronically, and money appears most often in the form of a line of a numbers on a computer screen or print-out.

This absence of limit or bound—which is what really underpins the loss of any sense of genuine ends, and so of real means also, as well as of any sense of proper value—is what sets the monetary and commercial so much against the philosophical, since it is precisely the attentiveness to limit and bound, and their exploration, that is central to philosophy. This is so not only because philosophy can be construed as an inquiry into the natures of things (and the nature of a thing is determined by the bounds that belong to it), but also because philosophy is just that mode of thinking that takes thinking as its object, and as such, it is essentially concerned with the nature and bounds *of thinking*, and may even be said to have its origin in the very recognition of thinking's own boundedness— in the recognition of its own limitation.

It is thus that Socrates, so often cited as the exemplary philosopher, whether in academic or popular discourse, puts such emphasis on ignorance, and the acknowledgment of ignorance, as the beginning of wisdom. If Socrates is wise, as the Delphic oracle declares, then it is because *he knows that he does not know*— and this is not only a recognition of a lack of knowledge (which otherwise one might suppose can be rectified simply by the gaining of knowledge), but also of the ever-present tendency to error and misunderstanding. We always remain in ignorance, which is why we are always committed to the project of thinking and knowing, because we always remain prone to error, misunderstanding, and misconstrual, and that is why the recognition of ignorance is and always remains so important. This is such a simple point that it is easy to forget or to overlook it, and yet it is with just this point that not only does philosophy have its origin, but so too does thinking.

---

tion can itself obscure the limitations of the commodity or commodities at issue. Thus, even though commodity wealth can be monetized, there is still an important difference between monetary and commodity wealth—although it is worth noting that this does not operate in quite the same way in respect of debt, which is not restricted, even if understood in commodity terms, by any considerations of limit that derive from issues of supply, storage, or spoilage. Indeed, when the notion of debt is coupled with the idea of interest on debt, so that debt (and so too wealth) becomes self-generating, then the possibility is opened up of forms of debt that constantly increase and so also of forms of debt that can never be discharged. Interest is itself facilitated by monetization, and one might argue, as does David Graeber, that debt and money themselves go together, since debt depends on the abstract quantification that money allows. See Graeber, 2011, chap. 2.

Thinking always arises out of something that calls us to think—perhaps some perplexity or problem, something that requires decision or action, something that provokes or reminds us, something that simply calls us to listen and respond. Thinking thus always stands in relation to something—something that thinking is turned towards, that thinking is "about"—and this is so even when our thinking is confused or vague and even when our thinking has a more contemplative character. What calls for thinking is that to which thinking itself has to respond and to which it must attend. Thinking falters when it forgets or loses sight, not only of that which calls for thinking, but also when it forgets or loses sight of the ground on which thinking already stands—when it ignores the prior judgments out of which it emerges and ceases to be mindful of the way in which its approach to its objects always depends on the inevitable particularity and partiality of thinking's own standpoint.[12]

When we think, we do so *from* somewhere and in relation *to* something, and this is already indicative of the necessary boundedness of thinking. That boundedness is not what prevents thinking, but is actually what enables it (one cannot think, no matter what is sometimes claimed, from nowhere at all—which is the hermeneutic point briefly noted in the discussion earlier), since it gives thinking an orientation and direction, as well as an object. The very distinction between thinking and what is thought about already indicates the way bound and limit are involved here, since *distinction* itself depends on bound and limit—for there to be a distinction is for there to be a mutual boundedness. One might say, in fact, that thinking arises only in the "between" of thinking and what is given to thinking. It is in that "between" that is opened up a space for thinking—and so for attending, responding, questioning, judging, deciding, connecting, identifying, inferring, hoping, desiring, believing and so on—in relation to something that is at issue in thinking. It is in the openness of this between that both ignorance and knowledge are possible, both error and veracity, since it is precisely the space that separates what we think from the reality of that which we think about. Inasmuch as thinking always presupposes this "between," and with it a sense of the "other" that calls upon thinking, so our own being as thinkers is a being "in" the world that is nevertheless also "apart from" the world. This being "in" and "apart" is what underlies the strangeness of human being—a strangeness that involves being both at home

---

[12] This is a key point in hermeneutics—although it is usually expressed in terms of the dependence of understanding on some prior understanding (the essence of the "hermeneutic circle"). I have argued elsewhere that this is a phenomenon itself best understood in terms of the placed character of thinking and understanding. See Jeff Malpas, 2017.

and not at home, in closeness and distance, on the earth and under the sky, in the midst of life and in the face of death.

There can be no thinking—nor anything *to be thought* or anyone who thinks —without bound or limit. To be bounded, to be limited, is also to be *placed*, and so when we talk of the essential relation between thinking and bound or limit we are also talking of the essential relation between thinking and place. It is in being-placed, which is to say being in the world in a certain way, here and now, that thinking is oriented, and it is in being oriented that thinking is opened to the world—and so is opened to that which calls upon thinking, opened to that which calls thinking into the world, opened *to that which calls us into thought*.

Moreover, when thinking is itself turned towards thinking, when thinking takes the form of a genuine philosophizing, then thinking must also turn itself to its own bound and limit, and so to its own place, and its relation to that place. Perhaps one might even say that this is what the most essential thinking actually is: just the thinking of the place of thinking which is also the thinking of our own place—which is to say, of that wherein we find ourselves, of the bounds and limits of our own being in the world. Of course, when we forget the place of our thinking, or when we try to think in a way that ignores the being-placed character of thinking, then, in all sorts of very ordinary ways, we tend to think "badly"—to become "thoughtless"—we over-generalize, we jump to conclusions, we become dogmatic, we ignore indeterminacies and ambiguities, we may even overlook the inadequacies and failures to which our thoughtlessness leads. In contrast, genuine thinking is also always alert to its own limitations, its own tendency to error and failure—which is also why genuine thinking so often takes the form of both a questioning and listening.

From this perspective, Heidegger's talk of the contemporary "flight from thinking" can be taken to refer to a flight from the engagement with our own bounds and limits, a flight from the very place in which we ourselves are, a flight from that in which our own being is grounded and, indeed, this is just the way Heidegger himself takes it. The flight from thinking is itself tied to a seeming loss of connectedness to those places in which our lives are supported and nurtured, and at the very same time, a loss of any sense of, or of any capacity to engage with the wider expansiveness of the world.[13] The flight from thinking and into thoughtlessness is thus also a flight into homelessness and worldlessness.

---

13 See Martin Heidegger, 1966, pp. 47–55. The language Heidegger uses here can all-too-easily be read as simply the invocation of a backward-looking and conservative clinging to tradition and native belonging. Yet it can also be read in a way that goes beyond this, and such a reading is supported both by Heidegger's emphasis on the growth beyond one's native ground alone and on his argument for the importance of the notions of "releasement" (*Gelassenheit*) and open-

This flight from thinking is one that Heidegger argues is itself inextricably bound to contemporary technology. Yet, in talking of technology, Heidegger is not concerned with particular devices or mechanisms, but instead with what the rise of what he himself calls "calculative thinking" and with the systems of organization that are part of it. Monetization, and the dominance of the financial and commercial, is an essential element in the forms of calculation and organization at issue here—and so contemporary technology has become deeply enmeshed with the structures of contemporary capitalism.[14] It is monetization, as a mode of pure quantification in which everything is rendered the same, that both enables and also drives the flight from thinking. Monetization erases any proper sense of the bounds within which human being is constituted and within which difference arises. It is thus that even the bounds within which the monetary itself operates—as a phenomenon that emerges out of and on the basis of human being—are obscured and forgotten, and by means of which the illusion of a generalized boundlessness is erected and maintained.

4 Thinking and the Primacy of the Non-instrumental

Although it may present itself as instrumentalist, the monetized instrumentalism of the contemporary world is indeed such that it has ceased to function, in any genuine sense, as instrumental. This is partly because its refusal of boundedness or limit is a refusal of the boundedness that constitutes even the instrumental itself—the instrumental being constituted through the contrast between the instrumental and that with respect to which it is instrumental. The result, however, is that, for all that the contemporary emphasis placed upon, for instance, efficiency, economy, or "value-for-money, it is arguably the case that there is now greater waste, greater dysfunctionality, greater difficulty in meeting even the most basic of goals.

---

ness. Both of these, I would suggest, involve exactly the sense of attentiveness to place and to bound, and one's own being given over to these, that I have emphasized here. For more on the idea of releasement, as it might be thought in relation to place, see Jeff Malpas, 2015, pp. 45–62; and also Jeff Malpas, 2017, pp. 119–126.

14 In diverse ways, new technologies have themselves enabled, among other developments, greater concentrations of wealth, the increased dominance of globalized corporations, the rise of unpaid work, de-skilling, and the disempowerment of labor. In their effect on financial and other systems, new technologies also contribute and are themselves reinforced by the rise of monetized forms of thinking and operation.

Even if we leave to one side the environmental breakdown that now appears directly linked to our current economic system (it is surely no accident that the environmental is so often set against the economic as if there were some sort of choice to be made between them[15]), the list of contemporary problems is many, and includes, among other things, not only the rise of a new and dangerous political populism (exemplified by Trump), but also a widespread breakdown in good governance across almost all institutions (but especially within the public sector), increasing social and political alienation and discontent, heightened levels of inequality and loss of social cohesion, a greater inability to manage economic and financial systems in the face of their volatility and unpredictability, and an increasing incapacity, in spite of higher wealth and productivity than ever before, to meet the basic health, education, and welfare needs of the majority of the world's population. The "public good" seems to have been overtaken by commercial interest, which now appears to drive even public institutions—if they have not already been marginalized, privatized, or simply disbanded.[16] There is one line of argument that would suggest that, in fact, this sort of dysfunctionality is itself part of the way modern capitalism must function—that it depends on a constant process of destruction and destabilization for its own maintenance.[17] Yet, even if this were so, what is seems simply to reaffirm is precisely the extent to which the system of which modern capitalism is an expression or which it embodies—namely, the system of monetized instrumentality—is a system that no longer operates instrumentally in the usual sense, since any instrumentality it has is now entirely internalized.

---

15 When properly understood the economic—the domain of the οἶκος, of the proper management, as one might say, of the immediate domain in which we live—must itself demand attentiveness to the environmental. The economic and environmental thus do not stand apart from one another, and it is only a narrowed down conception of the economic—one that is indeed tied to the monetized instrumentality of that has been the focus for the discussion here—that would suggest otherwise.

16 The imposition of monetized and commercialized systems of management and operation onto public institutions is effectively a way of bringing about a result similar to that which could have otherwise been achieved through privatization, but without the public outcry that such privatization would typically have provoked.

17 Such an idea echoes the Marxian notion, developed at length by Joseph Schumpeter, that capitalism depends essentially on processes of creative destruction—see esp. Schumpeter, 1942. Schumpeter saw such creative destruction as eventually leading to capitalism's own destruction, but others have seen it merely as part of the continuing process by which capitalism maintains itself—globalization being the latest instantiation of this process of destructive self-maintenance.

When thinking operates only instrumentally, then it already has a tendency to ignore its bounded character—and this is simply because the instrumental tends to lose itself in the focus on the instrumental relation itself and so on the relation between means and a particular end. Yet, so long as the instrumental does indeed operate in relation to some such end that is outside of the system of the instrumental, then the narrowness of instrumental thinking is not necessarily problematic. In effect, the boundedness of instrumental thinking is operative in such thinking, whether implicitly or explicitly, by the ends to which the instrumental is subordinated. What then becomes important are the ends that are at issue—and especially the relation between different ends and so the way the entire system of ends may constrain instrumental decision-making.

The monetization of instrumentality is problematic precisely because of the way it obliterates the distinction between instrument and end, and the very idea of there being different, distinct, and sometimes incommensurable ends. Neither as instrument nor as end does anything within the structure of monetized instrumentality appear as open to question, and so the legitimacy of that structure cannot be questioned without, as it were, already standing outside of the very structure that grants legitimacy to any question. When that structure appears to fail, then that failure is either not recognized or else it is seen as a function of some other interruption to its normal functioning—thus not even the global financial crisis of 2008, whose repercussions are still being felt, led to any radical and genuine change in the system of monetized instrumentality. If anything, that system is even more entrenched today than it was then. There simply is no space—no "between"—that the system of monetized instrumentality allows within which its own operation, its own bounds and limits, can be brought to salience, and so opened to any genuine inquiry; there is no "external" perspective, because there are no external ends, from which it can be examined and perhaps found wanting.

The "dysfunctionality" of the system of monetized instrumentality is not a dysfunctionality that appears within that system itself. It appears only if one allows that there may indeed be another standpoint from which that system can be viewed—most obviously, the perspective afforded by the human context in which that monetized instrumentality remains embedded and out of which it originally arose. From this perspective, the monetized instrumentality of the present—and, with it, the radicalized form of capitalism that it embodies—is itself *instrumentally* dysfunctional. Yet although this dysfunctionality is indeed connected with the way in which it has dissociated itself from any genuinely human ends, this dissociation is itself more a symptom than a cause. The dysfunctionality of the system of monetized instrumentality does indeed have its origin in its refusal of its own properly instrumental character, in its inability to recognize the inadequacy of the monetary to operate as a genuine end, in its blindness to its own bound and limit, in its essential thoughtlessness.

It is characteristic of genuine thinking that it is always failing—always being brought up short, always finding itself confounded by the things to which its attention is directed and yet which always exceed thinking. And this failing gives rise to the characteristic dynamic of thinking as a movement to and fro in that "between" that is essential to thinking—that "between" that belongs to thinking and its objects, to thinking and the thinker, to the thinker and other thinkers, to thinking and the world. The movement of thinking is a constant movement within and across various limits and bounds, and the movement of thinking is also a movement that looks to integrate at the same time as it also differentiates. Where the movement of thinking begins is with thinking's, and the thinker's, being placed within the world—the world of things and the world of ideas—in relation to other thinkers and things, and so with the fact of essential plurality and the thinker's own finitude in the face of that plurality. It is just such plurality and finitude that is effectively refused or ignored by the emphasis on forms of monetized instrumentality. Yet since that plurality and finitude remains an unavoidable feature of the world and of our own mode of being in it, so to refuse or to ignore it is to open oneself to even greater failure and breakdown than is ordinarily the case—and in such a way that the very fact of failure and breakdown will not itself be able to properly be addressed. The emphasis on the monetary and the instrumental thus turns out itself to be instrumentally dysfunctional.

One might be tempted to say, at this point, that what has actually been revealed, in spite of what might have been said earlier about the non-instrumental character of thinking or about thinking as "an end in itself," is precisely the instrumental value and significance of thinking. Thinking matters, and philosophy with it, one might say, because it allows us to recognize and explore the conditions under which thinking, and everything that follows from thinking, including even instrumental thinking, must operate, and so there can be no viable instrumental thinking without thinking in this broader sense—such broader thinking is itself *instrumentally valuable* even though it is *not instrumentally oriented.*

It is true that thinking has instrumental value, but the value and significance of thinking does not rest *primarily* in its instrumentality. It is characteristic of an instrument that it can be taken up or put down as the need serves. However, thinking cannot be taken up or put down in this way, and this is so even though it may be true that there is a contemporary "flight" from thinking. Thinking belongs to our very character as human, so much so that we might say that the "between" that thinking opens up is precisely the space in which human being finds its own place. The flight from thinking is thus an impossible flight—a flight from what we already are, a denial of that to which we are already committed. This is why the monetized instrumentality that has occupied so much of this discussion, and that dominates so much of contemporary discourse, turns out itself to be dysfunctional and contradictory: it operates in a way that is inconsistent with that in which it is itself grounded, in a way that fails to accord with the very bounds and limits by which it is constituted. As Heidegger points out, only that which can be a ground for growth can lie fallow, only those who have a capacity for hearing can be deaf, only those who have been young can become old, and only those who have a capacity for thinking, can be thoughtless.[18]

5 Thinking, Truth, and the Human

The rise of Trump seems to characterize the contemporary "flight from thinking" in a particularly powerful way. Yet one might argue that part of what has driven Trump's rise to power is popular reaction against the effects of exactly the monetized instrumentalism that has been at issue in the discussion here. In that case, does Trump's rise mark the decline of that instrumentalism?—If so, might it even mean, strange though such a suggestion might be, a stop to the flight from thinking? The seeming perversity of the latter idea, at least where Trump is concerned, ought to make us very cautious in our consideration of the former.

In fact, Trump's rise should *not* be taken to indicate that the sort of monetized instrumentalism at issue here is now itself in flight. It remains the case that the same structures that embody and reinforce the monetized and the instrumental remain in place around the world, and Trump has not shown a desire to contest those structures in any essential way—in fact, quite the opposite seems to be true. This should be not be surprising, since Trump is himself dependent upon, and a contributor to, the very same economic and financial order that is so much bound up with the contemporary dominance of the instrumental and the monetized. Ironically, much of Trump's support comes from those who have themselves been disadvantaged by that very order, but this merely shows that the system of monetized instrumentalism at issue here does not operate in ways that are entirely consist or indeed entirely functional, and that it may also operate through ideas or commitments that may, in terms of their content, even be antagonistic to it—and one might note that this seems an almost inevitable consequence of its instrumental character.

---

18 Martin Heidegger, 1966, p. 45.

In fact, this latter point, brings us directly back to the way in which the contemporary dominance of monetization and instrumentalism, including its manifestation in a figure such as Trump, is indeed tied up with the flight from thinking. When thinking itself becomes merely instrumental, then the very processes of thinking come to appear as themselves determined by that same instrumentalism—in its public forms, in public discourse and decision-making, thinking becomes simply a way of advancing or realizing an already identified outcome. What matters, then, is not consistency, which can just be ignored (as Trump himself shows), nor truth or evidence as such (the significance of which depends on a prior commitment to truth and knowledge, and so to thinking, as important in themselves and not merely as instrumentally valuable). What matters is simply the ability to get approval of or commitment to an outcome, and nothing more. If truth and evidence count all, it is only as they are themselves instrumental, and instrumentally, at least so far as gaining approval and commitment is concerned, all one needs is the *appearance* of truth and evidence. As monetization and instrumentalization tends to erase bounds, limits, and distinctions, so it erases or obscures even the distinction between good evidence and bad, between truth and what is taken to be truth, between truth and lie. So, we find ourselves in a world of "spin," a world of "alternative facts," a world that is "post-truth." Amidst this "confusion," it is easy to see how a populist figure like Trump, who is no friend of the dispossessed and the disempowered (as his record as a New York landlord and developer shows), might be taken for their champion.

Significantly, the era of "post-truth" did not begin in 2016, with the ascendency of Trump (or even with Brexit), but instead has its origins in earlier shifts in media, management, and organization that are not only part of the larger history of modernity,[19] but are also evident in developments over the last thirty to forty years. The undermining of professional authority, seen as a key instrument in public service reform beginning in the United Kingdom in the 1980s,[20] itself meant the establishing of the dominance of instrumentalist over other considerations, but it also implied a genericization of judgment and expertise. Questions of truth and evidence became part of the same instrumental calculation more reliably undertaken by a manager or administrator than anyone with more speci-

---

19 It is just such a history that Heidegger sketches in his own critique of technology so that although his talk specifically of the "flight of thinking" dates from 1955, the developments with which he connects it go back much earlier. What we see now is the further radicalization of trends and tendencies that have long been in play—trends and tendencies that may even be seen, as Max Weber pessimistically saw them, as tied up with the very nature of the human world in which we live, and so as trends and tendencies that cannot be avoided.
20 See, for instance, Max Travers, 2007.

alized capacities (who would anyway be liable to be distracted by concerns particular to their specialization). The attack on science that has been part of the conservative opposition to attempts to combat climate change over the last decade or so[21]—an opposition that itself derives largely from the prioritization of a set of narrow economic interests and is funded by them—has further contributed to the corroding of truth and the loss of any genuine sense of what constitutes knowledge, objectivity, or expertise. The concentration of power and authority —whether in the commercial sphere through the increasing dominance of large corporations, or in the governmental and public sphere through the erosion of institutional independence (partly through the use of audit and compliance mechanisms to ensure centralized control)—has resulted in both the increased capacity to "manage" information at the same time as it also made such "management" more and more instrumentally important. It is no accident that the role of the "media advisor" has become so prominent in governments and corporations, and increasingly so, from at least the 1990s onwards. The "media" has itself become a domain driven by the need to manage, control, and also to commercialize what is now generically understood as "information"—with such "information," and the media generally, more and more subject to manipulation and control by individuals and organizations according to their own agendas and interests. The rise of new forms of media has enhanced the capacity for management, control, and commercialization of information, but it has also hugely proliferated information at the same time as the overall quality and reliability of information has been degraded. Distinctions between is "real" and what is "constructed," between the "factual" and the invented, between "news" and entertainment, have all contributed to the loss of truth or of any commitment to truth that seems to characterize the present.[22]

The instrumentalist dismissal of philosophy in contemporary public discourse—whether directed at philosophy in its institutionalized forms or more generally—is almost always couched in terms that presuppose a form of mone-

---

[21] Attacks that nevertheless have an important precedent in the vitriolic and often *ad hominem* criticisms levelled, in the 1960s, against Rachel Carson and her ground-breaking book, *Silent Spring*. Rachel Carson, 1962.

[22] Heidegger warns of the "flight from thinking" in 1955, and the phenomena that constitute the "flight from truth" are clearly at issue in his own discussion, but his concern with the issues at stake here, especially as connected with modern technology, goes back much further. Many other thinkers have identified similar trends and tendencies, including those that relate to truth, in the rise of modernity itself. What we seen now is thus the further radicalization of developments that have long been in play—developments that may even be seen, as Max Weber saw them, as inextricably tied up with the very nature of the human world in which we live.

tized instrumentality as the basis on which any possible justification of the value or relevance of philosophy would have to be mounted. Such instrumentalism is not, however, directed at philosophy (or other forms of humanistic inquiry) in its institutionalized instantiation alone, nor even at the idea of thinking as that which philosophy exemplifies. Instead, it attacks the very idea of truth or of knowledge as apart from the system of monetization and of instrumentalization, thereby also attacking the idea of any limit to such monetization and instrumentalization.

Plato famously says in the *Republic* that the philosophers "are those who love the truth,"[23] and, although Plato contrasts the philosopher in this regard with those who love honor (soldiers) or money (merchants and traders), there is a sense in which we are all committed to truth, even if we may not all be its "lovers." The commitment to truth derives, in part, from certain simple facts about the relation that connects truth and thinking, but that also connects both to human life. Truth is that which is the ultimate concern of thinking as well as that which constrains it (it is thus both its ground and its limit). It is truth, and the concern with truth, that orients thinking in the space "between" in which thinking resides. "Truth" here does not name some eternal or unchanging transcendence, but rather the everyday sense at issue when, to paraphrase Aristotle, we say of what is that it is and of what is not that it is not.[24] Our own being as human is bound up with our character as *thinking* beings, and so also is it bound up with a commitment to truth. To be human is to find oneself in the space of thinking, in a space oriented towards truth, and it is in this space, this *place*, that we also find the possibility of *freedom*, of *self*, and of *commonality* that are themselves essential to a properly human mode of existence.

In Orwell's *1984*, a work that has acquired a new-found relevance with Trump's ascendency, the triumph of Big Brother involves *both* the assertion of Big Brother's control over truth itself *and* the destruction of any genuine humanity. In Orwell's novel, this is brought together in the use of the torture *which appears as both a violation of the human and a violation of truth*. The idea that "2 + 2" should equal whatever the Party or Big Brother says it equals, and the vision of the future that Winston's torturer O'Brien presents as "a boot stamping on a human face,"[25] are thus intimately connected[26]—as indeed the history of totalitarianism in the twentieth century demonstrates. Donald Trump's own endorsement of torture, reaffirmed in his first television interview as President in Janu-

---

23 Plato, 1961, *Republic* 4475e.
24 Aristotle, 1984, *Metaphysics* 1011b1.
25 George Orwell, *1984*, 1949, pp. 214–5.
26 See my discussion in Jeff Malpas, 2010, pp. 133–145.

ary 2017, is thus both chilling and unsurprising (so too was his refusal to take a firm stand against the Saudi Arabian killing of Jamal Kashoggi in October 2018). The flight from thinking is a flight from truth, and it is also a flight from the human. As such, it is a flight, not only into thoughtlessness, ignorance, and lie, but into violence and horror.[27]

The value and significance of philosophy is, indeed, not found primarily in any instrumental and monetized end to which it may contribute. The value and significance of philosophy, as with all of the humanities, as with science, with knowledge, with truth, lies in its intimate relation to our own human being. To refuse thinking, to refuse the bounds and limits with which thinking is itself engaged, to refuse truth, is to refuse that which makes us what we are. Moreover, since the value and significance of philosophy stands alongside the value and significance of questioning, of attending, of listening—all of which are at the very heart of thinking—so the denigration of philosophy, whether in its institutional or other forms, is also a denigration of just such questioning, attending, and listening. What have we become, one might ask, when we cease to question, cease to attend, cease to listen. Perhaps there is no question here—or at least it is a question to which we already know the answer all too well. What we become is what we see too much of in our contemporary world, what we have seen over too much of over the last one hundred years: we become deceivers as well as deceived, oppressors as well as oppressed, victims as well as executioners. The real question is not whether there is value or significance to be accorded to philosophy—or to thinking, truth, or the human. The real question, and the question that is most urgent, is whether we can regain a proper sense of the value and significance that philosophy already has; whether the contemporary world can be other than as determined by the instrumental and the monetized; whether we can restrain the flight from thinking, return to thinking, return to truth, return to ourselves.

---

27 One might argue, perhaps by setting Orwell's *1984* against Aldous Huxley's dystopic *Brave New World* (Huxley, 1932), in which a paternalistic state retains control through the effective drugging of its population, that the flight from thinking need not be a flight into violence or horror. There are different forms of violence and horror, however, and not all are immediately evident as violent or horrific—it is thus a moot point whether we should view Huxley's world as indeed free from either violence or horror. Moreover, the argument Orwell advances is that the antagonism between violence and truth is so deep and fundamental that there will always be a form of inhumanity that accompanies any denial or denigration of truth—even if it may sometimes be covered over or hidden. Although it may not be an inhumanity that will be experienced the same way by all, it will be an inhumanity nonetheless. In any case, truth and humanity are both also at issue in Huxley's novel, and, one might say, in similar ways even though by means of a very different narrative presentation.

Bibliography

Aristotle. *Metaphysics*. In vol. 2 of *The Complete Works of Aristotle: Revised Oxford Translation*. Jonathan Barnes (Ed.). Princeton: Princeton University Press, 1984.

Burawoy, Michael. "The Neoliberal University: Ascent of the Spiralists." *Critical Sociology* 42 (2016): pp. 941–942.

Carson, Rachel. *Silent Spring*. New York: Houghton-Mifflin, 1962.

Graeber, David. *Debt: The First 5,000 Years*. Brooklyn: Melville House, 2011.

Hénaff, Marcel. *The Price of Truth: Gift, Money, and Philosophy*. Jean-Louis Morhange (Trans.). Stanford: Stanford University Press, 2010.

Heidegger, Martin. *Discourse on Thinking. A Translation of* Gelassenheit. John M. Anderson and E. Hans Freund (Trans.). New York: Harper & Row, 1966.

Huxley, Aldous. *Brave New World*. London: Chatto & Windus, 1932.

Malpas, Jeff. "'Good Government Starts Today': On the Death of the Public, the Triumph of Private Interest, and the Loss of the Good." In *Reclaiming the Public: Working Papers in the Human Rights and Public Life Program, No.3: July 2016*, Anna Yeatman (Ed.), pp. 11–23. Parramatta, NSW: Whitlam Institute, 2016.

Malpas, Jeff. "Placing Understanding/Understanding Place." *Sophia* 55 (2017): 379–391.

Malpas, Jeff. "From Extremity to Releasement: Place, Authenticity, and the Self." In *The Horizons of Authenticity: Essays in Honor of Charles Guignon's Work on Phenomenology, Existentialism, and Moral Psychology*, Hans Pedersen and Lawrence Hatab (Eds.), pp. 45–62. Dordrecht: Springer, 2015.

Malpas, Jeff. "Truth, Politics, and Democracy: Arendt, Orwell, and Camus." In *Power, Judgment and Political Evil: In Conversation with Hannah Arendt*, Andrew Schaap, Danielle Celermajer, and Vrasidas Karalis (Eds.), pp. 133–145. Farnham: Ashgate, 2010.

Malpas, Jeff. "What is Architecture For?" In "Ethics in Architecture Festschrift for Karsten Harries," Eduard Führ (Ed.). *Cloud-Cuckoo-Land, International Journal of Architectural Theory* 22, no. 36 (2017): pp. 119–126. http://cloud-cuckoo.net/fileadmin/issues_en/issue_36/article_malpas.pdf.

Newman, John Henry. *The Idea of a University*. Daniel M O'Connell (Ed.). Chicago: Loyola University Press, 1927.

Orwell, George. *1984*. Harmondsworth: Penguin, 1949.

Plato. *Republic*. In *The Collected Dialogues of Plato*. Edith Hamilton and Huntingdon Cairns (Eds.). Princeton: Princeton University Press, 1961.

Schindler, D. C. "Why Socrates Didn't Charge: Plato and the Metaphysics of Money." *Communio: International Catholic Review* 36 (2009): pp. 394–426.

Simmel, Georg. *The Philosophy of Money*. T. Bottomore and D. Frisby (Trans.). London: Routledge, 1978.

Smith, Adam. *The Wealth of Nations*. A. Skinner (Ed.). New York: Penguin Books, 1980.

Schumpeter, Joseph. *Capitalism, Socialism, and Democracy*. New York: Harper & Brothers, 1942.

Travers, Max. *The New Bureaucracy: Quality Assurance and its Critics*. Bristol: Policy Press, 2007.

Contributors

Jon Askonas is 2nd year DPhil candidate in International Relations at the University of Oxford, where he is a Beinecke Scholar and a Healy Scholar. He is interested in the relationship between knowledge production/transmission and decision-making in large organizations. He has a BS in International Politics (summa cum laude) from Georgetown University and a MPhil (Merit) from Oxford. He has worked at the Council on Foreign Relations and the US Embassy in Moscow.

Babette Babich is Professor of Philosophy at Fordham University in New York City. Author of many articles, her books include, most recently, *Un politique brisé. Le souci d'autrui, l'humanisme, et les juifs chez Heidegger* (L'Harmattan, 2016), *The Hallelujah Effect: Music, Performance Practice, and Technology* [Routledge, 2016 (2013)], *La fin de la pensée? Philosophie analytique contre philosophie continentale* (L'Harmattan, 2012), *"Eines Gottes Glück, voller Macht und Liebe"* (Bauhaus-Universitätsverlag Weimar 2009); *Words in Blood, Like Flowers* (SUNY Press, 2006). Her *Nietzsche's Philosophy of Science* (SUNY Press, 1994) appeared in Italian (Cortina, 1996) and was revised for edition in German (2010). A four time Fulbright scholar, editor/co-editor of more than eight book collections, she edits the journal *New Nietzsche Studies* and, on behalf of the author, Patrick Aidan Heelan (1926–2015) S.J., *The Observable: Heisenberg's Philosophy of Quantum Mechanics* (Peter Lang, 2016).

Lisa Bortolotti is Professor of Philosophy at the University of Birmingham. She works in the philosophy of the cognitive sciences, and examines the philosophical issues emerging from psychology and psychiatry (such as belief, rationality, delusion, confabulation, optimism, responsibility, health and happiness). Her monograph *Delusions and Other Irrational Beliefs* (Oxford University Press, 2009) was awarded the American Philosophical Association Book Prize in 2011. Her most recent book is *Irrationality* (Polity 2014). Lisa is currently leading a major ERC-funded project (PERFECT, 2014–2019). As part of the project she developed the notion of epistemic innocence to characterize those beliefs that are false or irrational, but have epistemically relevant benefits that could not be attained otherwise. In 2013 Lisa founded Imperfect Cognitions, a group blog featuring research updates, conference reports, presentations of new books, first-person accounts of psychological distress, and interviews with experts.

Paolo Diego Bubbio is Associate Professor of Philosophy at Western Sydney University, Australia. His research is mainly in the area of post-Kantian philosophy. In particular he is interested in the relationship of the post-Kantian tradition (from Kant to Nietzsche) to the later movements of European philosophy, such as existentialism and hermeneutics, and in issues in philosophy of religion. He also has an ongoing interest in Rene Girard's mimetic theory. He is the author of *Sacrifice in the Post-Kantian Tradition: Perspectivism, Intersubjectivity, and Recognition* (SUNY Press, 2014); *God and the Self in Hegel: Beyond Subjectivism* (SUNY Press, 2017); and *Intellectual Sacrifice and Other Mimetic Paradoxes* (Michigan State University Press, 2018). He is the co-editor of *Religion After Kant: God and Culture in the Idealist Era* (with Paul Redding: Cambridge Scholars, 2012), and *The Relationship of Philosophy to Reli-*

gion Today (with Philip Quadrio: Cambridge Scholars, 2011). He also published articles in several philosophy journals, and he is a contributor to the New Philosopher magazine.

Robert Frodeman is Professor of Philosophy at the University of North Texas. His work ranges across environmental philosophy, the philosophy of science and technology policy, and the philosophy of interdisciplinarity. Frodeman is the author and/or editor of nine books, most recently *Sustainable Knowledge: A Theory of Interdisciplinarity* (Palgrave McMillan, 2013); and *Socrates Tenured: The Institutions of 21st Century Philosophy* (Roman and Littlefield), published in 2016.

Jacob Graham teaches philosophy at Bridgewater College, a small liberal arts college in Bridgewater, Virginia, USA. He is interested in ancient Greek and modern philosophy, particularly Spinoza. He has published two articles with the *Internet Encyclopedia of Philosophy*—one on the Presocratrics and an overview of ancient philosophy—and, among other projects, is co-editing a volume with Tom Sparrow on *True Detective and Philosophy* (Wiley-Blackwell).

David Macarthur is an Associate Professor in the Philosophy Department at The University of Sydney. He works at the interfaces of contemporary pragmatism, Wittgenstein's philosophy of language and psychology and philosophy of art and architecture. In addition to these topics, he has published articles in leading philosophy journals and books on liberal naturalism, metaphysical quietism, skepticism, common sense, perception, ordinary language, and philosophy of photography and film. He has co-edited three collections of papers with Mario De Caro (Roma Tre): *Naturalism in Question* (Harvard, 2004); *Naturalism and Normativity* (Columbia, 2010); and *Philosophy in an Age of Science: Physics, Mathematics and Skepticism* (Harvard, 2012); and recently edited Hilary & Ruth-Anna Putnam, *Pragmatism as a Way of Life: The Lasting Legacy of William James and John Dewey* (Harvard, 2017).

Jeff Malpas is Distinguished Professor of Philosophy at the University of Tasmania. The author of many books and articles on a wide range of topics, he is best known for his work on place and space, hermeneutics and philosophy of language, and twentieth century German philosophy. His most recent book is *Reading Heidegger's Black Notebooks*, with Ingo Farin (MIT Press, 2016).

Katherine Puddifoot is Research Fellow at the University of Birmingham. She works on issues at the intersection of the philosophy of psychology and epistemology, which have implications for feminist philosophy and the philosophy of medicine. She completed her PhD at the University of Sheffield and has since worked at the University of Bristol and the University of Glasgow. She has published in leading philosophy journals, including *Synthese, Pacific Philosophical Quarterly*, and *Philosophical Topics*.

Paul Redding is Emeritus Professor of Philosophy at The University of Sydney. He works broadly in the area of German idealist philosophy and its relation to analytic philosophy, most recently pursuing issues of logic and modality in Hegel's idealism. His books include *Analytic Philosophy and the Return of Hegelian Thought* (Cambridge University Press, 2007), *Continental Idealism: Leibniz to Nietzsche* (Routledge, 2009), and *Thoughts, Deeds, Words, and World: Hegel's idealist response to the linguistic "metacritical invasion"* (Noesis Press, 2016).

Patrick Stokes is senior lecturer in philosophy at Deakin University, Australia, where he works on issues of personal identity, moral psychology, and the philosophy of death. His publications include *The Naked Self* (Oxford University Press, 2015) and *Kierkegaard's Mirrors* (Palgrave, 2010). Stokes is a regular contributor to *The Conversation*, *New Philosopher*, and other media outlets.

Katherine Withy is an Associate Professor in the Department of Philosophy at Georgetown University. She specializes in the work of Martin Heidegger and is especially interested in world collapse and other sorts of breakdowns. Her book *Heidegger on Being Uncanny* was published by Harvard University Press in 2015.

Index of Names

Adler, Mortimer   129, 135
Alighieri, Dante   29
Anaximander   143
Anscombe, Gertrude Elizabeth Margaret   44
Aquinas, Thomas   44
Arendt, Hannah   127, 140
Aristophanes   ix f., xiv
Aristotle   41, 44, 90, 98, 126 f., 136 f., 167
Arvan, Marcus   137 f.

Bakewell, Sarah   122, 129
Barrett, William   129
Bateman, Chris   121, 125, 132
Baudrillard, Jean   137
Beckett, Samuel   36
Benjamin, Walter   38, 60
Berger, John   137
Bloom, Alan   130
Botton, Alain de   129
Brewer, William F.   59
Bubbio, Paolo Diego   27, 122
Bunge, Mario   125, 130
Buonarroti, Michelangelo   30
Burke, Edmund   117
Butler, Judith   135

Carman, Taylor   125
Carson, Rachel   166
Cavell, Stanley   43, 45, 122
Chinn, Chark A.   59
Churchill, Ward   117
Cleary, Skye   122, 129
Coleridge, Samuel Taylor   30
Croce, Benedetto   39
Crowley, Stephen   117

De Chirico, Giorgio   42
Debord, Guy   137
Descartes, René   41, 44 f.
Dewey, John   131
Douthat, Ross   110, 117

Elden, Stuart   132

Emerson, Ralph Waldo   141
Empedocles   126
Engels, Friedrich   34
Epicurus   12 f.

Feyerabend, Paul   28, 29 f., 124, 130, 139
Feynman, Richard   19
Findlay, John N.   95
Fish, Stanley   117
France, Anatole   94
Frank, Manfred   34
Frege, Friedrich Ludwig Gottlob   44, 90
Freud, Sigmund   37
Fuller, Steve   111, 117, 129 f., 134

Gadamer, Hans-Georg   34–38, 126
Galilei, Galileo   29, 130
Gelernter, David   108
George, Theodore   35, 37
Giedion, Siegfried   128
Goldstein, Rebecca Newberger   129
Graeber, David   76, 157

Haack, Susan   124
Hadot, Pierre   3, 129, 143
Hawking, Stephen   xiii, 15–18, 21–24, 124
Hayek, Friedrich August   91
Hegel, Georg Wilhelm Friedrich   32, 35, 44, 89, 94–98, 108, 133
Heidegger, Martin   34, 36, 38, 44, 66, 90, 110 f., 122, 125, 127 f., 132 f., 137, 141, 143, 149, 159 f., 164–166
Hénaff, Marcel   155
Hochschild, Arlie Russell   85, 91–93, 97
Holroyd, Jules   55
Hooks, Bell   127
Hume, David   25, 44, 87, 128, 141
Hunt, Elle   139
Hussein, Saddam   77
Husserl, Edmund Gustav Albrecht   66, 90, 122
Hutcheson, Francis   32
Huxley, Aldous   168

Index of Names

Illich, Ivan 137

Jaspers, Karl 15, 24 f., 90, 123, 129

Kaczynski, Ted 108
Kant, Immanuel xiv, 44 f., 87, 96, 116, 126, 130, 133
Kashoggi, Jamal 168
Kierkegaard, Søren 24 f.
Kimball, Roger 128, 130
Krauss, Lawrence 15–19, 21–24, 123 f., 143
Kuhn, Thomas Samuel 19–21, 25, 127, 133, 138

Langer, Suzanne 129
Lasch, Christopher 92 f., 95, 97
Latour, Bruno 123, 139
Leibniz, Gottfried Wilhelm (von) 44
Leiter, Brian 125, 131
Lilla, Mark 94, 98
Locke, John 32, 42, 141

Magee, Bryan 135
Malpas, Jeff 132, 152, 158, 160, 167
Manne, Kate 125, 141
Marx, Karl 33 f., 37 f., 89, 131, 133
Midgley, Mary 133 f., 142
Mill, John Stuart 8, 32, 44
Mlodinow, Leonard 16 f.
Moliere (Jean-Baptiste Poquelin) 25

Newman, John Henry 153
Newton, Isaac 20, 29, 97, 123, 141
Nietzsche, Friedrich 37, 44, 117, 122 f., 126 f., 129–131, 133, 137, 141 f.

Obama, Barack 81–83, 91
Oliver, Jamie 44
O'Rourke, Michael 117
Orwell, George 149, 167 f.

Parmenides 143
Payne, Keith 52
Peirce, Charles Sanders 83–87, 92, 141
Peterson, Jordan 130
Pirsig, Robert 129

Plato 4–6, 8–14, 41, 44, 46, 90, 98, 126 f., 129, 136 f., 156, 167
Popper, Karl 81, 86–92, 94–96, 98 f., 123
Postman, Neil 112
Protagoras 110
Putnam, Hilary 133

Quine, Willard van Ormond 90, 133

Rawls, John 42
Reich, Robert 93
Ricoeur, Paul 36–38
Rorty, Richard 41, 124, 142
Ruark, Jennifer 139 f.
Rubio, Marco 5

Sagan, Carl 21
Saul, Jennifer 54 f.
Scheler, Max Ferdinand 90
Schelling, Friedrich Wilhelm Joseph von 30
Schiller, Johann Christoph Friedrich von 96
Schrecker, Ellen 140
Schumpeter, Joseph 161
Schürmann, Reiner 125
Scruton, Roger 130
Sellars, Wilfrid Stalker 43, 86
Simmel, Georg 156
Singer, Peter 42, 117, 123
Smith, Adam 55, 123, 155
Snow, C. P. 131
Socrates ix f., 4–13, 15, 41, 113, 115–117, 155, 157
Sokal, Alan 123, 130, 139 f.
Soros, George 89
Stein, Jeff 29
Strauss, Leo 117

Thales 126 f., 136, 143
Thoreau, Henry David 43 f.
Trump, Donald xii, 81–83, 91 f., 108, 149, 161, 164 f., 167
Turing, Alan 42
Tyson, Neil Degrasse 15–17, 19–24

Vattimo, Gianni x, 38

Warburton, Nigel 129, 135

Wartofsky, Marx 131
Weber, Max 127, 165 f.
West, Cornel 127
Wittgenstein, Ludwig Josef Johann 23, 44–46, 66, 90, 95

Zabala, Santiago 38
Žižek, Slavoj 135

Index of Subjects

abstraction   92, 96 f.
academia   57, 89, 106, 115, 127, 132
academic philosophy   43, 46, 86
accountability   60
accumulation   156
affective states   57
Affordable Care Act   81
Afghanistan   29
agreement   36 f., 51
alienation   37, 154, 161
Amazon   133
American Philosophical Association   112, 131
amnesia   20, 57 f.
analytic-continental   125, 131, 135 f., 141
analytic philosophy   121 f., 124 f., 130, 132–134, 137, 141 f.
ancient philosophy   4, 33, 122
anglophonism   128, 138
animals   8, 42, 46, 70
anthropology   29, 65–67, 74
anxiety   13, 56
Apology   4, 8, 10 f., 41
appearance   46, 87, 89, 165
applied philosophy   113, 130
art   29 f., 45, 84, 93, 106, 126, 137
artificial intelligence   xiii
audit culture   104
Aufhebung   108
authority   ix, xiv, 35, 46, 75, 81–85, 140, 165 f.
avarice   156

baking   127 f.
BBC   135
being in   163
being in the world   159
being placed   163
belief   6 f., 9–12, 35, 42, 45, 51, 53 f., 57–61, 68 f., 73, 82–85, 87, 89, 91 f., 103, 131, 141
– fixation of belief   83 f.
– personal belief   x

bias   51 f., 55, 60 f., 117, 138
– implicit bias   xii, 51–57, 60 f.
Big Brother   167
boredom   133 f.
bound   84, 149 f., 156–160, 162–165, 167 f.
boundlessness   154, 160
bread   94, 126–128, 132
Brexit   xii, 82, 136, 165
business   69, 106, 130, 152, 155

calculation   153 f., 160, 165
calculative thinking   160
capitalism   90, 126 f., 152, 160–162
Caritas (charity)   x, 23, 38
causal ground   151
censorship   33
changing the world   27, 32–34, 38
circularity   134
citation   137 f., 141–143
citizenship   44
civil service   95
climate change   81 f., 85, 88, 92, 107 f., 140, 166
– global warming   84 f.
climatology   88
cognitive dissonance   151
colonialism   37, 77
commerce   152–157, 160 f., 166
commercialization   166
commodity   156 f.
– commodity wealth   156 f.
commonality   167
common sense   45, 87, 96
communication   44, 66, 82
– communication technologies   107
compassion   93, 150
competence   70
computer   42, 108, 139, 157
conformity   43, 46, 103
conservativism   103, 106 f.
consistency   165
continental philosophy   107, 121 f., 124 f., 132, 140–142

conversation 8, 11, 19, 22, 27, 32, 35–39, 68f., 85f., 125, 134, 142
corporation 56, 95, 160, 166
corruption 8
cosmopolitanism 90
Cotard delusion 58
counterinsurgency 65, 67–69, 73, 76f.
counterterrorism 29
creativity 153
– creative destruction 161
crime 60f., 81
– criminal insanity 60f.
culture xii, 9, 11, 28f., 31f., 39, 41–43, 58, 65–77, 104, 131, 133f., 137f., 141, 149
– cultural awareness 65, 70
– cultural literacy 68
– cultural sensitivity 65, 70, 75
curriculum 125, 136, 141
Cynics 12

death 4, 10f., 13, 15, 89, 111f., 127, 131, 138, 159
debt 156f.
decision making 60, 67, 81, 153, 155, 162, 165
delusion 13, 36, 58–61
– delusional beliefs 57, 59–61
dementia 57f.
depression 56f.
design thinking 153
desire 6f., 30, 117, 132, 136, 151f., 155, 164
dialogue 4, 7, 11, 35, 76, 84, 86f., 132
difference 10, 22, 29, 38f., 58, 65f., 72, 74f., 87, 97, 107, 109f., 125, 128, 130, 135, 157, 160
differentiation 156
digital 44, 123, 130, 132, 137, 141
disempowerment 160
distinction 22, 28f., 43, 83, 106, 110f., 121, 124, 129, 135, 140, 152, 156, 158, 162, 165f.
duty 10, 30, 44
dysfunctionality 160–162

eating disorders 57
economics 88, 106
economism 152

economy 33, 43, 74, 111, 153, 160f., 164, 166
– economic well-being 154
education 7, 21, 43, 45, 103f., 107, 111, 121, 142, 153, 161
efficiency 160
elite 82, 91–94
emotion xi, 13, 68, 92, 96
empirically informed philosophy 51
empirical methods 42
empirical sciences 84–86, 98
end 17, 82, 91, 98, 112, 114, 116, 155–157, 162f., 168
English 137–139, 141
Enlightenment xiv, 33, 37, 44, 84
environment 66, 91, 108, 110, 128, 161
– environmental breakdown 161
Epicureans 12f.
epistemology 7f., 20f., 23, 51, 54f., 59, 61, 85, 87, 103, 106f., 109f., 133
equivocation 135f., 142
error 113, 157–159
ethics 3f., 8, 13, 18f., 37, 51, 59, 77, 108f., 111, 122, 130, 143
European Union 83
evaluative framework 154
evidence 29, 51, 53–55, 57–59, 61, 82, 85, 87, 106, 108, 152, 154, 165
evolution 131
examined life 4, 10, 12, 41
executioner 168
existentialism 122f., 125, 129
expertise 103f., 108, 113f., 140, 153, 165f.
extremism 4f.

Facebook 112, 135, 149
Facts 44, 57, 67f., 87, 106, 113, 135, 167
– alternative facts 110, 165
– objective facts x
factual 93, 166
failure 8, 15, 28, 36, 57, 59, 65, 85, 94, 113, 115, 124, 126, 131, 135, 159, 162f.
fake news 110, 140
falsification 88
feeling xi, 12, 53, 73, 91f., 96, 103, 149
felt thoughtfulness 150
fideism 37

field philosopher 115 f.
financial 4, 33, 91, 153–156, 160 f., 164
finitude 10 f., 111, 163
flight from thinking 149, 159 f., 163–166, 168
flight into homelessness 159
forgetting 46, 149 f., 156
Fox News 135
France 96, 122, 124
– French Declaration of the Rights of Man and Citizen 32
– French Revolution 96
freedom 10, 12–14, 41, 43, 94, 122, 167
friendship 44

Gelassenheit 160
gender 31, 52–54, 74, 94, 114
genetic manipulation xiii
German Idealism 30
global financial crisis 162
globalization 82, 93 f., 106, 108, 161
goal 7, 18, 27, 31 f., 73, 76 f., 96, 112, 160
God 7, 9 f., 20, 29 f., 41, 45
governance 161
government 42, 44, 56, 75, 82 f., 89, 91 f., 110, 166
gravity 8
Great Depression 91
greed 156

habit 13, 43, 54, 103, 109, 112
hate-speech 93
hedonism 13
hermeneutics 35–38, 121, 123, 126, 130, 132, 136, 140–142, 152, 158
– hermeneutic circle 36, 158
himpathy 125, 138
history 21, 29, 31 f., 44, 61, 67, 72, 83, 98, 107 f., 115, 121, 124, 127 f., 133, 139, 141 f., 155, 165, 167
history of philosophy 23, 124, 133, 136, 138
hoax 82, 123, 139 f.
homelessness 159
honor 73 f., 167
horror 168
human 4, 7–9, 13, 16, 28–31, 39, 43, 45 f., 53, 66–68, 70–72, 96–98, 103 f., 109–111, 117, 127, 137, 139, 149 f., 153, 162–168
– human being 5, 8 f., 28, 31, 41, 43, 83, 97, 111, 158, 160, 163, 168
– human cloning 111
– human existence 84
– human mind 51, 57, 84
– human rights 31 f., 38
– violation of the human 167
humanities 4 f., 28 f., 103 f., 106, 111–116, 132, 137, 168

identity politics 94
– identity liberalism 98 f.
ignorance 4, 7, 9–11, 13, 157 f., 168
immigration 83
impact 18, 27, 31, 44, 51, 60, 108, 113, 115, 123, 125 f., 128 f., 134 f., 141, 149
imperialism 37, 77
industry 91, 95, 122, 140, 153
inequality 76, 154, 161
information 44, 54, 60, 67, 69 f., 82, 104, 107, 135, 166
inhumanity 168
innovation 106 f., 132, 153
institution 56, 77, 103, 107, 113, 117, 153, 161
instrumental desire 151
instrumentalism 116, 151 f., 155, 164 f., 167
– prioritization of the instrumental 152
instrumental justification 151
instrumental value 16 f., 163
interest 16, 67 f., 95, 125, 131 f., 151 f., 155, 157, 161, 166
interpretative methodology 28
interpreting the world 32, 34
iPhone 107 f.
Iraq 29, 65, 67, 69 f., 72, 75–77
– War in Iraq xiii, 65
– Human Terrain System 67
– Iraq Culture Smart Card 67, 69, 75
– The Minerva Initiative 67
irrationalism 125
irrationality 57–59
ISIS 4, 75, 89
Islam 60
– Salafism 75

– Shia Islam   29, 75
– Sunni Islam   29, 75 f.

jealousy   58
journal   81, 122 f., 125, 129, 133, 136 f., 139
judgment   4, 10, 27, 46, 54 f., 57 f., 60 f., 69, 151, 158, 165
justification   15, 29, 151, 167

knowledge   3 f., 6 f., 9, 11 f., 15, 17–19, 22 f., 28 f., 44–46, 51, 55, 57, 67, 70, 76, 84 f., 87, 95, 97 f., 106–108, 114, 130, 132, 139 f., 153, 157 f., 165–168
knowledge class   81, 91, 93, 95–97

labor   76, 93, 104, 111, 127, 160
language   4, 32, 43, 68 f., 71 f., 75, 90, 121, 129, 131, 134, 136–138, 140, 159
law   20, 29, 32, 41 f., 94, 96 f., 116, 131
legal systems   59
liberal education   107
liberalism   94, 99, 103
– liberal democracy   42, 82, 85
– liberal politics   98
– neo-liberalism   152
lie   110, 114, 165, 168
limit   7, 9, 11, 84, 96, 104, 138, 149 f., 154, 156–160, 162–165, 167 f.
listening   5, 159, 168
literature   5, 29 f., 41, 53, 56, 135, 139, 141
Logical Positivism   86
love   x, 6, 43 f., 46, 103, 108, 129, 136, 167

madness   58
mainstream   122–124, 129, 133, 135
management   115, 130, 154, 161, 165 f.
market   104, 107, 126 f., 130, 132 f., 136
Marxism   33, 91
meaning   11, 19, 30, 35–38, 46, 65, 70–72, 74–77, 111, 128, 133, 135, 141
media   xiii, 56, 61, 82, 108, 110, 115, 123, 132, 135, 137, 140 f., 165 f.
medicine   22, 42, 116
mental health   xii, 52, 56–58, 61
metaphysics   3, 8, 38, 41 f., 46, 84, 86, 90, 98, 107–111, 117, 167
methodology of the sciences   51

Middle Ages   33
milkmaid   127
mirrored-self misidentification   58
modernity   165 f.
money   28, 33, 73, 128, 150, 154–157, 167
– monetary wealth   156
– monetization   152 f., 157, 160, 162, 165, 167
– monetized instrumentalism   152, 155, 160, 164
morality   54 f., 93, 96, 126
– moral evaluations   93
moral philosophy   54
multiculturalism   93
music   29 f.

nanotechnology   xiii
nationalism   82
naturalism   20
natural philosophy   18, 142
nature   3 f., 6, 9–13, 19, 23, 25, 28, 41, 53 f., 57, 87, 89 f., 95, 98, 103 f., 109–111, 113 f., 116 f., 123, 126, 128, 139, 150, 157, 165 f.
nature of things   157
Neoplatonism   29 f.
news   110, 136, 166
non-instrumental   16, 155, 160, 163

obsolescence   107
οἶκος   161
openness   36, 158, 160
Open society   81, 88–91, 98
opinion   6, 9–11, 51, 81 f., 85
opioids   110
oppression   38, 149, 168
organization   160, 165 f.
outreach   113

particle accelerator   28
particularity   94–97, 158
Patreon   130
patriotism   93
persecution   58
Phenomenology   xiii, 66, 96, 125, 133
– phenomenological concept of 'world'   65

philosopher   3, 5f., 8, 10, 13–15, 18f., 21f., 25, 27, 29–36, 38f., 41–43, 45f., 51, 55, 57, 60, 65, 76f., 88–90, 98, 113–118, 121–127, 130–135, 137, 141–143, 156f., 167
– philosopher bureaucrat   115f.
philosophy as conversation   33
philosophy of art   21, 30
philosophy of science   18f., 21, 25, 87f., 90, 122–124
physics   13, 17f., 20, 22, 123f., 139, 141, 143
piety   5–7, 9–11, 13
plurality   163
poetry   30, 128
political correctness   93, 106
politics   4, 8, 88, 94, 98, 106, 108, 122, 126, 149
– political freedom   94
– political identity   84
– political justice   42
– political power   33
– political theory   114
popular culture   74
pornography   110
post-ethical   xiii
power   41f., 46, 65, 76, 108, 111, 116, 140f., 164, 166
practical philosophy   3, 51
practical use   19, 27f.
pragmatism   3, 83
prejudice   35–37, 52, 59–61, 140, 142f., 151
professorate   103, 107
prudence   118, 154
pseudophilosophy   125
pseudoscience   123
psychiatric disorders   51
public   15, 28, 31–33, 42, 67, 89, 94, 104, 109, 112f., 116, 118, 121, 125f., 128–132, 134, 142, 149, 153, 155, 161, 165
– public discourse   150, 155, 165f.
– public good   41, 161
– public intellectual   130f., 134
– public life   98, 131
– public policy   110
– public service   165
– public sphere   121, 136, 166
publishing   82, 128f.

quantification   153, 157, 160
questioning   9f., 25, 30f., 82, 133, 150f., 158f., 168

race   52f.
ranking   135, 153
rational structure   151
rational thought   x
real   4, 6f., 10, 14, 19, 31, 37f., 93, 96, 110, 113, 121, 128, 133, 136, 150–152, 154, 156f., 166, 168
realism   90, 133
reality   8, 29, 31, 38, 52, 57f., 69f., 84f., 111, 149, 158
– nature of reality   3f., 17, 51, 110, 122
reduction   37, 153
relation   20, 24, 36f., 44, 72, 89, 96f., 136, 149f., 158–160, 162f., 167f.
releasement   159f.
relevance   3, 41–43, 87, 95, 112f., 129, 133, 149–151, 167
religion   4f., 7, 9, 22, 29, 31, 44–46, 52, 58, 67f., 70, 73, 84, 87, 94, 131, 136
religious studies   29
reputation   89, 108, 153
research   15, 17, 20f., 23f., 51–53, 57, 66f., 83f., 103, 108, 110–112, 114f., 122, 125, 139f., 152f.
responsibility   30, 55
reverse discrimination   83, 93f.
revolution   21, 90, 96, 107, 138
rhetoric   109, 113
rituals   68

schizophrenia   57–59
scholarship   68, 122, 137f., 141f.
science   15, 17–23, 25, 28f., 41f., 44–46, 66f., 81–89, 93, 96, 98, 108–110, 113f., 116, 121–125, 128, 130f., 133, 137–140, 143, 166, 168
– normal science   20, 133
– objective science   28
– Science Wars   123, 130f., 139
– scientific achievement/discovery   28
– scientific knowledge   86f., 90
scientism   86, 124, 130
second World War   81, 91, 98

Index of Subjects

self 15, 17, 28 f., 36 f., 43, 45 f., 59, 75, 92, 117, 121 f., 129, 133, 139, 150, 154, 157, 161, 167
– self-conception 84, 97, 103, 112
– self-consistency 45
– self-determination 46
– self-interest 68, 95, 154 f.
– self-knowledge 46
sex 9, 68, 70, 110 f.
– sexual promiscuity 110
Skepticism 42, 46, 55, 98
Skeptics 12
skill 5, 16, 31 f., 51, 65, 82, 107
slavery 33
social cohesion 161
social contract 42
– social engineering 90
– social group 52–54, 61
– social isolation 57
social media x, 83
social sciences 29, 67, 106, 114, 123, 126
society 30–32, 38, 41 f., 46, 51, 56, 61, 68, 73, 75 f., 81, 85 f., 88–90, 92 f., 95, 97, 103 f., 106, 112, 115 f., 131, 153
– social benefit 31
sociology 5, 23, 29, 65–67, 106, 108, 115, 130, 132, 137
Socratic method 6 f., 28, 114
specialization 87, 124, 166
spectacle 137
spontaneism 37
state (political entity) 33, 90–92, 95–98, 104, 116, 168
– liberal state 85, 91
status quo 43, 103, 106, 116
STEM 104, 106, 108 f., 111, 115 f.
stigma xii, 51 f., 56, 58, 61
stoicism 122, 129
– stoics 12, 141
strangeness 158
string theory 17
style 69, 125, 133 f., 140–142
suspicion of philosophy 155

teaching 3, 45, 88, 114, 152 f.
Tea Party 85, 91 f.

technology xiii, 29, 44, 90, 103, 108–111, 121, 123, 132, 139, 160, 165 f.
– technological progress 46, 106
technoscience 107 f., 110
television 8, 21, 74, 93, 133, 135, 137, 149, 167
terrorism 4
theology 116
theoretical philosophy 51
the particular xii, 83, 97, 156
therapy 61, 130
the universal xii, 81, 83, 95, 97
thinking xiv, 5, 9, 16, 30 f., 43 f., 53 f., 65, 95–98, 111, 114, 116, 137 f., 142 f., 149–155, 157–160, 162–165, 167 f.
Thomism 30
thoughtlessness 149 f., 159, 163, 168
Toolbox Project 117
torture 167
Transhumanism 111, 117
truth x-xiii, 4, 12, 14, 21, 38, 45 f., 81–84, 116, 135, 140, 149 f., 154, 164–168
– post-truth x, xiii, 82, 92, 121, 129, 134, 140, 165
– search of the truth x
– truth and lie 165
– violation of truth 167
truthiness 92, 96
Twitter 82, 132, 135, 139, 149

United Kingdom 83, 90, 165
United States of America 67–69, 81, 86, 104, 110, 136, 149
– United States Army 65–68, 73–77
– United States Constitution 42
– United States Declaration of Independence 32
– U.S. 2016 Presidential Campaign 82, 108
universality 32, 83 f., 95, 97
universal point of view 81, 83, 95 f.
university 16, 31, 33, 35, 43, 66, 89, 93, 103 f., 106–108, 112–116, 124 f., 130 f., 133, 136, 138–142, 150, 152 f.
usefulness xiv, 3, 5, 13, 19, 27–29, 31, 35, 51, 58, 76, 121–125, 131, 151, 154

value   xiii, 5, 11, 16, 23 f., 27, 32 – 34, 43, 45, 57 f., 68, 77, 97, 109, 116, 131, 150 – 154, 156 f., 163, 167 f.
– value-for-money   152, 160
– value-in-itself   152
veracity   44, 158
victim   168
video games   110
violence   37, 52, 60, 72, 110, 149, 168

wager   36 – 38
Weak Anthropic Principle   17
wealth   153 f., 156 f., 160 f.
wisdom   3, 8, 13, 43, 46, 116, 126, 136, 157
work   15, 18 f., 28, 31 – 33, 35 f., 42, 44, 51, 54, 72, 74, 77, 82, 86, 88 – 90, 95 f., 104, 106, 113 – 117, 128, 132, 137 f., 142, 156, 160, 167
world   4 f., 7 – 9, 12 f., 17, 19, 27 – 30, 32 – 34, 36 – 38, 41 – 43, 46, 51, 65 – 77, 82 – 84, 88 f., 95 – 97, 103, 110, 115 f., 125, 129, 132, 134, 142, 149 – 151, 153, 155, 158 – 161, 163 – 166, 168
– world affairs   149
– world of ideas   163
– world of things   163
– world-view   31, 93
worldlessness   159
worthiness   4, 8 f., 14, 16, 28 f., 44, 46, 104, 134, 138, 157

YouTube   130, 133

www.ingramcontent.com/pod-product-compliance
Lightning Source LLC
Chambersburg PA
CBHW021734220426
43662CB00008B/851